The Spanish army
in the Peninsular War

War, Armed Forces and Society

General Editor: Ian F. W. Beckett

Editorial Board

Ian F. W. Beckett	Royal Military Academy, Sandhurst
John Childs	University of Leeds
John Gooch	University of Lancaster
Douglas Porch	The Citadel Military College of South Carolina
Geoffrey Till	Royal Naval College, Greenwich
John A. Lynn	University of Illinois, Urbana-Champaign

Also in the series

The army, politics and society in Germany, 1933–45
Klaus-Jürgen Müller

Troubled days of peace: Mountbatten and SEAC, 1945–46
Peter Dennis

The politics of manpower, 1914–18
Keith Grieves

The Commonwealth armies in the Korean War
Jeffrey Grey

The Commonwealth armies: manpower and organisation in two world wars
F. W. Perry

Kitchener's army: the raising of the New Armies, 1914–16
Peter Simkins

Charles J. Esdaile

The Spanish army in the Peninsular War

Manchester University Press
Manchester and New York
Distributed exclusively in the USA and Canada
by **St. Martin's Press**

Copyright © Imperial War Museum 1988

Published by Manchester University Press
Oxford Road, Manchester M13 9PL, UK
and Room 400, 175 Fifth Avenue,
New York, NY 10010, USA

*Distributed exclusively in the USA and Canada
by* St. Martin's Press, Inc.,
175 Fifth Avenue, New York, NY 10010, USA

British Library cataloguing in publication data
Esdaile, Charles
    The Spanish army in the Peninsular War.—(War, armed forces and society).
    1. Napoleonic Wars. Peninsular campaign. Army operations during Peninsular campaign of Napoleonic Wars. Spain. Ejército.
    I. Title II. Series
    940.2'7

Library of Congress cataloging in publication data
Esdaile, Charles J.
    The Spanish army in the Peninsular War / Charles J. Esdaile.
    p. cm. — (War, armed forces, and society)
    Bibliography: p. 212.
    Includes index.
    ISBN 0–7190–2538–9: $40.00 (U.S. : est.)
    1. Spain—History—Napoleonic Conquest, 1808–1813. 2. Spain—
    –History—Charles IV, 1788–1808. 3. Spain. Ejército—History—19th
    century. 4. Spain. Ejército—History—18th century. 5. Spain—
    –History, Military. 6. Sociology, Military—Spain. I. Title.
    II. Series.
    DP208.E82 1988
    946'.06—dc19   88-10274

ISBN 0–7190–2538–9 *hardback*

Phototypeset in Great Britain
by Northern Phototypesetting Co., Bolton

Printed and bound in Great Britain by
Anchor Brendon Ltd, Tiptree, Essex

Contents

	List of maps	*page* vi
	Preface	viii
	Acknowledgements	xi
Chapter 1	The Spanish army under the *ancien régime*	1
2	The era of Godoy, 1792–1808	36
3	The army and the revolution, May–September 1808	75
4	The war of the Junta Central	115
5	The army and the liberals, 1810–14	154
Epilogue	1814 and after	194
Appendix 1	Order of battle of the Spanish army, 1788	201
2	Order of battle of the Spanish army, 1808	203
3	Regiments of new creation, 1808	205
4	Order of battle of the Spanish army, 1814	209
	Select bibliography	212
	Index	223

Maps

1	The Iberian peninsula	xiv
2	The Spanish national uprising, May 1808	80
3	The campaign of Bailén	99
4	The military situation in northern Spain, October 1808	128
5	The Spanish War of Independence, 1808–14	160

For Alison, with love

Preface

The period from 1788 to 1814 is of immense importance in the history of the Spanish army, and thus, by extension, of Spain herself. Under the impact of the Revolutionary and Napoleonic Wars, the army was transformed from being the loyal servant of Bourbon absolutism to the intensely political 'king-maker' of the nineteenth century. Whereas a military coup would have been unthinkable before 1808, after 1814 Spain was never short of soldiers who were ready to intervene in politics, and to overthrow régimes which did not meet with their approval. The era of absolute monarchy had thus been effectively brought to an end, despite the efforts of Fernando VII to sustain it after 1814, for its chief prerequisite had been a reliable army. If Spain thereafter embarked upon a century of liberalism, it was to be characterised as much by the coup as by the constitution. The bourgeoisie may indeed have become revolutionary, but their revolutions in the last resort were made or unmade by the officer corps.

Considering that it was the wars of the Revolutionary Era that launched the army upon the interventionist course that has bedevilled Spanish politics almost until the present day, it is surprising that historians have not paid them more attention. Yet works dealing specifically with the political history of the army, such as those of Payne, Christiansen, Busquets, Fernández Bastarreche, and Seco, do no more than skim the surface of its involvement in the Revolutionary and Napoleonic Wars. Casado Burbano does treat the subject in more depth, but the chief emphasis of his work is on ideology and legislation. None of these historians has analysed the impact of the army's experience of war upon its composition, organisation or general outlook. Their reluctance to commit themselves to

Preface

the years before 1814 may in part be a reflection of their approach, for their aim has been to produce studies covering a very broad period in the history of the army. However, even authors who are concerned specifically with the military aspects of the Peninsular War have done little to broaden our knowledge of the subject. A particularly graphic example may be found in works dealing with the uniforms of the participants, which almost always spend far more time on the dress of the Spanish army as it was on the outbreak of war in 1808 than they do on the miscellany of costume actually worn during the war itself. As soon as the war begins, narrative is allowed to take the place of analysis, for reasons which were pinpointed by John Keegan in *The Face of Battle*:

Action is essentially destructive of all institutional studies . . . it damages the integrity of structures, upsets the balance of relationships, interrupts the network of communication which the institutional historian struggles to identify and, having identified, to crystallise. War . . . is the institutional military historian's irritant. It forces him . . . to qualify and particularise and above all to combine analysis with narrative – the most difficult of the historian's arts. Hence his preference for the study of armed forces in peacetime.[1]

Keegan's words are especially apposite in the case of the Spanish War of Independence of 1808–14, for the disruption normally attendant upon warfare was magnified a hundredfold by the total breakdown of central authority. With power in the hands of numerous provincial juntas and petty military dictators, for a time the army actually ceased to exist as a single entity. The formation of a new central government in September 1808 could do little to change matters, for one of the chief characteristics of the War of Independence was to be the complete inability of successive régimes to impose their authority upon the chaos which beset patriot Spain. Large parts of the armed forces therefore remained a law unto themselves. In view of these circumstances, the tendency of historians engaged in general studies of the Spanish army to shy away from detailed research into this period is entirely understandable. As Francisco Fernández Bastarreche has admitted, the Spanish army of the period before 1814 still awaits its historian.[2]

The failure of political historians to pay much attention to the military history of the War of Independence is equally glaring. The works of Artola, Anes, Domínguez Ortiz and most of their fellows display little interest in the military dimension of the struggle against the French. It has been suggested that this was in large part due to the difficulty of carrying out serious research into the army's history during the franquist era. Problematical though such investigations may have been, their lack of interest is also a reflection of the deep gulf that has separated the army from the rest of society – the general reaction of the author's Spanish friends to his interest in matters military was one of complete astonishment. However, if it is only to be expected that Spanish intellectuals would steer clear of affairs that could be held to be strictly military, the omission has not been rectified by foreign historians. Although both Lovett and Hamnett are more comprehensive in their coverage of the war, even they are somewhat conventional in their approach to many of its problems. Unfortunately, the latter's work, which has only been published in a limited edition in Mexico City, was unknown to the author until this study was in its final stages. It is of the first importance, however, and readers are urged to refer to it for a far more detailed examination of many of the social and political issues which form the context rather than the central concern of the present study.

Further justification for a study of the Spanish army may be found in the anglocentric approach which most British writers, with the exception of Sir Charles Oman, and, more recently, David Gates, have adopted with regard to the Peninsular campaigns. Basing their work solely on sources relating to the operations of Wellington's Anglo–Portuguese army, they have tended to present a distorted picture of the struggle, and to perpetuate the anti-Spanish prejudice evinced by so many of its British participants. Yet the object of the present work is not to pretend that British dissatisfaction with the Spaniards was unmerited, nor to minimise the role of Wellington's army. It is rather to suggest why the Spaniards were unable to satisfy their allies even in an auxiliary capacity, let alone to liberate themselves from foreign domination, and to examine the impact of that failure upon the later course of Spanish history. In reaching for those goals the author has striven for objectivity and accuracy in the firm belief that they cannot be allowed to take second place to rhetoric and myth. Yet he is all too well aware that what follows can only be a beginning, whose faults he is the first to acknowledge.

Notes

1   J. Keegan, *The Face of Battle* (London, 1979), p. 28.
2   F. Fernández Bastarreche, *El ejército español en el siglo XIX* (Madrid, 1978), p. 110.

Acknowledgements

After these brief words of introduction it only remains for me to embark upon the pleasant task of thanking the many people who have aided me along the long and difficult road to publication. In the first place, it would be dishonest of me to pretend that I am not indebted to the many historians whose work I have relied upon to provide a foundation for my own efforts, and whose ideas I have so frequently turned to as a source of inspiration. However, in personal terms, my greatest debt is undoubtedly to my supervisor, Dr. R. M. Blinkhorn. It is safe to say that this work would never have been brought to fruition without the kindness, generosity and patience with which he read through the endless reams of manuscript with which I flooded his groaning in-tray. My thanks are also due, albeit posthumously in the case of my father, to my parents for their constant encouragement and support. My superiors at the University of Southampton were unfailing in their patience at my frequent absences, and long incarceration at the keyboard. Amongst my friends and colleagues, Tony Kushner and Rory Muir both read versions of the manuscript and provided me with many useful suggestions and ideas, and John and Sue Zlosnik came gallantly to the rescue with a modern-day version of *bagajes y alojamiento* at a moment of desperate crisis. The editor of the series 'War, Armed Forces and Society', Dr. Ian Beckett, also proved most helpful, whilst the National Army Museum in London kindly supplied the cover photograph.

All the staff of the assorted archives at which I have worked have been polite and efficient without exception, but I should particularly like to mention those of the Biblióteca del Senado in Madrid, and of the archives of the University of Southampton. Of the former, the solicitude of Doña Rosario Herrera, Don José Luis Martín Consuegra, Don Roberto Carrasco Pérez, and Don Rafael Durán Aranda made my work there a real pleasure. At Southampton, Dr. Christopher Woolgar and his assistants, Sue Donnelly, Karen Robson, Mary Cockerill and Candy Godwin, have all contributed immeasurably to my work, and are to be congratulated on the success of their sterling efforts to catalogue and preserve the Wellington Papers.

I should also like to thank all the numerous people who smoothed my path during my research in Spain, especially Don Juan Balansó (Agencia EFE), Don Javier Pascual (Centro de Estudios Constitucionales), Coronel D. Juan Barrios, Coronel D. Fernando Redondo and Capitán D. Manuel Ramos (Servicio Histórico Militar), Don Amadeo Saguar Delgado and Don Julio Rodríguez Aramberri. On a personal level I was insulated from the loneliness of the long-distance researcher by many Spanish friends, of whom I should especially like to remember Doña Concha Bocos Rodríguez, Doña Marta Requena Martínez and Don Miguel Llopis. Their kindness has not been forgotten.

Finally, and above all, I must thank my wife, Alison, who has had to live with the consequences of this work for eight years, and to whom the result is humbly dedicated.

Charles Esdaile,
Southampton, September 1987.

1 The Iberian peninsula

Chapter 1

The Spanish army under the *ancien régime*

The standing army was the *sine qua non* of absolute monarchy. Without the emergence of such forces, no European monarch would ever have been able to exert any authority beyond that permitted to them by their subjects. Although other factors were also important, the growth of royal power was closely related to the formation of efficient professional armies financed through the medium of such bureaucracies as the French Intendance and the Prussian Generalkriegskomissariat rather than the Estates. Because they could now feed their armies and keep them within reasonable bounds, monarchs were freed from the spectre of another Thirty Years' War. As a result, they could engage in limited military campaigns that were designed to enhance the position of their dynasties. Territory gained through warfare provided taxes and recruits that could be used to expand the armed forces; by the same token, such victories undermined the power of rival rulers. Furthermore, the combination of regular armies with efficient civilian bureaucracies provided decisive advantages on the domestic front: hence the determination of every petty princeling to maintain an army of his own, even one so tiny as to be useless for any military purpose. Supported by disciplined armed forces, rulers could weld their possessions into a coherent state, impose their authority upon the nobility, ensure that revenue was collected, and overawe a frequently recalcitrant populace. Nor was the standing army solely an instrument of coercion. The constant demand it furnished for arms, uniforms and equipment provided a considerable stimulus for the national economy, just as the existence of a garrison provided a guaranteed market for local farmers and traders. Soldiers could also be mobilised to provide cheap labour for capital projects of all sorts. Finally, the army also furnished the nobility with an outlet for their military traditions and their social aspirations that at the same time served to reinforce their subordination to the throne.

The attractions of a standing army applied as much to Spain as they did to any other European country. However, the circumstances surrounding the accession to the throne of the Bourbon dynasty in 1700 had lent such a force redoubled importance. When Felipe V arrived in Spain he discovered that the Hapsburg army had dwindled away almost to nothing. Furthermore, large parts of the country, together with a majority of the upper nobility, refused to accept his rule and rallied instead to the cause of the Archduke Charles of Austria. Felipe's very survival was therefore bound up with the creation of a new army, for which naturally enough he chose the forces of Louis XIV as a model. Even when the war ended in a Bourbon victory, Felipe continued to rely heavily upon the army as the central pillar of his rule. Not only was the officer corps loaded with privileges of every sort, but the military administration was utilised as the basis for the entire Bourbon government. In addition to the creation of a French-style Intendance, Spain was divided into a number of Captain Generalcies whose incumbents were as much provincial governors as they were military commanders.

Yet in thus exalting the army the Bourbons had created a rod for their own backs. Because the officer corps was dominated by the upper nobility, its privileges were guaranteed to become a source of considerable social tension. In addition to the jealousy which was generated by this situation among the petty *hidalguía* and those men who though *notable* were not *noble*, such a policy proved counter-productive. One of the central aims underlying the formation of all standing armies had been the political emasculation of the nobility. However much they now exercised authority at the behest of the Spanish King rather than as of right, the *grandeza* had been elevated to a position of great power. Yet Louis XIV had specifically counselled Felipe V 'to allow the grandees to retain all the external prerogatives of their dignity whilst excluding them from all affairs that might augment their credit'.[1] By allowing the magnates to dominate the army, the Bourbons had given them a means of resisting the efforts of the monarchy to restrict the power of the nobility. Although the ability of the grandees to subvert the officer corps was restricted by the serious tensions which their predominance had engendered within its ranks, those same tensions constituted a further source of danger: years of frustration were to create the possibility of the subaltern officers being exploited by opponents of the régime. Riddled by social and economic tensions, detested by much of civilian society, and dominated by that section of the nobility with most reason to oppose the Bourbons – for the general trend of government policy was to erode the influence of the aristocracy – the Spanish army was transformed into a veritable 'Trojan Horse'.

For all the importance which the Bourbons placed upon the army, it suffered from numerous defects, of which one of the most important was the complexity and inefficiency of its administration. In theory, the authority of the King as Commander-in-Chief was exercised through the medium of the Supreme Council of War, which comprised the War Minister, the senior officers of the various branches of the army, and a number of other officers who were appointed by the King to represent military opinion as a whole. Originally this body had been the supreme authority in all matters pertaining to the army, as well as the highest court in the system of military justice. However, by the late eighteenth century most of its administrative functions had been taken over by the Ministry of War, and it had essentially become a simple court of justice.[2] In recognition of this development, in 1803 Carlos IV ordered a considerable reduction in its membership: henceforth it was to consist only of a President, six officers and four civilian legal advisers.[3] With the increasing marginalisation of the Supreme Council of War, the administration of the army was centred upon the Minister of War, who transmitted the orders of the sovereign to the Inspectors who headed its different branches. These numbered ten – line infantry, Swiss infantry, cavalry, dragoons, artillery, engineers, provincial militia, Guardias de Corps, Guardias de Infantería, Carabinieros Reales. The Inspectors had the task of implementing the decisions taken in the Ministry of War, presided over the administration of the *fuero militar*, and dealt with all personnel matters. They also watched over the internal economy of the units for which they were responsible, and ratified all recommendations for promotion.[4]

The centralisation of authority in the hands of the Ministry of War was vitiated by the fact that its staff was too small to be able to cope with the burdens with which it was faced. Nor was its authority total, for the chief responsibility for the army's pay and supply lay with the Ministry of Finance. The administration was therefore disproportionately expensive, and prone to considerable duplication of function. Factionalism was also endemic, particularly as the division of the army into so many separate branches was a recipe for the emergence of powerful vested interests. Ironically enough, there existed a perfectly satisfactory alternative to the Inspectorates in the Captain Generalcies. Although there was good reason why the Captains General should not have been the Inspectors of the forces they commanded, which consisted of all the troops who were garrisoned within their particular regions, there was none why these putative divisions should not have taken the place of the separate Inspectorates: to maintain both was simply to generate unnecessary expence.

Matters were not improved by the situation with regard to the command of the army. Ultimately, of course, this lay in the hands of the monarch, who in peacetime delegated his functions to the Captains General. This arrangement was logical enough, except for the fact that as soon as war broke out, the troops were mobilised into field armies commanded by specially appointed generals, who might or might not also be Captains General. Whilst this system was reasonably satisfactory as long as the army operated outside Spain, should it ever be called to do so within the national frontiers it was clear that the potential for confusion would be immense, as the Captains General would continue to wield their territorial authority independently of the commanders in the field. No attempt was made to use the Captain Generalcies as the basis for a system of permanent divisions, nor was there any general staff, despite the fact that both institutions had existed in France since 1763. Instead, on the outbreak of hostilities the commander of each field army had to appoint an *ad hoc* temporary headquarters of his own, as well as to improvise the organisation of his fighting forces. The result was that the operations of the Spanish army were certain to be marred by poor staffwork, for there was no means to prevent a general from appointing his immediate subordinates from the ranks of his own relations and protegés.

There was nothing unique in these administrative problems; indeed, they were shared by many other European armies. In other respects the Bourbon armed forces were far less deficient. With the accession to the throne of the new dynasty in 1700, the cumbersome Hapsburg *tercios* disappeared, to be replaced by a modern system of regiments. The army's tactics were also brought into line with those used in the rest of Europe. The original model for these changes was the French army, with which the Spaniards were to retain close contacts throughout the eighteenth century. Not only were numerous Spanish officers trained in French military academies, but a number of them also saw service with the French forces during the Seven Years' War.[5] These contacts were to some extent perpetuated by the Family Compact of 1761, but the victories of Frederick the Great increasingly made Prussia the chief focus of attention.[6] When a military commission was sent on a tour of Europe in 1787 to examine the state of military science, the report published on its return consisted of a treatise on the Prussian military system.[7] By then, however, the Spanish army had already been ruled by Prussian norms for almost twenty years: following the end of the Seven Years War, Carlos III had commissioned the Conde de O'Reilly to reform the Spanish army along Frederician lines; the result had been the publication of the Ordenanzas of 1768, which were characterised by a slavish devotion to Prussian military practice.[8]

On the death of Carlos III in 1788 there were twenty-seven Spanish and twelve foreign line infantry regiments, each of which was supposed to consist of two battalions. Each battalion was divided into eight musketeer and one grenadier companies, but in wartime the grenadiers were drawn off to form separate elite battalions. As in Prussia, the three-deep line was adopted as the standard tactical formation, its role being steadily to advance upon the enemy, firing successive volleys as it did so, before closing with the bayonet.[9] Frederician tactics were also adopted by the twelve regiments of line cavalry, which were henceforth trained to rely upon shock action rather than the French-style volleys of pistol and carbine fire that had been favoured in the first half of the century. Only the eight regiments of dragoons stood out against the general trend: whereas in Prussia the dragoons had increasingly been absorbed into the ordinary cavalry, in Spain they were theoretically still expected to function in their original role as mounted infantry.[10] As far as the quality of these troops is concerned, although the infantry were comparable with most of their contemporaries, the cavalry were placed at a serious disadvantage by the quality of their horseflesh. Centuries of mule breeding had greatly reduced both the size and the quality of Spain's horseherds, so that it became increasingly difficult to provide for the cavalry's requirements. Not only could few horses be obtained, but those that did become available were too small and weak to be suited to the use of shock tactics, even had their strength not been sapped still further by the army's perennial shortage of fodder.[11]

Although the majority of the Spanish army was organised in accordance with the requirements of the formal tactics of the Frederician era, by 1788 it also contained three regiments of light infantry and two of light cavalry.[12] The origins of these troops were two-fold. In forming these units the Spaniards were on the one hand responding to the contemporary vogue for *chasseurs*, *jagers*, hussars and light dragoons. Trained to fight in a more irregular fashion than ordinary troops, these forces were designed to harass the enemy at all times, and were a response to the experience of colonial warfare and the campaigns against the Turks. In addition, however, Spain's rugged terrain and the depredations of bandits, smugglers and Barbary pirates had given rise to a clear need for forces of mobile troops who were able to carry out police duties, small units of light infantry and cavalry being formed for this purpose from the 1730s onwards.[13] As a strong tradition also existed that in the event of invasion the many regions exempt from conscription – Aragón, Catalonia and Valencia, Navarre, and the Basque *señoríos* – should provide bands of irregular *somatenes* and *miqueletes*, it was but a short step to the formation of regular units of light troops.[14]

Another area in which the Spanish army kept pace with developments abroad was the artillery. The Seven Years' War had seen considerable advances in the employment of this arm. The numbers of cannon had increased enormously, horse artillery batteries had been introduced for the first time, and the guns had begun to be used in concentrated masses rather than being dispersed in support of the infantry. In line with these developments experiments with horse artillery were carried out in South America, the strength of the artillery was increased, and an academy established at Segovia, whose director, Tomás de Morla, gained considerable renown through the publication of a comprehensive manual on the gunner's craft.[15] The actual guns themselves were also improved in line with contemporary advances in the design and production of cannon. Various improvements in metallurgy had enabled guns to be cast lighter and to a more exact calibre. The resulting improvements in mobility and accuracy, which had also benefited from the invention of tangential sights and the elevating screw, had been incorporated into the Gribeauval system of artillery equipment. Arguably the best

Under the ancien régime 7

in the world, this equipment was introduced into the Spanish army in 1792. Even before this date, however, Bourbon interest in science and industry had ensured that they paid much attention to the new techniques. With the aid of foreign experts, in the 1780s the new methods of casting were introduced in foundries at Seville and Barcelona which between them were soon producing five hundred modern guns per year.[16]

Nevertheless, some problems remained with both the artillery and the engineers. Even supposing that the provision of guns and artillerymen had been sufficient, the absence of permanent train detachments forced the army to hire all the necessary teamsters and draught animals from the civilian populace at the start of each campaign. Although this system was very economical, amassing sufficient animals proved an exceptionally slow process even when the interior of Spain was at peace, as was discovered when the army mobilised against Portugal in 1801.[17] Once Spain had been plunged into a major war, the system became all but unworkable: suitable animals were few and far between, civilian contractors were able to charge prohibitively high rates of hire for their beasts, and the teamsters were undisciplined and prone to desert with their animals at every possible opportunity. Further difficulties were caused by the fact that the mainstays of the agricultural economy were the ox and the mule, both of which were notoriously slow moving and intractable.[18] As for the engineers, the entire corps only consisted of 150 officers, there being no units of trained sappers or miners.[19]

The Spanish army's technical deficiencies were far less important than the problems afflicting its logistical system. The maintenance of the armed forces was the responsibility of the Intendance. Each wartime field army and each Captain Generalcy had an Intendant who paid and supplied the troops, audited the military accounts, levied patriotic contributions, administered the hospitals and magazines, and imposed the dues of *bagajes, alojamiento y utensilios* (whereby the civilian population were theoretically responsible for providing the troops with transport and accommodation whenever it was required).[20] However, curiously enough the state did not accept that it had the responsibility to feed its forces. In normal circumstances the troops only received a minimum bread ration, which they were expected to supplement with the aid of their daily wage of nine *cuartos*. Every day each man paid seven *cuartos* over to a member of his squad whose responsibility it was to purchase food from the local populace.²¹ The army was equally dependant on the civilian population for its transport, which had to be hired at the start of each campaign. The cost varied, but rates were supposed to average twenty to twenty-four *reales* per day for a draught mule, fourteen for a cart, and fourteen to fifteen for a pack mule. Carts being infrequent in Spain, the mainstay of the system was the pack mule; since a single cart could transport as much as a dozen mules, the costs were thereby greatly increased.²²

Although it was always open to abuse by civilian contractors, this system could be expected to function reasonably well in peacetime so long as it was complemented by a regular supply of money and a prosperous agriculture. What it could not be expected to do was to operate successfully in the context of the sort of war that was to engulf Spain after 1808. Yet such a conflict would have been impossible to envisage in the latter half of the eighteenth century. In 1761 Spain signed a treaty with France known as the Family Compact which effectively ended the possibility of her army becoming involved in a major European conflict in anything other than an auxiliary capacity. With the Pyrenean frontier secured by France's friendship, the only tasks that faced the Spanish army were the defence of Spain's coasts against British raids, the blockade of Gibraltar, and the occasional punitive expedition against the Moors and the Portuguese. Because Spain's strategic concerns were henceforth to be directed towards her colonies and the endless maritime rivalry with Great Britain, the rest of the reign of Carlos III was marked by a heavy programme of naval building: between 1761 and 1778 the number of ships of the line was increased from thirty-seven to sixty-seven.²³ The cost of this programme was immense: in 1778 the navy consumed 100,000,000 *reales* out of a total expenditure of 489,000,000. At this point over twice as much money was still being spent on the army as the navy, but the outbreak of war with Britain in 1779 soon forced the government to reduce the size of its land forces.²⁴ Even before this date the damaging effect of excessive concentration on the navy had been made brutally apparent by the chaos that accompanied the Conde de O'Reilly's abortive expedition to Algiers in 1775. The arrangements for supplying the invasion force had totally broken down, there had been much muddle and confusion, and the number of troops which Spain could actually send into action had proved inadequate to deal with their opponents. Brave though the individual soldiers may have been, the fact remains

Under the ancien régime

that the army had been shown to be unable to carry out even the limited role assigned to it under the Family Compact.[25]

Political and economic considerations are also apparent in the manner in which the army was recruited. Because it was believed that armies were inherently unproductive and wasteful, soldiers were deliberately recruited from those groups who were assumed to have least to contribute to society. As was the case with most other European armies, the ranks were therefore filled with the urban and rural poor, criminals and foreigners. Whether or not this policy fulfilled its economic aims, the army as a result became regarded as a sink of iniquity that 'spread throughout the kingdom the vices of the soldiery, poisoning the seed of future generations and perverting morals'.[26] Military service eventually became so unpopular that the regime was forced to abandon the idea of conscription altogether. The outcome was a shortage of manpower that was to dog the army right up until 1808.

Until 1770 the army was chiefly recruited from volunteers. In so far as was possible the ranks were filled with foreigners, for such a policy not only reduced the need to force native Spaniards into the army, but also increased the population of the state, which was then held to be the key to its prosperity. Though the proportion of foreigners in the Spanish army never reached the same level as that attained in some other forces, the Bourbons sent out recruiting parties to scour Catholic areas for suitable volunteers. The early years of the eighteenth century had also witnessed the arrival of a considerable of number of Irish refugees who were eager to gain revenge against the British. A further source of recruits was provided by deserters from the French army who had fled across the Pyrenees. Thanks to the steady influx of Frenchmen, Irishmen, Germans, Walloons, Flemings and Italians, Felipe V had been able to form as many as twenty-three foreign regiments, but by the late eighteenth century the number had been reduced to eight – three Flemish, three Irish and two Italian. In addition, there were six battalions of Walloons amongst the Royal Guards, and four infantry regiments that were recruited by contract from the Catholic cantons of Switzerland. In 1788, the whole force of twenty-eight battalions amounted to some 23,000 men out of a total establishment for the regular army of 95,000.[27]

The problem with these recruits was that they were 'deserters and vagabonds from all over Europe, a most wretched crew'.[28]

Notoriously drunken and dissolute, it was also suspected that their ranks contained large numbers of Protestant heretics.[29] The evil reputation with which the army was in consequence imbued ensured that only the most desperate Spaniard would enlist in the army of his own free will. This, of course, served only to worsen the army's reputation still further, for its ranks became filled with what were commonly regarded as the dregs of society. Since the number of foreign recruits could never have been sufficient to meet all the army's needs, the outcome was a shortage of manpower so severe that when war threatened with Britain over the Falkland Islands in 1770 not even a draft of 12,000 men from the provincial militia could fill up the gaps in the ranks.[30] The only solution seemed to be to the reintroduction of some form of conscription. Conscious of the unpopularity of this measure, the regime decided to make the system as equitable as possible by keeping the number of exemptions to a minimum. In addition, for the first time the whole of Spain was to be made liable for military service, a measure that had the added virtue of striking a useful blow against provincial privilege. As a result of these reforms it was hoped that the ranks would henceforth be filled with 'men of property and probity' rather than 'drunken mechanics and dissolute vagrants'. Military service would thus be rendered more respectable, leading to an improvement in both the number and the quality of volunteers. The need for conscription would in this manner eventually be obviated altogether.[31]

In accordance with this thinking a new system of conscription was established in 1770. A quota was assigned to each province which the Intendant then apportioned amongst its various *corregimientos* according to their population. Having compiled a register of all men who were eligible for service (essentially all those aged between seventeen and thirty-six, who were single, of good health, and over five feet tall, and who could not prove their entitlement to exemption), the local magistrates selected the requisite number of conscripts by means of a ballot known as the *sorteo*. The whole process was strictly codified and many safeguards were built into it to ensure that justice was seen to be done.[32] But the hopes placed upon the new system were not to be fulfilled, military service remaining as unpopular as ever. At the announcement of a *sorteo*, young men would flee from their homes to the haven provided by areas that were still free of conscription, such as Madrid. Alternatively, they would hastily get married in order to qualify for

Under the ancien régime

exemption. Those unfortunates who were finally chosen had to be dragged away from their distraught families by armed guards.[33] Popular hostility to military service was a natural reflection of general perceptions of the army. Reputedly moral, sober and 'seldom given to inebriety', ordinary Spaniards despised soldiers as drunken, evil brutes. Their prejudices were confirmed by the fate of ex-soldiers in civil life, who invariably became characterised by 'misery and mendacity . . . idleness and vice'.[34]

The miserable conditions endured by the rank and file were equally discouraging as an advertisement for the army. Some reforms had been effected in this area by Carlos III, who had attempted to house all his troops in modern barracks as well as to guarantee them certain basic necessities.[35] These improvements were only relative, however. After paying for their food, soldiers were left with a mere two *cuartos*, or enough for a little tobacco or a glass of wine.[36] Described by one observer as 'dirty, melancholy dwarfs', they were forced to endure appalling conditions in their barracks and hospitals.[37] To add to their troubles, they were also subjected to a host of petty regulations that were designed to uphold the decorum of the military estate, and to exclude the soldiery from polite society: soldiers had to wear full uniform and to keep their hair properly powdered and curled at all times; they were forbidden to smoke, or even to sit down, in the streets; and they were banned from areas that were fashionable venues for the *paseo*.[38] Finally, in line with common practice elsewhere, they were subjected to a brutal code of discipline, all NCOs carrying canes the thickness of a finger with which to 'encourage' their men.[39]

The manner in which the new system was introduced did nothing to increase its popularity. Although it had originally been intended that there should be as few exemptions to the *sorteo* as possible, in the event the government could not bring itself to allow the energies of the 'useful' classes to be squandered in so unproductive an activity as military service. Nor could it afford to abrogate the privileges of either the Church or the nobility. The regulations for the *sorteo* therefore exempted *hijosdalgo*, clerics, officials of all sorts, members of the liberal professions, skilled industrial workers and artisans, stock breeders, tenant farmers who worked their own land, merchants, entrepreneurs and master craftsmen. In addition, the number of exemptions was steadily increased thereafter, whilst it was also stipulated that commoners could not hold positions that normally conferred freedom from the *sorteo*.[40] The main burden of conscription was therefore certain to fall upon the poorer classes of society, whose only protection lay in a few humanitarian clauses which laid down that sole breadwinners should should never be liable for service. Nor was the burden especially equitable even then: many towns and cities and the foral provinces continued to be exempted from the *sorteo* altogether. Carlos III had certainly not intended to allow these privileges to remain intact, but his attempts to extend the system for the most part proved a failure. Only Navarre submitted to this further erosion of its *fueros*: in the Basque provinces the local magistrates refused to co-operate, whilst in Barcelona the announcement of a *sorteo* in 1773 led to a furious outbreak of rioting.[41] Almost the entire weight of the *sorteo* had therefore to be borne by the rural poor of the Castiles, León, Asturias, Galicia and Andalucía, the same provinces which already had to provide the 39,000 men required by the forty-three regiments of provincial militia (recruited by a very similar system of conscription that had been introduced in 1767).[42]

The introduction of the *sorteo* in consequence tended to increase rather than diminish the unpopularity of military service. Instead of implementing measures designed to attract a better class of volunteer, improve the conditions of the rank and file, and lessen the social stigma that was attached to soldiering, the régime responded to the problem by turning to repression. Draconian punishments were imposed on deserters and their accomplices.[43] Marriages whose banns had not been read at least fifteen days before the announcement of a *sorteo* were annulled, and attempts to seek safety in flight were frustrated by empowering magistrates to impress into the army all *vagos* – criminals, beggars, and the unemployed. Such a *leva* was supposed to be implemented every time that a *sorteo* was decreed: as young men who fled to such cities as Madrid were unlikely to have been able to find work immediately, the chances were that they would be swept into the army after all. As well as dealing with fugitives from the *sorteo*, the *leva* had other advantages for it served to reduce the hordes of beggars who infested all Spanish cities. In addition, although the conscription of *vagos* did nothing to improve the image of the army, their presence in the ranks did at least reduce the number of soldiers who had to be provided by the rest of the population.[44]

Given the hostility of the general populace, it is clear that the success of the *sorteo* in the last resort depended upon the attitude of the local magistrates who were charged with its imposition. Yet it was almost as unpopular with the propertied classes as it was with its intended victims. So many young men were supposed to have fled their villages that agricultural production fell dramatically, whilst the fugitives were also regarded as a threat to social stability, since they gave themselves over to 'idleness and libertinage'.[45] Much alarm was also evinced at the sexual impact of conscription: on the one hand, the removal of so many healthy young men into the ranks of the army was held 'to propagate celibacy more than is convenient for the good of the state'; on the other, the *sorteo* was supposed to encourage early marriages, which were believed to result in the birth of handicapped children.[46] Finally, it was felt that 'the vices of the army' would inevitably spread to civilian society, corrupting the 'industry and simple manners' of the mass of the population.[47] Numerous magistrates and clergymen therefore sought to frustrate the imposition of the *sorteo* and to abet the large numbers of fugitives and deserters.[48]

With no means of overcoming this hostility, the régime abandoned the *sorteo* in 1776, leaving the army to rely on voluntary enlistment and the *leva*. The latter does not seem to have been put to much use, however, for in 1801 the line infantry contained only 4,771 men who had been pressed in this fashion.[49] As far as the flow of volunteers was concerned, there was a steady decline in the number of foreign recruits who reached Spain. In 1792 the Milán, Flandés, Brabante and Bruselas regiments had consequently to be disbanded, their rank and file being distributed amongst the other foreign units.[50] The shortage of recruits was less acute in the Swiss regiments, but even they were only kept up to strength by extending the area of enlistment beyond the borders of Switzerland, obtaining recruits 'by artifice and by force', and defrauding men of their discharges once they had actually been inducted into the army.[51] Yet few Spaniards came forward to take the place of the foreigners. Despite the financial incentives offered by re-enlistment, most serving soldiers thought only of 'the happy moment when they would gain their liberty'.[52] As for the civilian population, most regiments could only gain fresh blood by sending their recruiting parties to the spots where they would find the most 'dupes and libertines'. In short, soldiers remained 'the refuse of society'.[53]

The abandonment of the *sorteo* was therefore a serious blow. The last conscripts which it produced finished their eight years' service in 1784, after which there was a yearly shortfall in the infantry of some 17,500 men out of a full establishment total of 59,000. So bad was the situation that only six of the forty-one line regiments could muster the two battalions laid down by the Ordenanzas.[54] The gaps in the ranks were partly camouflaged by a series of decrees that cut the establishment of most units by as much as fifty per cent in order to save money.[55] However, the effect of these measures was to leave the army in too weak a condition to fulfil any requirements other than those imposed by the Family Compact. The full extent of its debility was revealed in 1792, when it was estimated that Spain could put no more than 36,000 men into the field.[56] Compared with this situation, the poor quality of the army's human material was irrelevant: in every country in Europe it had been shown that the proverbial 'scum of the earth' could be drilled and flogged into a perfectly satisfactory battlefield performance. However, that process could not be completed overnight. By allowing their military cadres to dwindle away so dramatically, the Bourbons ensured that in the event of a major war the Spanish army would be swamped by a mass of raw recruits. No other single factor was to be so influential in its humiliation during the War of Independence of 1808–14.

That humiliation might not have been so great had it not been for the deficiencies which marred the Spanish officer corps. Often technically unskilled, its members had also incurred the wrath of the rest of society for the exalted position to which they had been elevated by the Bourbons. Yet the officer corps lacked the professional unity necessary to sustain its predominance. The Prussian army, whose officers were united by a powerful sense of their common status as *junkers*, was able not only to survive the cataclysmic trauma of 1806, but afterwards to strengthen its influence in society. In Spain, by contrast, the army proved totally unable to defend itself against attack – and thus to maintain its influence – when the growing civilian antagonism was finally unleashed by the events of 1808. Totally lacking in any sense of corporate unity, it disintegrated in fratricidal strife at the very moment when its solidarity was most essential.

The heterogeneity that marked the Spanish officer corps was in the first place the result of the influx of foreign officers who had entered Spain under the Bourbons. Large numbers of foreigners had accompanied Felipe V and Carlos III when they came to Spain, whilst the

Irish, Italian, Flemish and Walloon regiments all continued to be officered by men of foreign descent long after their rank and file had been hispanicised. In the Guardias Walonas, for example, 176 officers were still of non-Spanish origin in 1791 out of a total of 185.[57] Moreover, a disproportionately number of foreigners achieved high rank: in 1792 they accounted for no fewer than seventy-seven of Spain's 327 generals.[58] In 1775 the considerable resentment caused by this situation was ignited by the abortive campaign in Algiers. When the Conde de O'Reilly attempted to blame his defeat on the cowardice of his troops a number of Spanish officers mutinied in protest.[59] By the late eighteenth century, however, the foreigners had largely been assimilated into the Spanish nobility, the tension occasioned by their presence being as nothing compared to that which stemmed from the social composition of the officer corps. As in most European armies, the nobility enjoyed privileged access to the military estate. Not only had the Bourbons seized upon military service as a means whereby the *hidalguía* could be bound to the throne, but it was traditional to argue that the sword was its chief *raison d'être*.[60] In consequence, only *hijosdalgo* could become officer cadets (with the exception of sons of commoner officers of the rank of captain and above). For the artillery, the engineers and the Royal Guards, this meant that all officers would be noblemen, for it was impossible to gain a commission in these units without having first served in them as a cadet. In the infantry and the cavalry, however, one third of the officers could be promoted from the ranks. Those eligible for such promotion included *hijosdalgo*, young men who were serving in the rank and file of regiments in which their fathers held a commission, and finally sergeants who had displayed 'the spirit . . . customs and application that make up a good officer'.[61]

The difficulties faced by commoners in obtaining commissions should not be underestimated. Because relatively few non-nobles could hope even to reach the rank of captain, the number of commoners who could become officer cadets was small. As for promotion from the ranks, it was only permitted after all officer cadets awaiting promotion had themselves been given their commissions, whilst even then any *hijosdalgo* serving in the ranks took precedence over non-noble candidates.[62] Yet a substantial number of commoners still succeeded in obtaining commissions, if only because a resourceful man could always forge the patents of nobility required for acceptance as a cadet, or seek to bribe his way into the service.[63] However, perhaps the most important factor that encouraged the recruitment of commoners was the reluctance of the nobility, or at least its richer sections, to endure the dreary servitude of life in a garrison town, let alone the indignity of being commanded by men of a lower social class. Wherever possible the nobility therefore sought to use their influence at court to gain rapid promotion. In consequence, according to some estimates, at least two thirds of the line officers were drawn 'from the least powerful and even less noble part of the population'. Taking the officer corps as a whole, the proportion of non-nobles was probably nearer to one quarter.[64]

In general, the result of this situation was that the nobility 'are rapidly promoted and rise suddenly to the highest rank while meritorious, old and experienced officers are left in subaltern situations and tend to vegetate in obscure garrisons'.[65] A list of thirty captains in the Fourth Army who were awaiting promotion in the year 1813 shows that of the twenty-two who had been officers before 1808, six had enlisted as common soldiers, nine as cadets, four as sublieutenants in the provincial militia, and two as gentlemen-volunteers (the last had been a royal page who had been commissioned directly as a captain). The six ex-rankers took an average of fourteen years to reach the rank of sublieutenant, and the four who had been promoted further by the outbreak of the War of Independence had then had to wait a further seven and a half years before becoming lieutenants. By contrast, it took an average of just over two years for the cadets to be appointed as sublieutenants, and only five more for them to make lieutenant.[66] It would nevertheless be misleading to regard the divisions which accordingly began to emerge within the officer corps solely in terms of a clash between nobles and non-nobles. The *hidalguía*, which in 1787 numbered 480,592 out of a total of 11,000,000 inhabitants, covered a very broad range of social classes. Because money was as important as rank in becoming an officer cadet, it was in consequence only its upper sections that were in any position to dominate the officer corps. All cadets had to be provided with an allowance of at least four *reales* per day, whilst in the military academies they had to pay fees, and to provide their own books, linen and household necessaries. Finally, even in the provincial militia prospective officers had to show that they enjoyed a reasonably decorous standard of living.[67]

These economic requirements could not be met by a proportion of the petty *hidalguía*, but even those who could afford to become cadets were placed at a disadvantage by the system of promotion. Except in the engineers and the artillery, where promotion depended entirely upon seniority, all patronage was in the hands of the King, to whom the Minister of War passed on the recommendations of the Inspectors. Carlos III, in particular, took a very close personal interest in these duties, in one instance vetoing the promotion of an officer for thirty years simply because he had appeared at a parade with a parasol.[68] Given the upper nobility's close association with the court, the lower nobility and the ex-rankers were placed at a serious disadvantage. Whilst they languished in the lower ranks, the scions of the *grandeza* received commissions whilst they were still children, and in some instances before they were out of their mother's arms: the Duque de Rivas even became an officer in the Guardias de Corps at the tender age of six months. Once they were embarked upon their careers, their promotion was frequently meteoric, the Duque de Alburquerque advancing from the rank of captain to that of lieutenant general in just four years.[69] By 1792 eighty generals out of 327 were *titulados* even though that group represented less than one quarter of one per cent of the nobility as a whole.[70]

Although the privileged position of the aristocracy would have caused considerable resentment at the best of times, it was exacerbated by the severe inflation that gripped Spain after 1780. Prices rose by some fifty-nine per cent in the period 1780–98, but the wages of the officer corps remained pegged at their 1768 level until 1791 when they were raised by an average of sixteen and one half per cent.[71] Pay had never been especially high in the junior ranks of the officer corps: in 1788 a sublieutenant received only 250 *reales* in basic pay every month, compared with a skilled artisan who could earn as many as 180.[72] This level of payment was soon eroded by the spiralling inflation. As early as 1775 it was noted that no officer could survive on his pay without the command of a company or some other emolument.[73] Twenty years later it was alleged that 'prices have reached such a level that for some time the officer has not been able to subsist on the pay which is accorded him', as the minimum monthly expenditure of a sublieutenant came to 392 *reales*, and his pay to only 272.[74] An officer without independent means could only hope to escape from the poverty with which he was increasingly threatened by achieving promotion: aside from the obvious increase in salary, the command of a company offered substantial opportunities for financial peculation.[75] As these perquisites were effectively monopolised by the richer *hijosdalgo*, tension within the officer corps was certain to mount in proportion with inflation.

The advantages of the upper nobility were reinforced still further by their domination of the Royal Guards, which in 1788 consisted of the Guardias de Corps and Carabinieros Reales cavalry regiments, two regiments of Guardias de Infantería, one of them Spanish and the other Walloon, and a company of halberdiers. Most of these units had been formed by Felipe V in 1702 as an exact replica of the French Guards, Louis XIV having warned his nephew that he would never be a real king unless he possessed such troops.[76] Designed to cement the hold of the new dynasty upon the throne, they had consequently been showered with honours and privileges, and their numbers increased until by 1788 they had reached the enormous figure of 10,500 men.[77] Most favoured of all were the Guardias de Corps, whose close attendance upon the royal family offered them many opportunities of gaining its patronage, as witness the spectacular rise of Manuel de Godoy. Service in this regiment, of which membership was restricted to the nobility, may only be descibed as having been idyllic. Many of its wealthier troopers lived in private lodgings, whilst even those who were in barracks had servants and rooms of their own. Their duties were confined to escorting the royal family on its periodic journeys between the various palaces around Madrid, and to accompanying the Bourbon monarchs on their daily hunting parties.[78] These excursions were not entirely free of danger, for Carlos IV in particular insisted in riding at such a pace that his escort were frequently injured in falls from their horses.[79] Even this was not without its compensations, however, for it was just such a fall that first brought Godoy to the attention of the Queen. For those who were less favoured, there was still plenty of feminine comfort: the guardsmen were much in demand as *cortejos* (see below), and were often supplied by their ladies 'with the means of their extravagance'.[80]

The French Revolution led to an enhancement of the already privileged status of the Guardias de Corps. Alarmed by the wholesale defection of the Gardes Françaises, Carlos IV sought to ensure the loyalty of his personal bodyguard by flattering its ego. The regiment's pay was increased, a fourth company was added to the existing three, and, most importantly, troopers and cadets were given the right to be commissioned directly into the regiments of the line.[81] Yet the privileged position of the Royal Guards was seemingly not merited by any outstanding military prowess. The Guardias de Corps had the reputation of being a 'pacific phalanx of pure ostentation', and were slightingly referred to as 'the chocolate soldiers'.[82] As for the rest of the Guards, they were recruited from exactly the same unpromising material as the line regiments; not surprisingly, contemporary observers found them to be ill-trained, dirty and slovenly.[83] This failure to justify themselves did not increase the household troops' popularity with their humbler colleagues, particularly in view of the aristocratic nature of their officers. Commoners were completely excluded from the officer corps, whilst the lower *hidalguía* were also effectively debarred by regulations requiring guards officers to maintain a decorous standard of living: in the Guardias de Corps even simple guardsmen had to have an allowance of at least 240 reales per month.[84]

The triumph of what the eighteenth-century soldier and writer, José Cadalso, scathingly called *el regimiento de la grandeza* was particularly galling to the under-privileged mass of regimental officers.[85] In view of the difficulties experienced by these officers in obtaining promotion the decision to allow members of the Guardias de Corps to be commissioned directly into the line regiments was most unwise. Such aristocratic queue jumping was not the only obstacle facing their advancement. Upward mobility within the officer corps was greatly reduced by the tendency of many brigadiers to retain the command of their regiments even after they had been elevated to the *generalato*, whilst many officers were forced by the inadequacy of their pensions 'to continue to serve ... till age or infirmities obliged them to retire'.[86] The role that seniority played in recommendations for promotion also tended to work against the interests of officers without connections at the court, for men who had been promoted from the ranks had generally taken so long to achieve their commissions that they were at a permanent disadvantage *vis à vis* their *hijodalgo* rivals. Serious difficulties were also occasioned by the *grado* system whereby brevet ranks were conferred on officers who were deemed worthy of particular reward. Under this system a lieutenant who was given the *grado* of captain would continue to serve in his former rank, but would take precedence over his fellow lieutenants as soon as a vacant captaincy occurred. Needless to say, like everything else, the benefits of this system were gleaned by the better connected officers.

Although firm evidence is lacking, it is likely that in the late eighteenth century an increasing premium was being placed upon membership of the military estate, for a commission was of considerable economic and social value. For the nobility in particular, service in the army provided a means by which they could reassert their status in the face of its steady erosion by the monarchy. At the same time, the financial advantages which it offered, such as freedom from all ordinary taxation, were a safeguard against the onward march of inflation. In addition, the *fuero militar* brought many judicial advantages. All those to whom it applied had the right to be tried by military tribunals, which were not only quicker in their proceedings than the civil courts, but also notoriously partial in their judgements in any case where an officer was in conflict with a civilian. Furthermore, the *fuero* also secured a certain amount of protection against the Inquisition.[87] A commission was also a valuable social commodity, for, aside from being entitled to the deference of their fellow citizens, officers enjoyed the right to wear uniform and bear arms. Although much valued by Spaniards for its own sake, the significance of this privilege only becomes apparent when it is viewed in the context of the *cortejo*. This custom seems to have arisen as a response to the unhappiness engendered by arranged marriages. With the tacit consent of their husbands, married women would select some eligible young man to be their *cortejo*, or champion, confidant and general escort.[88] Thanks to their ability to cut a more dashing figure than any of their rivals, officers naturally enjoyed a considerable advantage.[89]

In the latter half of the eighteenth century all these factors combined to produce a considerable revival of interest in a military career amongst the nobility.[90] At the same time, however, membership of the military estate was becoming equally attractive to that section of the population which lacked *hijodalgo* status, but yet enjoyed a certain degree of prosperity and education. The ranks of this group had been swelled in the course of the eighteenth century by the emergence of the characteristic figure of the *cacique*, rural notables who had rented the estates of absentee grandees, dipossessed their poorer neighbours, or acquired the lion's share of the common lands in those towns where it was customary to share them out among the inhabitants. Other factors favouring the domination of this incipient rural bourgeoisie was their *de facto* control of local government, and their ability to exploit their poorer neighbours, and turn both inflation and harvest failures to their own economic advantage.[91] Nor were the *caciques* the only group that were emerging to challenge the traditional division between the *hidalguía* and the *estado llano*. The multiplicity of councils and courts by which Spain was governed had spawned a large class of bureaucrats and officials, whose ambitions had been inflated by the tendency of Carlos III to appoint many of his leading ministers from amongst their number. Finally, the rapid economic growth of the late eighteenth century gave considerable stimulation to the commercial community. Given the perquisites enjoyed by the officer corps, it was only natural that the nascent middle classes should have looked upon it with eyes that were increasingly covetous.

The increasing pressure on the officer corps inevitably created serious tensions within its ranks. Although the Ordenanzas limited the number of cadets to a maximum of only two per regiment, many colonels allowed themselves to be persuaded to ignore these restrictions.[92] Yet the growing numbers of cadets could not be accommodated by the limited opportunites for promotion offered by a peacetime army. The only means by which surplus officers could be found a niche was to attach them to regiments as supernumeraries. Known as *agregados*, these men drew full pay and were automatically entitled to any vacancy which occurred for an officer of their rank. Not surprisingly, they were intensely disliked by the *efectivos*, one of whom wrote: '... the difference between an *agregado* and an *efectivo* lies in the work: an *efectivo* has to take care of everything pertaining to his company and carry out his duty, whilst the *agregado* does no more than take the pay'.[93]

The only officers who could hope to cut their way through this accumulation of obstacles were those with influence at court, commoners and poor *hijosdalgo* for the most part being left to suffer a life that was both harsh and frustrating. Few could hope to rise above the rank of captain; they had no say in the running of their regiments; and they were exposed to the jeers of their wealthier fellows, who referred scathingly to the ex-rankers as *los pinos* in what was presumably a reference to the height requirements of the rank and file.[94] To make matters worse, the life that they led was often 'such as to benumb all their faculties'.[95] They were overwhelmed with paperwork, their pay was inadequate, their garrisons were frequently 'lonely places without resources either in respect to instruction or genteel amusements', they received little leave, and the regulations of the army's contributory pension fund, the Monte Pío Militar, forbade them to marry until they had obtained a captaincy. Even though they might not reach this rank before the age of sixty, officers without private means could not afford to disobey, for to do so would be to forego the only income to which they could look forward in their old age.[96] There were other possibilities, such as the grant of a *señorío* belonging to one of the four military orders, or membership of the Order of Carlos III (which conveyed a substantial pension). Some officers were also able to find posts in the bureaucracy, the Resguardo (a heterogeneous collection of local police units), or one of the numerous companies of invalids and urban militia. Yet the more worthwhile of these rewards were only open to the nobility, whilst all of them depended upon the royal favour. Many officers were therefore forced back upon the increasingly inadequate payments of the Monte Pío Militar.[97]

If the social and economic divisions that characterised the officer corps were in the long term to be fatal to the army's domination of civilian society, in the short term they could not but impair its efficiency. Although the officers promoted from the ranks were poorly educated, their conditions did not provide them with any incentive to improve themselves. On the contrary, as one observer noted, thanks to their 'dull, monotonous round of daily obscurity, they become stupefied, lose all their energy and activity, and contract habits of apathy and insociability which have an unhappy and permanent influence upon their minds'.[98] The low rate of promotion at the same time served to increase the average age of the officer corps: by 1806 this was sixty-one for colonels, fifty-nine for captains and fifty-eight for lieutenants, one cavalry regiment even having a squadron commander aged seventy-nine.[99] If the bulk of the officer corps was ignorant and aging, the quality of its more privileged members was little better. Carlos III had established a number of military academies for the training of officer cadets, but they were simply too small to have had any real impact.[100] In any case, in 1790 Carlos IV closed most of them down in the belief that they were potential foci of progressive thought.[101] Most cadets were posted directly to their regiments and placed in the charge of an experienced officer who was supposed to watch over their morals, teach them the basis of military science, and instil in them the principles of honour and subordination. The formal teaching of the academy was thus to be replaced by emulation, observation and experience.[102]

This system of instruction was never likely to produce outstanding results. On the contrary, it was liable to perpetuate all the evils from which the officer corps already suffered, for military life was simply not conducive to the education of adolescent boys. The heart of the problem was the constant emphasis on personal honour. Although originally based upon the principles of chivalry, the need which it imposed on each and every officer constantly to be mindful of his standing with his fellows had produced an atmosphere of pride, jealousy and rivalry. The 'honour' of many officers in fact became an exaggerated *amour propre*: duelling became frequent, and reprimands from superiors came to be regarded by some officers as personal insults for which they were prone to demand instant satisfaction.[103] The cult of honour also inspired much womanising, encouraged of course by the custom of the *cortejo*, and this in turn led to the adoption of ever more flamboyant styles of dress.[104] As many officers simply did not have the money to live in the style which was required of them, gambling also became widespread.[105] Thanks in large part to their feeling of superiority with regard to the civilan population, many officers indulged in all sorts of daredevilry. In Madrid the guards officers spent their free time in obstructing the authorities, picking fights with the swashbuckling *majos*, and disrupting balls and fiestas.[106] The baiting of the civilian population often reached extreme limits. For example, one English traveller has an amusing story of how a group of young officers decided to teach a notoriously licentious monastery a lesson by bringing a party of whores within its walls in the guise of society ladies. Knowing what the sequel was likely to be, they asked the monks to entertain the ladies whilst they themselves went hunting. The result was exactly what they had intended – 'The hot-livered monks . . . smarted so severely for the favours which they obtained from the good humoured nymphs that for many months afterwards the chief dignitaries of the house were dispersed about in the neighbouring towns under the care of the barber surgeons.'[107]

Despite the existence of a minority of intellectual and cultivated officers, such as the *ilustrados*, Cadalso and Aguirre, for the most part studying was looked upon with scorn, and promotion sought by toadying to superiors. If a certain interest was sometimes evinced in the ideas of the Enlightenment, this was generally merely the product of a desire to appear fashionable.[108] To expect the cadets to receive a reasonable education whilst serving with their regiments was therefore naive in the extreme. As the Marqués de Casa Cagigal pointed out in 1798, 'As youths separated from their parents with full liberty at the age when this is most prejudicial to them, they acquire every vice, weaken their health with licentious disorders, and ruin their . . . families with exorbitant expenses stemming from gambling and other expences.'[109]

Spain was to reap a bitter harvest from the mediocrity of so many of her officers in the War of Independence of 1808–14. In the meantime their vanity and egotism could not fail to effect the army's standing with the civilian population, particularly given the dominant position enjoyed by the military in Spanish society. Thanks to the institution of the Captain Generalcy, the army had been elevated to a central position in the governance of Bourbon Spain. As the personal representatives of the monarch, the Captains General stood at the head of the administrative and judicial machine in every part of the Kingdom, sitting as the *ex oficio* presidents of the Audiencias and Chancillerías which handled the day-to-day business of government at a provincial level.[110] Their civil functions were reinforced by the supervisory functions which had been allotted to the Supreme Council of War with regard to the economy, particularly in matters relating to the production of armaments.[111] The extent to which individual Captains General actually made use of these functions obviously varied according to their personality and disposition, but numerous examples may be found of their involvement in massive programmes of public works such as those carried out by Mina, O'Reilly and Socorro in Cádiz and Barcelona. When the last of these officers invaded southern Portugal in 1807, it was entirely in character that his first action should have been to plan a similar improvement for the town of Elvas.[112]

The civil powers enjoyed by the Captains General were not simply a reflection of the Bourbons' complete dependence on the army in the first years of their reign, for this force was used as one more element in their efforts at etatist economic development. Just as artillery officers administered Spain's arsenals, so the corps of engineers superintended the construction of the never-to-be-finished Canals of Aragón and Castile, and the improvements that were made in the highway between Madrid and Andalucía in the 1780s. Furthermore, these projects were carried out with the labour of thousands of common soldiers.[113] The very organisation of the army was an additional testimony to the determination of the régime that it should not constitute a complete drain on the resources of the state, if it could not actually be made to augment them: men who could contribute to society in some more useful way were exempted from military service, soldiers were released from the service for several months in every summer in order that they could help bring in the harvest in their home villages, and devices such as the *leva* employed to find occupation for the destitute. Above all, however, it was as much the responsibility of the Intendants to promote agriculture, industry and trade as it was to provide for the upkeep of the army; indeed, they may safely be regarded as the lynchpins in the Bourbon policy of *fomento*.[114]

Finally, military influence was also strong in the judiciary, and in matters relating to the protection of society. Although the Captains General did not preside over the Audiencias and Chancillerías when they were sitting as courts of law, the extension of the *fuero militar* to many cases in which civilians were involved brought the army squarely into the judicial process.[115] In addition, the army provided the only means by which the state could maintain law and order, or take action in cases of natural disaster. Soldiers could be summoned by the civil magistrates to put down outbreaks of rioting, whilst in rural areas they also established a precedent for the later activities of the Guardia Civil, fighting numerous skirmishes against bands of smugglers and bandits (to ensure that the troops remained reliable in such situations they were rotated in their garrisons every three years).[116] Similarly, it was the army that was turned out to fight the huge fire that broke out in Madrid in September of 1804, and to man the *cordon sanitaire* which prevented the spread of yellow fever from Andalucía to the rest of Spain between 1801 and 1804.[117]

The very ubiquity of the army's presence was bound to inject civil-military relations with a certain degree of tension. Such friction can be seen in most European countries in the latter half of the eighteenth century, but in Spain a number of factors coincided to ensure that it was particularly intense. The ordinary inhabitants hated the imposition of military service and of the traditional dues of *bagajes*, *alojamientos*, *y utensilios*, whilst they also disliked the soldiers themselves, the Motín de Esquilache of 1766 being in large part the consequence of the general hatred of the Guardias Walonas.[118] Popular detestation of the army was shared by the more affluent classes of society, although this might not have been the case had the increasingly powerful rural bourgeoisie enjoyed freedom of access to the military estate and equality of promotion within its ranks. In theory, however, only *hijosdalgos* could enter the officer corps without first serving a painful apprenticeship in the rank and file, whilst promotion was dominated by the aristocracy. Finally, for all the privileges with which it had been loaded by the Bourbons, perceptive observers could see that the army was suffering from serious defects.

A letter published in the *Correo de Madrid* in March 1788 is highly indicative of the manner in which the army was regarded by the rest of society. It was occasioned by a series of articles written by Lieutenant Colonel Manuel de Aguirre in support of the Spanish Enlightenment against its traditionalist critics. The author confessed himself to be astonished that Aguirre had ventured to express an opinion on matters that were had nothing to do with 'a profession that I . . . thought barbarous, ignorant, unjust, libertine, arrogant, bloodthirsty', and whose members consisted of 'the worthless and criminal scum of the nation'. As some of the greatest republics and empires in history had been governed by the force of arms, he was forced to conclude that this view might be unjust, but it was impossible to deny that the army's numerous failings had produced 'the greatest scorn for the military profession, and all those who follow it'. Signing himself as *el medio convertido*, he therefore challenged Aguirre to provide an explanation of the army's organisation and the role that it should play in the civilian government.[119] Aguirre's response can hardly have been regarded as satisfactory. After pointing out that to answer his critic's challenge in full would require a complete treatise on the military art, he began by lamenting the manner in which the various professions had become separated up from one another. The dangers of such a situation were shown by the example of ancient Rome. At first, all men had served in the army, and Rome had prospered, but then society had become corrupted by luxury, and the military profession had become looked upon as the preserve of mercenaries and wrong-doers. Because the professional soldiers lacked the motivation of the citizens' militia that they replaced, Rome had ultimately been overthrown. In the light of this experience later nations had always sought to ensure that their armies were accorded the greatest honour and respect, and that they were properly trained and equipped, thereby ensuring their own prosperity. However, the honour with which the military estate was treated was not simply merited on the grounds of national self-interest, but also on the grounds of admiration: after expatiating at great length upon the qualities and skills that could only be learnt by bearing arms, Aguirre went on to proclaim that 'armies and warfare have been the seminary of the greatest men and the most wonderful virtues'. Furthermore, as 'the character of the military estate is the sum of the social virtues elevated to the highest grade of perfection that the efforts of human policy can attain', it followed that 'if there are societies or nations ... that do not achieve in the particular character of their armies all the circumstances that are so essential to their well being, they should attribute it to their own unthinking ineptitude, their lack of basic principles, and the confusion and stupidity of their ideas'.[120]

In short, Aguirre was not only wholeheartedly in favour of the privileged status of the military estate, but he also refused to accept that it could possibly be worthy of criticism. That such views could be held even by an *ilustrado* is indicative of the extent to which the officer corps' thinking had become distorted by its own immoderate pride. Many officers were sincerely convinced that the safety and prosperity of Spain rested upon their shoulders. Furthermore, they were expected to be ready to bear the harshest privations and even to lay down their lives for their country. Since no other section of the citizenry had to face such demands, it followed that officers, who had after all chosen the military profession of their own free will, must be *españoles escogidos*. As the cream of the nation, they therefore deserved to take precedence over all their fellow citizens. A variety of more-or-less specious arguments was advanced in justification of this position, of which Aguirre's exposition of the connection between military privilege and national well-being is only one example. In addition, it was claimed that in order to maintain his honour an officer had to enjoy a position in society that was commensurate with his status. With amazing cynicism, it was even argued that men would only risk their lives in battle if they could be assured of an adequate reward, including, of course, the esteem of their fellow citizens – or rather a position of supremacy amongst them.[121]

The flaws in such arguments are obvious: for one thing, given the conditions of the Family Compact, few officers ever had to risk death in battle. Yet that did not prevent them from adopting a most insolent and arrogant attitude towards all civilians, who they treated as 'abject beings ... whose sole purpose was to provide for their comfort'.[122] Such behaviour was certain to inflame the state of civil-military relations. Students and soldiers came to blows in the streets over who should have the right of way, whilst local officials excluded army officers from their meetings, refused them the correct honours, obstructed the levying of *bagajes y alojamiento*, and aided the escape of deserters.[123] Several orders were issued enjoining moderation on both sides, but they seem to have had little effect.[124] Harmony could only have been restored if the officer corps was thrown open to the notables, but such an assault on the structure of society would have been far too radical for even the most enlightened monarch or minister. The army therefore continued to be unpopular with the classes who provided the bulk of the administration's personnel. Without their support the régime could not overcome popular opposition to conscription, and thereby to ensure that the army was provided with an adequate supply of manpower. In short, government policy coincided with the widespread anti-militarism provoked by the pretensions of the officer corps in allowing the army to fall into decay.

In terms of its military quality, for all its deficiencies, the Spanish army of the eighteenth century was comparable to most of its European rivals. Contemporary observers were for the most part satisfied that the troops would do their duty. Although it was noted that they were on occasion liable to sudden outbreaks of panic, as well as being cruel to their prisoners, it was generally accepted that they were 'brave and patient of hardships', and that 'wherever their officers lead them, they will follow without flinching'.[125] Nor would it be correct to view the Spanish army as being obsolescent: if it lacked such units as sappers and miners or a permanent artillery train, so did almost every other army in Europe. Even the ignorance, frivolity and arrogance that marred the officer corps was replicated in many other countries. The central problem facing the army was rather the role that it played in Bourbon foreign policy. Thanks to the Family Compact, it was never likely to have to field more than a small expeditionary force of a size that could easily be accommodated by its cumbersome command structure and rudimentary logistical arrangements. Furthermore, it could safely be neglected and allowed to fall below strength whilst Carlos III concentrated on building a powerful navy with which to fight the British. Nor was there any obstacle to giving the army a system of recruitment whose chief aim was to ensure that military service should inflict as little harm as possible on the civilian economy. However, with the outbreak of the French Revolution in 1789, a major European war once more became a possibility. As this was precisely the eventuality for which the Spanish army was least prepared, its inadequacies were now to be revealed with brutal clarity. Indeed, in view of the dramatic developments in warfare unleashed by the French Revolution, they were even to be magnified.

The challenge facing the Spanish army was as much political as it was military, however. In response to the expectations that had been fuelled by the Spanish Enlightenment, Bourbon reformism, and the economic growth of the late eighteenth century, the rising civilian oligarchy of petty *hijosdalgo* and prosperous non-nobles could not but regard the army's privileged status with jealousy and resentment. Nor were their feelings assuaged by the arrogance affected by so many officers. Yet the officer corps was even less ready to meet this hostility than it was to embark upon the Revolutionary Wars. In place of the solidarity that was required to overawe its civilian critics, the military estate was characterised by division and mutual hostility: condemned to a life of poverty and frustration, the subaltern officers resented the predominance of the upper nobility, whilst the line officers were affronted by the privileges enjoyed by the guards. Rather than uniting with their aristocratic fellows in defence of the army's privileges, the increasingly disaffected subaltern officers were likely to ally themselves with the notables against their superiors. In 1788 the army therefore already stood on the brink of catastrophe, for the imposing facade of military power masked tensions which threatened to bring about its downfall. Accentuated by the events of the reign of Carlos IV, in 1808 they were to precipitate a revolution that led not merely to the eclipse of the army, but also to the destruction of the *ancien régime*.

Chapter 1   Notes

1   Louis XIV to Felipe V, 2 September 1705, cit. G. Desdevises du Dézert, 'La societé espagnole au XVIIIème. siécle', *Revue Hispanique*, LXIV, p. 489 (hereafter Desdevises du Dézert, *Société espagnole*).
2   Real Cédula, 4 November 1788, cit. *Extracto puntual de todas las pragmáticas, cédulas, provisiones, circulares, autos acordados y otras providencias publicadas en el reinado del Señor Don Carlos III*, ed. S. Sánchez (Madrid, 1794), I, 302–12 (hereafter Sánchez, *Extracto puntual*); A. Laborde, *A View of Spain* (London, 1809), IV, 496–7; J. F. de

Bourgoing, *A Modern State of Spain* (London, 1808), I, p. 176.
3 *Real Cédula en que S.M. se sirve dar nueva planta a su Consejo Supremo de Guerra*, 16 May 1803, Servicio Histórico Militar, Museo de Literatura (hereafter SHM. ML.) 1803/8.
4 Laborde, *op. cit.*, IV, 455–6; Bourgoing, *op. cit.*, II, p. 65.
5 J. Ramón Alonso, *Historia política del ejército español* (Madrid, 1974), p. 39; J. Vicens Vives (ed.), *Historia de España y América social y económica* (Barcelona, 1979), IV, p. 214.
6 J. Serrano Valdenebro, *Discursos varios del arte de la guerra. Tratan el buen uso de la táctica de tierra con relación y crítica de la batalla de Almansa* (Madrid, 1796), i–ii; A. von Schepeler, *Histoire de la révolution d'Espagne et de Portugal, ainsi que de la guerre qui en résulta* (Liège, 1829), I, lxii.
7 F. Gil Ossorio, 'Morla de artillería', *Revista de Historia Militar*, No. 51, p. 35.
8 H. Swinburne, *Travels through Spain in the Years 1775 and 1776* (Dublin, 1779), p. 268.
9 *Ordenanzas de Su Majestad para el régimen, disciplina, subordinación y servicio de sus ejércitos* (Madrid, 1768), I, i, 2–6; *ibid.*, IV, iii, x, xi, xii (hereafter *Ordenanzas*).
10 Vizconde Dambly, 'Memoria sobre la caballería' (MS), Real Academía de Historia (hereafter RAH.) 2-MS135, No. 5 (hereafter Dambly (MS)); *Ordenanzas*, V, x, xi;
11 Bourgoing, *op. cit.*, II, 76–7; W. Dalrymple, *Travels through Spain and Portugal in 1774* (London, 1777), 43–4; Schepeler, *op. cit.*, I, xlvii.
12 Conde de Clonard, *Historia orgánica de las armas de infantería y caballería españolas* (Madrid, 1851–62), V, 280–83, 307–9, 334–5 (hereafter Clonard, *Historia orgánica*).
13 G. Desdevises du Dézert, *L'Espagne de l'ancien régime* (Paris, 1897–1904), II, p. 247 (hereafter Desdevises du Dézert, *Ancien régime*); Clonard, *Historia orgánica*, V, p. 333 ; J.M. Bueno, *El ejército y la armada en 1808* (Madrid, 1982), 136–9.
14 C. Oman, *A History of the Peninsular War,* (Oxford, 1902–30), I, p. 70.
15 C. Peñalosa y Zuñiga, *Memoria sobre la artillería volante o de a caballo* (Segovia, 1796), 18–20; Bourgoing, *op. cit.*, I, p. 71; R. Salas, *Memorial histórico de la artillería española* (Madrid, 1831), p. 43; Ramón Alonso, *op. cit.*, 52–3; Gil Ossorio, *op. cit.*, 39–42.
16 Bourgoing, op. cit., IV, p. 40; J. Vigón, *Historia de la artillería española* (Madrid, 1947), II, p. 323; Desdevises du Dézert, *Ancien régime*, II, p. 281.
17 Godoy to María Luisa, 15 May 1801, Archivo Histórico Nacional, Sección de Estado (hereafter AHN. Estado), 2821/1;
18 Doyle to Castlereagh, 2 August 1808, Public Record Office, War Office Papers (hereafter PRO. WO.) 1/227, p. 87; Graham to Liverpool, 26 March 1810, PRO. WO.1/247, 85–6; Leith to Castlereagh, 13 September 1808, PRO. WO.1/229, p. 206;

Semanario Patriótico, 25 May 1809, Hemeroteca Municipal de Madrid (hereafter HMM.) AH1-6(195); M. de Godoy, *Memorias de Don Manuel de Godoy* (Madrid, 1836–46), III, p. 110; G. García de la Cuesta, *Manifiesto que presenta a la Europa el Capitán General Don Gregorio García de la Cuesta sobre sus operaciones militares y políticas desde el mes de junio de 1808 hasta el doce de agosto de 1809* (Palma, 1811), p. 35.

19 'Estado militar de España', *Kalendario manual y guía de forasteros en Madrid* (Madrid, 1792), 43–4 (hereafter *Estado Militar*); *Ordenanzas*, II, xvii, 40–6; J. Townsend, *A Journey through Spain and Portugal in the Years 1786 and 1787*, II, p. 278.

20 P. Alvarez, *Espíritu militar o principios teóricos y prácticos del arte de la guerra, acomodados al servicio de los estados mayores generales y divisionarios de los ejércitos nacionales* (Madrid, 1814), 180–2.

21 *Ordenanzas*, II, i, 10, 19; T. González Carvajal, *Del oficio y cargos del Intendente del Ejército en campaña* (Valencia, 1810), 24–31 (hereafter *Intendente del ejército*); there were eight and one half *cuartos* to the *real*, which in 1808 was worth approximately 2¼d (i.e. 100 *reales* were equivalent to £1).

22 González Carvajal, *Intendente del ejército*, 68–9, 79–81.

23 Bourgoing, *op. cit.*, II, p. 110.

24 Townsend, *op. cit.*, I, 409–12; J. Priego López, *Guerra de la Independencia, 1808–14*, (Madrid, 1972–81), I, 115.

25 Swinburne, *op. cit.*, 29–44.

26 *El Espactador Sevillano*, 27 December 1809, p. 343, HMM. AH2-4 (347).

27 *Estado militar*, 1792, p. 41; Bourgoing, *op. cit.*, II, p. 71; Clonard, *Historia orgánica*, VI, 45–6; A. Carner, 'Las tropas suizas al servicio de España', *Revista de Historia Militar*, No. 7, 75–6.

28 W. Dalrymple, *op. cit.*, p. 65.

29 Marqués de Casa Cagigal, 'Prospecto de un plan de ejército suficiente a hacer respetable a España según exigen las actuales circunstancias' (MS), RAH. 2-MS135, No. 6 (hereafter Casa Cagigal (MS)); C. A. Fischer, *A Picture of Madrid*, (London, 1808), p. 63 (hereafter Fischer, *Madrid*); Bourgoing, *op. cit.*, II, p. 72.

30 Godoy to Carlos IV, 26 February 1796, RAH. 2-MS135, No. 7.

31 Conde de Aranda to Carlos III, 21 December 1770, RAH. 2-MS135, No. 1; W. Dalrymple, *op. cit.*, p. 64.

32 Real Cédula, 3 November 1770, cit. Sánchez, *Extracto puntual*, I, 186–214.

33 Reales Cédulas, 22 June 1773 and 13 May 1775, *cit. ibid.*, I, 288, 321–33; Bourgoing, *op. cit.*, II, p. 79; A. Alvarez Valdés, *Memorias del levantamiento de Asturias en 1808* (Oviedo, 1889), p. 38.

34 'Representación de D. Manuel de Binos a Carlos III' (MS), RAH. 2-MS135, No. 2 (hereafter Binos (MS)); Laborde, *op. cit.*, IV, p. 505.

35 Townsend, *op cit*, II, p. 15; W. Dalrymple, *op. cit.*, p. 67.

36 *Ordenanzas*, II, i, 19–22.

37 González Carvajal, *Intendente del Ejército*, 254–8; Swinburne, *op.*

cit., 26, 254.
38 Ordenanzas, II, i, 12–16; Periódico Militar del Estado Mayor General, 13 February 1812, p. 96, Servicio Histórico Militar, Colección Documental del Fraile (hereafter SHM. CDF.) CXVI.
39 Ordenanzas, II., i, 23.
40 Reales Cédulas, 3 November 1770 and 17 March 1773, cit. Sánchez, Extracto puntual, I, 186–214, 256–82.
41 Townsend, op. cit., II, p. 15; Swinburne, op. cit., p. 15; Desdevises du Dézert, Ancien régime, II, 236–7.
42 Real declaración sobre puntos esenciales de la ordenanza de milicias provinciales de España que interin se regla la formal que corresponde a estos cuerpos se debe observar como tal en todos sus partes, 30 May 1767, Biblióteca del Senado (hereafter BS.) 011634 (hereafter Real declaración sobre milicias provinciales).
43 Reales Cédulas, 17 March and 28 November 1773, cit., Sánchez, Extracto puntual, I, 256–82, 313.
44 Reales Cédulas, 22 June 1773 and 13 May 1775, cit. ibid., I, 288, 321–3.
45 J. del Castrillo Villamayor to Carlos III, 25 July 1787, RAH. 2-MS135, No. 3; El Espectador Sevillano, 27 December 1809, p. 343, HMM. AH2-4(347).
46 B. M. de Calzada, Pensamientos militares que da a luz por si fuesen útiles el Teniente Coronel Don Bernardo María de Calzada, Capitán del Regimiento de Dragones de Granada (Madrid, 1814), p. 18.
47 W. Dalrymple, op. cit., p. 64.
48 Real Cédula, 24 November 1770, cit. Sánchez, Extracto Puntual, I, 93–4; Real Cédula, 20 June 1796, cit. Colección de todas las pragmáticas, cédulas, circulares, autos acordados, bandos y otras providencias publicados en el reinado del Señor Don Carlos IV, ed. S. Sánchez (Madrid, 1794), II, 176–7 (hereafter Sánchez, Colección).
49 Clonard, Historia orgánica, VI, 80–1.
50 Ibid., VI, 51–5; B. Pardo de Figueroa, 'Voto del Señor Pardo acerca del plan de ejército y de una constitución militar' (MS), RAH. 2-MS135, No. 16 (hereafter Pardo de Figueroa (MS)).
51 C. A. Fischer, Travels in Spain in 1797 and 1798 (London, 1802), p. 268 (hereafter Fischer, Travels in Spain).
52 Binos (MS), op. cit., RAH. 2-MS135, No. 2; W. Dalrymple, op. cit., p. 371.
53 Laborde, op. cit., IV, p. 505; W. Dalrymple, op. cit., p. 76; Casa Cagigal (MS), op. cit., RAH. 2-MS135, No. 6; Bourgoing, op. cit., II, p. 72.
54 Godoy to Carlos IV, 26 February 1796, RAH. 2-MS135, No. 7; Swinburne, op. cit., p. 25.
55 Clonard, Historia orgánica, V, 505–9; ibid., VI, p. 287.
56 Bourgoing, op. cit., II, p. 69.
57 G. Guillaume, Histoire des gardes wallonnes au service d'Espagne (Brussels, 1858), 189–90.
58 Estado militar, 1792, 8–16.

59 Swinburne, *op. cit.*, p. 28; W. Dalrymple, *op. cit.*, p. 186; Ramón Alonso, *op. cit.*, 58–9.
60 C. Peñalosa y Zuñiga, *El honor militar: causas de su origen, progresos y decadencia, o correspondencia de dos hermanos desde el Ejército de Navarra de S.M.C.*, (Madrid, 1795), 34–5.
61 *Ordenanzas*, II, xviii, 12.
62 *Ibid.*, II, xviii, 13.
63 Laborde, *op. cit.*, IV, p. 506; J. Blanco White, *Letters from Spain* (London, 1825), p. 26.
64 Pardo de Figueroa (MS), *op. cit.*, RAH. 2-MS135, No. 16; Laborde, *op. cit.*, IV, p. 503; F. Fernández Bastarreche, 'El ejército español en el siglo XIX: aspectos sociales y ecónomicos', *Revista de Historia Militar*, No. 50, p. 79.
65 Laborde, *op cit.*, IV, p. 503.
66 'Subinspección de Infantería del Cuarto Ejército: relación de los capitanes que no han sido promovidos a jefes' (MS), 1 February 1813, University of Southampton, Wellington Papers (hereafter US. WP.) 1/382, f. 2.
67 *Ordenanzas*, II, xviii, 3; *Instrucción para los pretendientes a plaza en el Real Colegio Militar de Caballeros Cadetes del Real Cuerpo de Artillería establecido en la ciudad de Segovia*, 12 July 1800, SHM. ML.1800/7; *Real declaración sobre milicias provinciales*, 104–5.
68 Lady Holland, *The Spanish Journal of Elizabeth, Lady Holland* (London, 1910), p. 167.
69 A. Alcalá Galiano, *Memorias* (Madrid, 1886), I, 154–5; A. Carrasco y Saiz, *Iconobiografía del generalato español* (Madrid, 1901), p. 215; F. Moya y Jiménez and C. Rey Joly, *El ejército y la marina en las Cortes de Cádiz* (Cádiz, 1913), 414, 601–2.
70 *Estado militar*, 1792, 8–17, 66–87; G. Anes Alvarez, *El antiguo régimen: los Borbones* (Madrid, 1975), p. 48.
71 Vicens Vives, *op. cit.*, IV, p. 214; Clonard, *Historia orgánica*, V, 294–7; *ibid.*, VI, 56–7.
72 Vicens Vives, *op. cit*, IV, p. 34.
73 Swinburne, *op. cit.*, p. 27.
74 'Plan sobre organización de dos batallones por regimiento y sobre sueldos' (MS), RAH. 2-MS135, No. 9.
75 J. Childs, *Armies and Warfare in Europe 1648–1789* (Manchester, 1982), p. 79; A. Corvisier, *Armies and societies in Europe 1484–1789* (London, 1979), 64–6.
76 Bourgoing, *op. cit.*, I, p. 117.
77 *Ordenanzas*, II, xxvi, 7; Laborde, *op. cit.*, V, p. 461.
78 Fischer, *Madrid*, p. 64; C. Pardo González, *Don Manuel Godoy y Alvarez de Faría, Príncipe de la Paz*, (Madrid, 1911), p. 10.
79 R. W. Southey, *Letters written during a Journey in Spain and a Short Residence in Portugal* (London, 1808), I, p. 211 (hereafter Southey, *Letters*); W. Dalrymple, *op. cit.*, 43–4.
80 W. Dalrymple, *op. cit.*, p. 45.
81 J. Ordovas, 'Estado del ejército y armada de S.M.C., año de 1807'

(MS), SHM. ML.1807/8 (hereafter Ordovas (MS)); Fischer, *Madrid*, p. 64; Laborde, *op. cit.*, IV, p. 459; Conde de Clonard, *Memorias para la historia de las tropas de la casa real de España* (Madrid, 1828), p. 163 (hereafter Clonard, *Memorias*).
82 A. Muriel, *Historia de Carlos IV*, ed. C. Seco Serrano (Madrid, 1959), I, p. 94; E. D'Auvergne, *Godoy, the Queen's Favourite* (London, 1912), p. 20.
83 W. Dalrymple, *op. cit.*, 32, 64–5.
84 Pardo González, *op. cit.*, 9–10.
85 J. Cadalso, *Obras inéditas de Don José Cadalso*, ed. R. Fouché Delbosc (Madrid, 1894), p. 80 (hereafter Cadalso, *Obras inéditas*).
86 Schepeler, *op. cit.*, I, p. 82; W. Dalrymple, *op. cit.*, p. 64.
87 Southey, *Letters*, I, p. 26; Bourgoing, *op. cit.*, I, p. 376; *ibid.*, II, p. 65; Laborde, *op. cit.*, IV, 495–7.
88 Blanco White, *op. cit.*, p. 48; Fischer, *Travels in Spain*, 171–3.
89 Townsend, *op. cit.*, I, p. 385.
90 Laborde, *op. cit.*, IV, p. 504; Bourgoing, *op. cit.*, I, p. 154.
91 R. Herr, *The Eighteenth Century Revolution in Spain* (Princeton, 1958), 102–10; A. Domínguez Ortiz, *Sociedad y estado en el siglo XVIII español* (Barcelona, 1976), 413–17.
92 *Ordenanzas*, II, xviii, 5–6; Laborde, *op. cit.*, IV, p. 503.
93 F. Guervos to his parents, 4 May 1814, RAH. 11–5–7:9003, No. 50.
94 Laborde, *op. cit.*, IV, p. 503; *Ordenanzas*, II, xxvii, 1–7; W. Dalrymple, *op. cit.*, p. 65; Blanco White, *op. cit.*, p. 25
95 Bourgoing, *op. cit.*, II, p. 75.
96 Moya y Jiménez, *op. cit.*, 71, 280; *Ordenanzas*, II, xxx, 1–3; Bourgoing, *op. cit.*, II, p. 75; Laborde, *op. cit.*, IV, p. 504.
97 Laborde, *op. cit.*, IV, 98–9, 102–3; W. Dalrymple, *op. cit.*, 64–5; Moya y Jiménez, *op. cit.*, 279–80.
98 Laborde, *op. cit.*, IV, p. 505.
99 Moya y Jiménez, *op. cit.*, 27–8.
100 Bourgoing, *op. cit.*, I, 71, 307; W. Dalrymple, *op. cit.*, 57–8.
101 Desdevises du Dézert, *Ancien régime*, II, p. 225.
102 *Ordenanzas*, II, xviii; *Periódico Militar del Estado Mayor General*, 6 February 1812, p. 80, SHM. CDF.CXVI.
103 *Ordenanzas*, II, xvii, 1–26; J. Cadalso, 'El buen militar a la vióleta', *Obras de Don José Cadalso* (Madrid, 1818), 265–8 (hereafter Cadalso, *El buen militar*); J. Sánchez Cisneros, *Ideas sueltas sobre la ciencia militar* (Valencia, 1814), 12–14.
104 Alcalá Galiano, *op. cit.*, I, 60–71; Cadalso, *El buen militar*, 265–8; Clonard, *Historia orgánica*, V, 309–10.
105 Schepeler, *op. cit.*, I, p. 16.
106 Alcalá Galiano, *op. cit.*, I, 156–7.
107 Swinburne, *op. cit.*, p. 82.
108 Alcalá Galiano, *op. cit.*, I, p. 158; Cadalso, *El buen militar*, 264–6.
109 Casa Cagigal (MS), *op. cit.*, RAH. 2-MS135, No. 6.
110 Anes, *Antiguo régimen*, 314–5.
111 Real Cédula, 4 November 1788, cit. Sánchez, *Extracto puntual*, I,

301–2.
112 Swinburne, *op. cit.*, 16–19; Bourgoing, *op. cit.*, III, 146–51; W. Jacob, *Travels in the South of Spain* (London, 1811), p. 26; Conde de Toreno, *Historia del levantamiento, guerra y revolución de España* (Madrid, 1836), I, p. 24.
113 Bourgoing, *op. cit.*, III, p. 76.
114 Anes, *Antiguo régimen*, 316–17.
115 Laborde, *op. cit.*, IV, 495–7; Reales Cédulas, 23 April 1789 and 8 March 1793, *cit.* Sánchez, *Colección*, I, 27, 345–7.
116 Pragmática, 17 April 1777, *cit.* Sánchez, *Extracto puntual*, I, p. 315; Townsend, *op. cit.*, II, 186–9; Clonard, *Historia orgánica*, V, p. 310.
117 Godoy to María Luisa, 26 September 1804, AHN. Estado, 2821/5; Moya y Jiménez, *op. cit.*, 82, 456.
118 L. Rodríguez, 'The riots of 1766 in Madrid', *European Studies Review*, III, No. 3 (1973), 223–42.
119 M. de Aguirre, *Cartas y discursos del militar ingenuo al Correo de los Ciegos de Madrid*, ed. A. Elorza (San Sebastián, 1973), 287–8.
120 *Ibid.*, 289–95.
121 *El ejército español destruido por las leyes o manifestación de los efectos que debe producir el decreto que separa de los gobiernos militares la intervención en lo político, y de las Capitanias Generales la presidencia de las Audiencias, dejando al ejército aislado en sus empleos interiores* (Alicante, 1813), 7, 9–10, 23; Calzada, *op. cit.*, 89–91; T. Finestra, *Exposición que hace un oficial subalterno a sus compañeros de armas sobre la decadencia de los ejércitos españoles* (Cádiz, 1813), 12–13.
122 Alcalá Galiano, *op. cit.*, I, p. 156; Cadalso, *El buen militar*, 263–4.
123 Real Cédula, 30 May 1775, *cit.* Sánchez, *Extracto puntual*, I, p. 334; Circular, 4 August 1792, *cit.* Sánchez, *Colección*, I, p. 300; Circulares, 14 March 1795 and 18 February 1796, *cit. ibid.*, II, 111, 164–5; W. Dalrymple, *op. cit.*, p. 76.
124 Reales Cédulas, 25 February 1772 and 1 August 1784, *cit.* Sánchez, *Extracto puntual*, I, 246, 334; W. Dalrymple, *op. cit.*, p. 76.
125 Bourgoing, *op. cit.*, IV, 267–8; Swinburne, *op. cit.*, 391–2; Fischer, *Travels in Spain*, p. 266.

Chapter 2

The era of Godoy, 1792–1808

The history of the Spanish army during the reign of King Carlos IV (1788–1808) was dominated by the royal favourite, Manuel de Godoy. An obscure scion of the Extremaduran petty nobility, Godoy had first come to Madrid in 1787 as a private soldier in the Guardias de Corps. Once he was there, his handsome bearing soon brought him to the attention of the Queen, María Luisa, and it was not long before he had assumed the role of her official *cortejo*. His rise thereafter was spectacular. Doted upon by both the King and Queen, by 1792 Godoy held the rank of Captain General of the Army and was a grandee of the first class with the title of Duque de la Alcudía. In November of that year he was appointed to be Secretary of State, whereafter, except for a brief interlude in the period 1798–1800, he was the virtual dictator of Spain until his overthrow in the Motín de Aranjuez of March 1808. History has not been kind to Godoy, however, for he became a classic scapegoat for all the ills that beset Spain after 1808. Twentieth century historians have done something to rescue his reputation by pointing to the manner in which he sought to continue the enlightened policies favoured by Carlos III, but as far as military affairs are concerned the common view is still that propounded by the Conde de Toreno – that Godoy reduced the army to a mere plaything and allowed it to slide into complete decrepitude.[1]

It would be absurd to pretend that Godoy was perfect, but he was by no means solely the frivolous incompetent of legend. Pitchforked into a position of power that was far beyond his talents, his response to the crisis in Spain's international position engendered by the French Revolution displayed a degree of realism and intelligence for which he has never been given credit. When Godoy came to power in November 1792, Spanish policy was essentially to conciliate the revolutionary régime in the hope of saving both the hapless French royal family and the Family Compact of 1761. The new Secretary of State continued these efforts, but the French rejected his advances, and not only sent Louis XVI and Marie Antoinette to the guillotine, but declared war on Spain on 7 March 1793. It was a conflict from which she was far from ready despite the attempts that had been made since 1791 to increase the size of the army. A depot battalion was added to every line infantry regiment in an attempt to provide them with a steady flow of recruits, and the army's order of battle had been strengthened by the addition of the Málaga line infantry and Gerona and Tarragona light infantry regiments. The light regiments and the cavalry also received an increase in their personnel.[2] The shortage of manpower nevertheless remained as acute as ever: with most infantry regiments below half strength, Spain could deploy only 55,000 men on the Pyrenean front.[3] To some extent the shortfall was made up by the volunteers who came forward in large numbers in response to the Church's presentation of the war as a crusade against the enemies of religion. The regular army was also supplemented by a number of irregular units, such as the traditional *somatenes* and *miqueletes* of Catalonia. Entire bands of smugglers from the Sierra Morena were even formed into 'free corps' on the German model, albeit with limited success as they showed more interest in pillaging the civilian population than in harassing the enemy.[4] The wave of enthusiasm was nevertheless insufficient to overcome the general dislike of military service: the call for volunteers had to be sweetened by the offer of extremely advantageous terms of service, and even then a *sorteo* had to be imposed in February 1793, to the accompaniment of the wholesale impressment of *vagos*.[5]

Such enthusiasm as there was was soon dissipated by the course of the war, whose strategy was controlled by a council of generals sitting in Madrid. It was decided that the Spaniards should adopt a defensive stance in the western Pyrenees, whilst a large army under General Antonio Ricardos struck into the French province of Roussillon. Yet so many men were tied down in the static defence of the western frontier that Ricardos was left with insufficient troops. Although he was able to brush aside the polyglot levies who faced his veteran troops without difficulty, the Spanish general was also hampered by a want of heavy artillery: as usual, the Spaniards had found it all but impossible to amass the draught animals that they needed to bring forward their siege guns. As a result, the advance petered out under the walls of Perpignan, and Ricardos went into winter quarters. Although the Spaniards ended the campaign by winning two minor battles at Trouillas and Boulou, the operations of 1793 represented a squandered opportunity. With France beset by foreign invasion and internal revolt, she had been wide open to a Spanish attack, but by the end of 1793 the great crisis was over. The invaders been driven back, the counter-revolutionaries crushed, and the French armies reinforced by the *levée en masse*.

Strengthened by the arrival of large numbers of fresh troops, in April 1794 the French launched a counter offensive which soon bundled the outnumbered Spaniards back over the frontier. This initial success was followed up by fresh attacks, which by the end of the year had over-run the province of Guipúzcoa and the important fortress of Figueras. Meanwhile, the Spanish army continued to be dogged by a want of recruits. After a call made in March 1794 for 40,000 fresh volunteers had failed, Godoy therefore had no choice but to impose a second *sorteo* in 1795.[6] The use of conscription was very much a last resort, for the populace was increasingly war weary. Revolutionary propaganda was beginning to make some headway, whilst attempts to draw more heavily on Catalan and Valencian manpower had met with fierce popular opposition.[7] The *sorteo* was therefore palliated by limiting the number of men taken in any one area to one in every fifty inhabitants and promising that the conscripts would only serve for the duration of the war.[8] Other sources of manpower were also raided to reduce the need for conscription to a minimum: generous amnesties were offered to deserters who would re-enlist, two new Swiss regiments were formed, bringing the total in the army up to six, and several units of French *emigrés* were incorporated into the army as the Borbón line infantry regiment.[9]

Godoy's achievements were not unimpressive in view of the war's growing unpopularity. Sufficient men were raised to form no fewer than ten new Spanish regiments. The light infantry received the First and Second Regiments of Barcelona, the Second Regiment of Voluntarios de Aragón, the Cazadores de Barbastro, and the Voluntarios de Valencia. The new line infantry regiments were those of Jaén, Ordenes Militares, Voluntarios de Castilla, Voluntarios del Estado, and Voluntarios de la Corona. Finally, the cavalry gained the Husares de María Luisa and the Husares Españoles. Nor was this accession of strength made only on paper, for the censuses of 1787 and 1797 show that the number of soldiers in Spain rose in the intervening decade from 77,884 to 149,340.[10] Yet it was obvious that the army's ramshackle logistical system could not support such an increase in the size of the armed forces, or at least to maintain them in the rugged border regions in which the war was fought, for the troops were all too often ragged, shoeless and half-starved. The British were later to claim that they could not have kept the field in Catalonia at all but for the supplies convoyed for them by the Royal Navy.[11] As the war dragged on into 1795, it became clear that peace was rapidly becoming a necessity. Spain's finances were exhausted, a republican conspiracy had been uncovered in Madrid, the Basque provinces and Catalonia were showing disturbing signs of separatism, and the French armies were once again on the advance. On 22 July 1796 Godoy therefore made peace with France by means of the Treaty of Basle. All of Spain rejoiced, including the King and Queen, who rewarded Godoy with the title of Príncipe de la Paz. The title was not undeserved: not only was peace most welcome, but Spain's losses were restricted to the island of Santo Domingo.

Although he had succeeded in extricating Spain from a difficult position at a very moderate cost, Godoy still faced the problem of the attitude which Spain should adopt towards Britain and France in the light of the collapse of the Family Compact. His response was to revert to the classic Bourbon position of the eighteenth century. With Britain and France still at war with one another, the ideal position for Spain would have been one of armed neutrality. However, as it was clear that neither of the two belligerents could be relied upon to respect the neutrality of any country, let alone one that was situated so close to the seat of the conflict, Godoy reasoned that Spain could only remain neutral if she possessed 'forces that are superior, or at least equal, to those which can be deployed against [her] by the warring powers'; otherwise her neutrality would be 'no more than an illusion, a chimera to excite laughter and scorn'.[12] As Spain did not possess such forces, she would clearly be forced to choose between one or other of the two belligerents. In Godoy's eyes, the logical choice was France. If the Spanish army had just shown itself to be unable to contain the French on land, Spain still had the powerful navy bequeathed to her by Carlos III; added to the French fleet, it might yet bring victory in a war against Great Britain. At the same time, 'perfidious Albion' had proved herself to be a most unreliable ally, harassing Spanish trade and stirring up revolution in the colonies whilst yet denying Spain adequate assistance in the campaign against France.[13]

Encouraged by the growing moderation that had become apparent in France with the advent of the Directory and the ever more threatening attitude adopted by the British government, it was but a short step to the resurrection of the Family Compact by means of the Treaty of San Ildefonso of 18 August 1796. This offensive and defensive alliance against Great Britain has been castigated as 'the origin of the ruin and desolation of Spain'.[14] With the benefit of hindsight, it is obvious that, for all its promises of mutual support, in reality the treaty threatened ultimately to reduce Spain to the status of a mere satellite. Yet Godoy was not as foolish as he has been portrayed: as he wrote to María Luisa in 1801, he was only too well aware that 'France can be trusted with nothing, nor ... will the French ever be allies of anything other than their own interests'.[15] Hence the strenuous efforts that he made to limit the obligations that Spain was placed under by the alliance. As far as he was concerned, in fact, the Treaty of San Ildefonso was a mere stratagem that would allow Spain to buy the time necessary to achieve the armed neutrality that was counselled by her interests.

Despite the incontestably disastrous results of this foreign policy, none of Godoy's numerous critics have been able to suggest an alternative course of action. Moreover, the reformism that characterised his rule suggests that Godoy was perfectly serious in his desire to escape the French, even if the movement was ultimately unsuccessful. Following the precedent already established by Carlos III, he made a serious attempt to promote agriculture, trade, industry and education, to encourage the arts and sciences, and to curb the power of the Church. Above all, however, Godoy was determined to achieve the reform of the army: even though he probably did not realise the full extent of the changes in warfare that had been wrought by the French Revolution, he certainly regarded military reform as essential if Spain was to have any chance of retaining her political independence. Together with a number of progressive officers, including Tomás de Morla, Benito Pardo de Figueroa and the Marqués de Casa Cagigal, he mapped out a programme of reform which he laid before Carlos IV in a long manifesto dated 26 February 1796. Its main elements were that the army should be given an adequate system of recruitment, that the columnar tactics used by the French with such success should be introduced, that training and discipline be improved through the establishment of 'camps of instruction' and new military academies, that the army be pruned of corps such as the Royal Guards and provincial militia whose dubious military value was far outweighed by their cost, and finally that significant changes be effected in the supply system, the officer corps, the cavalry, the artillery and the engineers. To achieve these ends, Godoy urged the King to establish a special commission charged with the task of producing a specific plan of action.[16]

Still pleased with his favourite for ending the war, on 16 April 1796 Carlos IV duly appointed twenty-three senior generals and bureaucrats to be members of the Junta de Constitución y Ordenanzas del Ejército (more commonly known as the Junta de Generales y Ministros). Their task was to examine the size, composition, organisation, recruitment, training, tactics, provisioning, maintenance, privileges, and rewards of the army, the role of the provincial militia, the condition of Spain's fortifications, armaments and munitions works, and, in short, 'all matters concerning war'.[17] The breadth of this purview seemed to presage the sort of root and branch reform of the military estate that was so desperately needed, but the chance was to be lost, thanks very largely to the controversy that was engendered by the perennial problem of manpower.

The very size of the forces that the French had shown themselves able to deploy made a solution to this problem a matter of the first importance, for it was clear that the army would not only have to be brought up to strength but also increased in numbers. Added emphasis was given to the question by the manpower shortage that was revealed in the immediate aftermath of the war. Most of the soldiers who had volunteered during the war had to be released in 1795 as they had only enlisted for the duration of hostilities. Godoy reported that 24,000 men had been killed in the course of the fighting and that at least as many had deserted. There were no means to replace these losses nor even to fill the gap that would soon be left by the release of the wartime *quintas*.[18] As experience had shown that there were never sufficient volunteers to keep the army up to strength, the Junta de Generales y Ministros was charged with the design of a new system of conscription that would produce the requisite supply of manpower but at the same time cause 'the least possible prejudice' to agriculture, industry and the population as a whole.[19] Had they been able to do so, the reformers would have preferred to forgo the use of conscription altogether because of the drain which it imposed on the national economy. Godoy in particular always demonstrated considerable awareness of the influence which military policy could have on both agriculture and manufactures. In 1795, for example, he had flirted with the idea of abolishing the system of exemptions, only to abandon it for fear of the damage that would thus have been caused to the 'productive' classes of the population.[20] In February 1796, he had told the King that the size of the army had to be governed by the proportion of the budget and the population that could be mobilised in its service without prejudice to the navy, the merchant marine, and 'industry and agriculture, the principal nerve of our strength and wealth'.[21] Similarly, after the War of the Oranges had been brought to a close in 1801, he showed himself to be most anxious to demobilise the provincial militia and to restore the army's carts and mules to their original owners in the shortest possible time.[22] So strong was the reformers' dislike of conscription that they even rejected the *sorteo*, which was condemned on the grounds that it 'makes [military] service odious and leads to the depopulation of entire provinces'.[23] They also expressed much interest in plans that would have obviated the need for conscription altogether, such as the establishment of military orphanages from which foundlings could be drafted into the army, and improvements in the conditions of the rank and file designed to encourage voluntary enlistment and discourage desertion.[24]

Forced to turn to conscription despite themselves, the reformers immediately demonstrated their refusal to recognise the realities of the new warfare by rejecting the idea of universal conscription. Unable to accept the economic and political consequences of organising an army that was large enough to allow Spain to hold her own against the massive forces that could now be deployed by France, they cited a long series of historical precedents to demonstrate the military superiority of a regular army.[25] Rather than transforming Spain into a nation-in-arms, the reformers instead sought to reform her on the model of Frederician Prussia, to which their attention had been drawn by a visit to that country in 1787 on the part of Tomás de Morla. Prussia had been divided into a series of cantons, each of which was assigned the task of supplying a specific regiment with an annual quota of recruits. In order to reduce the burden on the economy to the greatest degree possible, after receiving their basic training the conscripts only served with their units for two months of each year, for the rest of the time being dismissed to their homes. In accordance with this model, it was proposed that the Spanish army should be divided into two halves, the *ejército permanente* and the *ejército de campaña*. The former was to be composed of all the foreign troops, the third battalions of the line infantry regiments, the light infantry, the cavalry, and the artillery. Recruited from a mixture of foreigners, *levas* and volunteers, these troops would be permanently under arms and would perform all the duties required of a standing army in peacetime. In contrast, the *ejército de campaña*, which was to be composed of the first and second battalions of the Spanish line infantry regiments, would consist of conscripts who would be raised and trained according to a copy of the Prussian system.

Manifold advantages were claimed for this plan. The financial savings it entailed would enable Spain to maintain a much larger army. The agricultural labour force would not be denuded. The troops would be healthier in mind and body because they would be spared the corrupting and slothful monotony of barrack life. The division of Spain into cantons would facilitate the organisation of a system of permanent divisions, just as the annual 'camps of instruction' which the conscripts would have to attend would provide an opportunity for the introduction of the tactical innovations of the Revolutionary Wars. Hostility to conscription would be reduced because the conscripts could rely on serving in their home districts in the company of their friends and neighbours. They would only be away from their homes for a very short space of time, whilst they would no longer have to serve with the 'scum of the earth' who had hitherto constituted the bulk of the rank and file. Because of the reduced effect on the economy, the call-up could be made more equitable as it would be possible to reduce the number of exemptions. Reducing the unpopularity of the *sorteo* would allow the government to impose it with greater frequency, thereby unleashing a further chain of advantages. An annual *sorteo* would allow a reduction in the number of men taken in each ballot. The authorities charged with its imposition would become more familiar with their duties, and would in consequence be less likely to commit the abuses that had helped make the *sorteo* so unpopular in the past. The new-found ability to rely upon this measure for the recruitment of the army would also have a favourable effect upon its quality: in future, the bulk of the soldiery would be drawn from the peasantry, the class which it was conventional to regard as that which was most imbued with the martial virtues. One last advantage of the new scheme concerned the provincial militia. Many of the reformers had expressed grave doubts as to the value of this force, and their plan offered the opportunity of abolishing it altogether since its duties could now be carried out by the *ejército permanente*. In this manner, both the cost of the armed forces and the burden of conscription would be reduced still further.[26]

Predictably enough, the reformers' enthusiastic support for the new scheme was not shared by the more conservative members of the commission, or by those whose special interests were threatened by the disappearance of such units as the provincial militia. Some of the arguments that were advanced against the scheme were so specious as to suggest an absolute predisposition against any reform whatsoever, but the reformers' ideas were nevertheless marred by serious flaws. Not only could it justifiably be argued that the training received by the *ejército permanente* would be less than adequate, but previous experiments with the release of conscripts had been a complete failure as the men had simply deserted *en masse*.[27] As far as the conservatives were concerned, the solution was to disband the third battalions of the infantry regiments, which they had always regarded as being decidedly new-fangled, and to draft their members into the rest of the army. Left intact, the provincial militia could then be used as a trained reserve.[28]

The reformers' plans were therefore rejected, but not before Carlos IV had become thoroughly alarmed. Terrified of revolution and surrounded by aristocratic courtiers who were all too anxious to denounce the favourite, the King allowed himself to be persuaded that Godoy's plans constuted a dangerous threat to the stability of the régime. On 7 July 1796 he accordingly ordered the commission to suspend its sittings, and two months later dissolved it altogether.[29] Thus was lost Spain's best opportunity for a comprehensive reform of the military estate, but, for all that reform was now certain to be piecemeal, Godoy attempted to continue with his plans. Packing the administration of the army with his supporters, including several members of his own family, he sought to tackle the problem of recruitment with the tools that were already to hand. Fresh sources of foreign recruits were found in the large numbers of prisoners who had been captured by the French in the Italian campaign of 1796, as well as in deserters from the four *emigré* regiments in the Portuguese service. Indeed, so many of the former were sold by their captors to the Spaniards that one third of the rank and file of some regiments were said to be made up of Austrians.[30]

As these reinforcements could be little more than a palliative, Godoy seized upon a suggestion originally put forward by his conservative opponents for the army to be kept up to strength by drafts from the provincial militia rather than by conscription.[31] If this plan was to work, it was essential that conscription for the militia should be extended to the foral regions. The favourite had always stated this to be one of his objectives, and had already attempted to make more use of their manpower by increasing the number of light infantry regiments traditionally recruited from them. As the war of 1793–95 had produced plans for a Valencian homeguard, it was logical that that province should be chosen for the formation of six new provincial regiments of provincial militia in 1798.[32] In addition, Godoy sought to introduce many of the other reforms that had been lost by the collapse of the commission of 1796. 'Camps of instruction' were established at Cáceres, Algeciras and San Roque, where Pardo de Figueroa and Casa Cagigal commenced the introduction of French tactics.[33] At the same time a topographical bureau was added to the corps of engineers, and experiments were carried out with horse artillery batteries and pontoon bridge companies.[34]

Yet for all the importance placed by Godoy upon military reform, all this activity amounted to little more than tinkering with details. The fundamental problems facing the army – the establishment of an adequate system of recruitment and the logistical infrastructure necessary to support large scale military operations – were not addressed. Writing in 1798, the Marqués de Casa Cagigal could therefore complain, 'At present our army is a weak skeleton, incapable of taking the field should this become necessary, small in numbers, lacking in training, and unprovided with everything that is necessary for its operations.'[35] Given time Godoy might have been more successful, notwithstanding the immense economic difficulties that had been occasioned by the Spanish involvement in the Revolutionary Wars, but in March 1798 he was forced temporarily to retire from public life. Always regarded as an upstart who owed his position solely to his prowess in the Queen's bedchamber, Godoy stood little chance of obtaining the support of the most respected figures of Spanish society, such as the famous *ilustrado*, Gaspar Melchor de Jovellanos. The favourite's standing in the political nation was also severely damaged by the shortcomings of his financial policy. In order to finance Spain's rearmament, the government had had recourse to the wholesale issue of government bonds. The British naval blockade imposed after 1796 cut off the colonial revenue that was the sole guarantor of these *vales reales*. Inflation therefore soared and the government's credit collapsed, leaving Godoy with no option but to attempt to finance his activities by imposing a series of new taxes on the wealthier classes of Spanish society, from which even the Church was not exempt.[36]

The growing isolation experienced by Godoy left him extremely vulnerable to the intrigues of his many enemies in the Spanish court. Led by a leading official of the Supreme Council of War, José Antonio Caballero, the growing anti-Godoyist clique sought to persuade the paranoid Carlos IV that all reform was unwise in an age of revolution. Meanwhile, the King was also coming under pressure from the French Directory to renounce his favourite, for Godoy had persistently opposed every French attempt to draw Spain deeper into the war. In particular, he had refused to agree to an invasion of Portugal (which officially remained at war with France until August 1797), and to send a Spanish fleet to take part in a descent on Great Britain. By early 1798 Franco–Spanish relations were close to breaking point. Rather than risk a rupture with the Republic, on 28 March Godoy resigned from his post as Secretary of State.[37] There immediately followed a purge of his supporters: accused of being 'dangerous innovators of sinister intent', they were replaced by generals such as Gonzalo O'Farrill and Antonio Cornel, who were later to prove themselves to be among the favourite's most bitter enemies.[38]

For all the criticism that its members had heaped upon Godoy, the new government proved even less capable of meeting Spain's problems. Whilst pursuing precisely the same foreign and domestic policies that had marked the régime of Godoy, they yet neglected the well-being of the army. Meanwhile, the Queen was now showering her favours upon a pale substitute for the ousted Manuel in the figure of another young guardsman named Mallo.[39] So serious did the situation in the army become that some officers were reduced to begging for alms in the street.[40] The extent of the problem was only revealed when Spain went to war against Portugal in 1801 thanks to the growing pressure that was being exerted by Napoleon to eliminate British influence in that country: several Spanish generals refused to accept the command on the grounds that the army was not in a fit state to take the field even against the weak opposition likely to be mounted by the Portuguese.[41] Their refusal cleared the way for Godoy's rehabilitation. With his interest reawakened in military affairs, Carlos IV appointed the favourite to command the 60,000 men that had been mobilised against Portugal. There followed the brief War of the Oranges (so-called because Godoy sent back to the Queen a branch of an orange tree plucked under fire at Elvas as a trophy). After a number of minor sieges and skirmishes, the Portuguese capitulated after only three weeks. Delighted with Godoy's achievements, and alerted to the problems of the army by the furious complaints the favourite had dispatched to him, Carlos IV rewarded him with the unprecedented rank of Generalísimo, and ordered him to undertake a comprehensive reform of the military estate.[42]

It seemed that Godoy now had *carte blanche* for his programme of reform, but he almost immediately ran into fresh difficulties. In October 1800 new regulations had been issued for the *sorteo*, which had sought to make this more effective and equitable by reducing the number of exemptions, ending the purchase of substitutes, and officially extending conscription to the foral provinces.[43] The abolition of their privileges in this respect had been already been presaged by the establishment of six regiments of provincial militia in Valencia in 1798. Amongst the propertied classes this measure had been relatively popular as commissions in the militia, which were in the gift of the Ayuntamientos of the towns from which its regiments were drawn, brought considerable social prestige as well as access to the coveted *fuero militar* without at the same time incurring the hardships of active service.[44] However, the enthusiasm of the notables was not shared by the general public, whose determination to defend what little remained of the Valencian *fuero* after a century of Bourbon centralisation was reinforced by economic distress and the same virulent opposition to military service that marked every other section of the Spanish people. In September 1801 the growing unrest burst into open rebellion.[45] Fearing that the revolt would spread to Aragón and Catalonia, Godoy acted quickly 'to contain the evil and punish the insurgents', dispatching troops to Valencia under the command of the Marqués de la Romana.[46] When local magistrates subsequently complained that the repression was being conducted with unnecessary savagery and demanded the arrest of troops who had fired on civilians, Godoy tartly replied, 'Justice demands the punishment of the malcontents, and it is against them and not the troops that charges should be brought.'[47] Order was duly restored, but it was nevertheless clear that the attempt to extend the militia system to Valencia was extremely impolitic. The offending regiments were therefore disbanded on the face-saving pretext that the exempt provinces already provided their quota of troops through recruitment to the existing light infantry regiments.[48]

Despite this setback to his plans, in July 1802 Godoy issued new regulations for the provincial militia. This force was now to consist of forty-three regiments, each consisting of one battalion with one grenadier and four fusilier companies. However, the grenadiers were permanently drawn off to serve in four élite regiments, with two battalions apiece.[49] The regulations also provided for the militia to be used as a source of manpower for the army, and in 1804 Godoy once more sought to extend it to the exempt provinces, this time choosing Vizcaya as his target. Another severe outbreak of rioting forced the favourite to abandon the project, but in 1806 he revived the issue yet again, proposing that 30,000 militia should be raised from the exempt provinces. In practice, however, the scheme was dead. Even where the militiamen had been drafted into the regular army, as in the lands of the Crown of Castile, all that had been achieved was to make the militia ballot as hated as the *sorteo*. As for the ex-militiamen themselves, they were despised by the regular soldiers, who referred to them scathingly as 'the innocents'.[50]

For all Godoy's efforts, the army was consequently forced to rely upon its traditional sources of recruitment, to which recourse continued to be had whilst the new measures were under consideration: for example, in 1805 a general *leva* of *vagos* was carried out in Madrid.[51] Other than this, the best that Godoy could achieve was to introduce new regulations for the line infantry that confirmed the existence of depot battalions in each regiment. Each of the thirty five Spanish and four foreign line regiments was now to consist of two field and one depot battalions. The first battalion was to have two grenadier and two fusilier companies, and the other two four fusilier companies.[52] However, useful though the depot battalions undoubtedly were, they could not act as a substitute for new recruits. Reliance on the traditional sources of recruitment merely reinforced civilian hostility to military service, and thereby discouraged enlistment. As desertion also continued to be as high as ever, in 1808 Spain could muster only 46,402 line infantrymen out of a theoretical establishment of 87,984.[53]

Godoy proved equally unsuccessful in his attempt to improve the quality of the army. For example, the favourite had hoped to raise the standards of the officer corps through the establishment of a network of military academies. Although his support for this measure had been one of the factors that had been instrumental in his temporary fall from grace in 1798, he had nevertheless continued to press it upon the King and Queen.[54] Following his appointment as Generalísimo, Godoy was enabled to open general military academies at Alcalá de Henares, Valladolid and Granada. Access was still largely limited to the nobility (commoners were only admitted if their fathers had attained the almost unheard of rank of lieutenant colonel), but some attempt was made to cater for the petty *hidalguía*: one hundred places at each school were subsidised and reserved for the sons of deceased *hijodalgo* officers and officials.[55] The value of these institutions was reduced by their small size – only 200 places apiece – and their excessively theoretical curriculum. In any case, in 1805 financial difficulties forced their amalgamation into a single college at Zamora. The new institution had only sixty places, and even then it only catered for serving officers who were seconded to it from their regiments.[56] With the opportunities for their instruction reduced still further by the refusal of Carlos IV to permit the annual 'camps of instruction', the bulk of the officer corps remained as ill-educated as ever. In the absence of such diversions, military life continued in its usual dreary and monotonous fashion. Many officers were too burdened with paperwork to be able to carry out their other duties; significantly, the reformers had proposed an increase in the staff of each regiment to relieve the pressure of administration.[57] Meanwhile, discipline and morale all remained at a low ebb. The richer officers continued to be foppish and extravagant, the latest fashion being to sport fancy sabres and magnificent whiskers, but the events of 1808 suggest that such martial posturing was not accompanied by a corresponding sense of duty: not only were the French able to seize many of the Spanish border fortresses through the culpable negligence of their garrisons, but out of a total of 4,511 line infantry and militia officers, only 2,751 were actually present with their regiments when the French struck.[58]

The reform of the Spanish army's tactical system had been another of Godoy's priorities, especially with regard to the introduction of the columns of attack used by the French infantry. This had been one of the chief purposes of the 'camps of instruction' that had been established after 1796. Following the restoration of the favourite's influence, three new camps were set up in 1800, but the opening of hostilities against Portugal led to their dissolution without any significant progress having been made.[59] A number of progressive army officers, such as Francisco Xavier de Castaños and Pedro Agustín Girón, continued to experiment with the new tactics, but conservative resistance was strong enough to prevent Godoy from officially introducing the French system until late in 1807.[60] Even then he was only able to do so because of the general desire not to be shown up in front of the French armies that by then were moving into Spain in accordance with the terms of the Treaty of Fontainebleau.[61] It took some time before the new tactics penetrated throughout the army, however, the old system continuing to be used until well into the War of Independence.[62]

Matters were not helped by the fact that the *Reglamento para el servicio y maniobras de la infantería* of 1807 gave almost no guidance as to how the new tactics should be employed. In particular, it was not realised that the infantry column was unlikely to achieve its objectives unless the enemy was first battered by concentrated artillery fire and harassed by a strong skirmish screen. Horse artillery might also be brought up in close support, and cavalry sent in to exploit any breakthrough achieved by the infantry. Yet the few treatises on the subject that were published in Spain merely conducted an arid debate on the relative merits of column and line without making any attempt to place them in their proper context.[63] The attitude that was taken towards the light infantry is particularly indicative of the manner in which the reformers failed to grasp the full implications of the tactical debate. Godoy certainly increased the proportion of light infantry in the Spanish army – indeed, in 1802 he formed two new regiments, Campo Mayor and Navarra – but the continued organisation of these troops into separate units suggests that they were still regarded as agents of the *petite guerre* of the eighteenth century, rather than as a battlefield adjunct of the line infantry, as was increasingly the case in the rest of Europe. The old distinction between light and line infantry was fast disappearing, each battalion instead being provided with its own integral light company or simply being expected to send out a proportion of its strength as skirmishers as required, independent of its precise nomenclature.

In the Spanish army, by contrast, the provision of skirmish cover was woefully inadequate. The regulations of 1802 had left the army with twelve light infantry regiments, each of which consisted of a single battalion of six companies, but without a proper divisional organisation it was impossible to distribute these units on an even basis. The line infantry, meanwhile, were not trained to fight in open order. Nor were they provided with their own light companies, except in the case of a few units commanded by progressive officers who acted on their own initiative.[64] The only official concession made in this direction by the new infantry regulations of 1802 was to adopt the Prussian practice of detailing a few men in each company – in this case eight – to act as skirmishers. A Spanish battalion of some 750 men could consequently deploy only thirty-two skirmishers compared with the 100–150 of its French counterpart.

The absence of a proper tactical manual concerning their use ensured that the few skirmishers that the Spaniards could deploy would be very ill-trained.[65] In addition, in 1806 the light infantry were deprived of the simple and practical costume by which they had hitherto been characterised in favour of the conventional bicorn and tailcoat of the rest of the army. The result, as a later critic noted, was that the *cazador* became impeded by 'a stiff cravat that does not let him turn his head, a coat whose useless tails get caught on branches, a cartridge box that continually bangs against him, a sabre that gets between his legs, tripping him up at every instant, and above all a pack that impedes his progress even when he is walking normally'.[66]

If Godoy's failure to pay proper attention to the role of the skirmisher marred the reforms he effected in the Spanish infantry, his efforts with regard to the cavalry had almost no effect whatsoever. In 1796 he had stated his intention to merge the dragoons, an arm which he regarded as having long outlived its original function, with the rest of the cavalry, and to increase the proportion of light horse. By new regulations that were issued in 1803, he duly added the eight regiments of dragoons to the existing force of four regiments of light cavalry to create six regiments of hussars and six of chasseurs. The twelve regiments of line cavalry were left untouched except that, in common with all the mounted units, they each received a fifth squadron that was designed to act as a depot.[67] The reorganisation certainly made administrative sense in that the dragoons had hitherto been organised as a separate branch of the service, a wholly unnecessary expense in view of the fact that they had long since become totally indistinguishable from the rest of the cavalry. Yet changing the nomenclature of particular regiments did nothing to address the army's shortage of mounted troops, let alone the fundamental problems that afflicted the Spanish cavalry. After 1795 the number of regiments remained static at twenty-four. Furthermore, in 1808 they could only muster 14,440 rank and file out of an establishment of 16,164.[68]

The difficulty was not so much one of manpower as of horseflesh. To Godoy's credit, he did make every effort to remedy the deleterious effects of centuries of mule breeding: horses were imported from Normandy, Africa and Denmark to improve the breeding strains; a royal stud was established at Aranjuez; horse breeding was encouraged by financial and legal concessions; and the privileges of the mule breeders were reduced.[69] Yet for the time being the quality of the horses available to the army remained as poor as ever. It was perhaps for this reason that the few cavalry units engaged in the War of the Oranges do not seem to have distinguished themselves: indeed, the María Luisa hussar regiment even earned itself the scornful nickname of 'Mari huye' ('run-away Mary').[70] Horses were also in such short supply that when Godoy briefly sought to declare war on France in 1806, he was forced to appeal to the general public to donate remounts to the army.[71] This appeal was unavailing: when the army took the field against Portugal in 1807, most cavalry regiments could only mount one or two squadrons, and in 1808 the army possessed only 9,526 horses out of an establishment of 13,296.[72] Compared with these issues, the changes brought about by Godoy in 1803 were purely cosmetic, but even these did not survive for long: much to the favourite's annoyance, in 1805 he was forced to restore the dragoon regiments to their original state.[73] On the eve of the War of Independence the cavalry therefore consisted of twelve line regiments, eight dragoon regiments, two hussar regiments and two chasseur regiments; each regiment consisted of five squadrons.

The reform of the technical branches of the army proved somewhat less nugatory. Godoy's promise to María Luisa in 1804 that he would create '*cuerpos facultátivos* such as Frederick himself would not have been able to establish' was not entirely an idle boast.[74] In 1802 the engineers were provided with a regiment of sappers and miners to act as a reliable source of skilled labour for their operations, and a general reform of the whole corps the following year increased its size, raised its pay, and created an engineering academy at Alcalá de Henares.[75] Similar encouragement was given to the artillery, of which Godoy himself was titular commander from 1803 to 1808. New regulations were introduced for the artillery school at Segovia, a central artillery park was established in Madrid, the corps was reorganised and increased in size by the Ordenanzas of 1802 and 1806, and some measures were taken to place its civilian drivers under military discipline.[76] As a result of these changes, in 1808 the artillery consisted of four field regiments, each of ten batteries of six guns. Two of the batteries in each of the first three regiments consisted of horse artillery. There were also nineteen companies of garrison artillery and five companies of pioneers. A comprehensive tactical manual was also produced which included many of the tactical innovations seen on on the battlefields of the Revolutionary Wars, with the artillery being enjoined to employ their guns in concentrated masses rather than in scattered individual batteries.[77] The value of these reforms was seen at Bailén, where the Spanish gunners quickly succeeded in silencing their opponents and dominating the battlefield.[78]

Many problems remained, however. For example, British officers who served in the Peninsula frequently found the Spanish engineers to be obstinate, opinionated and ignorant of anything other than the construction of permanent works of fortification.[79] Except in the case of the horse batteries, nothing was done to provide the artillery with its own transport, with the result that it was still left at the mercy of civilian contractors and teamsters. Once again, in short, Godoy had merely interfered in matters of detail whilst leaving fundamental problems unaddressed. Nowhere was this more visible than with the organisation of the army taken as a whole. To be fair to Godoy, the papers submitted to the Junta de Generales y Ministros in 1796 show that he had had every intention of establishing both a general staff and a system of permanent divisions. The War of the Oranges of 1801 afforded him an opportunity of putting both these ideas into practice, but with the return of peace Carlos IV ordered him to abandon them.[80] In the same way, the military administration and the supply system remained as cumbersome as ever. The overall result of Godoy's rule was, if anything, to make matters worse than before. The ranks of the *cuerpo político* became swelled by placemen appointed as a result of Godoy's favour: to take just one example, the number of Comisarios de Guerra grew from sixty-nine in 1792 to 190 in 1807.[81] Godoy's rule also saw a further proliferation of the army's administrative organs. Although on the one hand the favourite streamlined the organisation of the Supreme Council of War, on the other he removed the artillery from the competence of the Intendance in an attempt to increase its privileges *vis à vis* the rest of the army.[82]

However sincere was Godoy's devotion to the cause of military reform, it is clear that he did little to prepare the army for involvement in a struggle of the magnitude of the Napoleonic Wars. Although it continued to suffer from many problems – shortage of manpower, inferior officers, defective organisation, and a chaotic administrative system – the trouble was not its quality. Contemporary observers were by no means unimpressed with the troops of the old army: for example, after its escape from Denmark in 1808 Sir James Leith wrote of the division of the Marqués de la Romana: 'They are indeed very fine troops, and I conceive their coming ... of great importance.'[83] Indeed, wherever the forces of the *ancien régime* were able to fight the French without their ranks having been excessively diluted by the masses of raw levies unleashed by the rising of 1808, they were able to acquit themselves with honour. The greatest weakness of the army was not its courage, but the complete inability of the military system to support a major war. Even had the army been made capable of rapid expansion, it was doubtful whether a larger force could have been maintained in the field. As was demonstrated by the expeditions against Portugal of 1801 and 1807, Spain could hardly deploy forces of the limited size available before 1808, let alone the mass armies of the War of Independence: in the War of the Oranges, Godoy's operations were gravely delayed by the problem of providing the army with adequate transport, whilst in 1807 the invasion forces only avoided starvation by resorting to wholesale pillage.[84]

The responsibility for this lamentable situation must in part rest with the favourite. It is extremely unlikely that he ever fully grasped the extent of the changes that were necessary before Spain could face a war with France, and had he done so it is unclear that he had either the energy or the personal authority necessary to force an acceptance of such radical reform upon an unwilling Spanish establishment. Furthermore, if the government was unable to find the finance that was necessary to underwrite his reforms and to ensure that the army was adequately paid and supplied, it was in part because of the undoubted venality of Godoy's régime. The favourite's incontrovertible taste for riches, and the general extravagance of the court placed a heavy burden upon Spain's slender resources. Furthermore, his régime was marked by a huge upsurge of nepotism, of which his family were the first beneficiaries. Godoy's brother-in-law, brothers and uncles were all appointed to the rank of lieutenant general or above; in several cases they also occupied important positions in the military hierarchy. In addition, between 1793 and 1795 alone Godoy appointed eight captains general, fifty-five lieutenant generals, and 101 *mariscales de campo*; by 1808 he had raised the total number of generals from 330 to 411.[85]

Such prodigality undoubtedly had a most debilitating effect. The large number of promotions was a heavy burden on the treasury, incompetence and corruption were widespread, and the court itself became a scandal. The favourite was constantly bemoaning both the decline in the standards of public life and his own isolation.[86] Yet he failed to see that matters would not improve whilst he allowed himself to be surrounded by 'a crowd of flatterers', and showed himself to be especially accommodating to 'those who appear at his public levees attended by a handsome wife or blooming daughter'.[87] The sycophantic atmosphere of the court, Godoy's personal greed and ostentation and the persistent rumours of his liaison with María Luisa made his claims to be leading a national renaissance sound exceedingly hollow. The *ilustrados* whose support was essential to the favourite if he was ever to lend real authority to his rule therefore stayed aloof: all too often the 'reformers' were mere opportunists who had attached themselves to Godoy to further their personal ambitions.

Godoy's undoubted failings contributed to his difficulties, but the foreign policy to which he had committed Spain in 1796 proved to be incompatible with the programme of reform that it was supposed to facilitate. Although none of its numerous critics have yet suggested a viable alternative, the fact remains that by plunging Spain into a maritime conflict with Great Britain, the alliance with France compounded the blow already dealt to the treasury by the conflict of 1793–95. The concomitant British blockade disrupted Spain's trade with her colonies and ended the flow of bullion that had hitherto formed the central basis of her revenue. The result was an acceleration of the already severe rate of inflation, and the depreciation of the *vales reales*.[88] In order to reduce the pressure upon it the government sought to cut its expenditure – a measure that was in itself a serious obstacle to reform – but it was prevented from doing so by the ever growing demands of the alliance with France: aside from the costs of the naval campaign against the British, between 1796 and 1808, Spain was twice compelled to invade Portugal as well as to dispatch expeditionary forces to Italy and Denmark. After October 1803 she was also supposed to be paying France a monthly subsidy of six million francs. Even the two and a half years of peace with Great Britain that Spain was granted following the Treaty of Amiens of March 1802 were insufficient to allow a restoration of her finances.

With the government perpetually teetering on the verge of bankruptcy, Godoy was unable to effect a significant change in the position of the army. At the same time, the alliance was inflicting severe damage on the domestic political situation. The massive inflation caused by the war was not matched by a corresponding increase in wages. Commerce and industry slumped, a series of bad harvests produced widespread distress, and in some areas the general misery was increased by serious epidemics of yellow fever.[89] Meanwhile, Madrid, in particular, experienced a steady influx of immigrants from the provinces fleeing poverty, starvation and pestilence. The huge numbers of paupers who clogged the city constituted a distinct threat to public order, as shown by the outbreak of severe bread riots in 1802.[90] They were also ripe for exploitation by the hostile *camarilla* that had emerged in the Spanish court around the figure of the jealous and embittered heir to the throne, Prince Fernando.

The origins of the *fernandino* party lie in the hatred which Fernando had conceived for his parents' favourite. Deeply resentful of the manner in which Godoy had usurped their affections, the Prince became convinced that he intended to seize the throne for himself, or at the very least to alter the order of succession in favour of one of the younger *infantes*, who were reputedly the offspring of the supposed liaison between María Luisa and Godoy. His jealousy made him a natural focus for all those who bore a personal grudge against the favourite or who opposed his policies, most notably Fernando's erstwhile tutor, Juan de Escoiquiz, and Godoy's inveterate enemy, José Antonio Caballero. A large number of noblemen, many of them with commissions in the Royal Guards, also became supporters of Fernando. If some of them, such as the Conde de Montijo and the Duque del Infantado, had personal reasons for their hostility, it is also by no means impossible that they saw the weak figure of Fernando as an ideal puppet king whose accession to the throne would enable them to turn back the gradual erosion of the privileges of the nobility at the hands of the Bourbon monarchy. The disparity of their motives did not prevent the *fernandinos* from uniting in a programme of action designed to blacken the reputation of the régime. To spread their propaganda, the favourite's enemies were able to avail themselves of the current fashion amongst the nobility for adopting popular dress and mingling with the Madrid crowd. Fortified by an armoury of scurrilous broadsheets, it was easy for them to bring the reputation of the court into ever greater disrepute and to paint an exaggerated picture of the 'Golden Age' that would follow the accession to the throne of Fernando as *el rey deseado*.[91] By November 1803, Godoy was complaining to María Luisa that it was unsafe for him even to appear in the streets.[92]

It was also increasingly apparent that the French alliance was doing nothing to check the maritime power of Great Britain. In 1797 the British defeated a Spanish squadron at Cape St. Vincent, and seized the island of Trinidad, a gain which they followed a year later by that of Menorca. Seaborne assaults on Cádiz, Santa Cruz de Tenerife, El Ferrol, and Puerto Rico were only beaten off with difficulty. Following the renewed outbreak of hostilities in November 1804, Franco–Spanish sea power was shattered at the battle of Trafalgar in October 1805, and in June 1806 a British force occupied Buenos Aires. Even the subsequent expulsion of the invaders the following year was of little comfort for it had been achieved entirely by the efforts of the creole militia, much to the stimulation of colonial self-confidence. The alliance was just as unsatisfactory in a political sense, for France had shown herself to be quite prepared to trample on her ally's diplomatic interests whenever it suited her. Rather than reinforcing Spain's independence in the international arena, the Treaty of San Ildefonso had brought about her subordination to a foreign power. Godoy was by no means unaware of the disadvantages of the continued liaison with France, but his ability and wisdom were unequal to the hazardous task of extricating Spain from the Napoleonic embrace. His blundering efforts to provide her with an alternative foreign policy, first of all by building a power-bloc of neutral states and then by a singularly ill-timed attempt to join Prussia in the campaign of 1806, only succeeded in hastening direct French intervention in the Peninsula. However, although Napoleon was well aware of Godoy's readiness to betray France, his initial reaction was to attempt to buy the favourite's continued loyalty by exploiting his cupidity, a policy which tallied with the Emperor's determination to force Portugal to enter the Continental System. Acting with the agreement of the Spanish government, in October 1807 Napoleon dispatched an army of 25,000 men to invade Portugal under General Junot. The details of the enterprise were finalised by the Treaty of Fontainebleau (27 October 1807). Spain was to furnish Junot with the support of an army of 27,000 men, in return for which Portugal was to be dismembered, and large portions of it given to Godoy and Carlos IV's son-in-law, the erstwhile King of Etruria, as independent principalities.

The introduction of French forces into the Peninsula sparked off the chain of events that led to the outbreak of the War of Independence. Godoy's military reforms were thus to be put to the test in dramatic fashion. Another aspect of the effect of his rule on the army was also to be revealed: in March 1808 disaffected elements of the Royal Guards mounted a successful *pronunciamiento* against his rule in the so-called Motín de Aranjuez. The army had clearly been politicised, and in a sense that was hostile to Godoy. That this should have been the case seems extraordinary in view of the importance which he had placed upon military affairs. Had the officer corps been entirely the preserve of the upper nobility, then its hostility might have been understandable: not only could the favourite be regarded as an interloper, but he had also shown himself to be firmly opposed to the ambitions entertained by certain grandees of turning back the advance of the monarchy at the expence of the magnates. For example, when the Conde de Montijo published a manifesto in 1794 which combined a panegyric of the nobility with a fierce critique of the manner in which their authority had been usurped by the throne, Godoy had him arrested and sent into internal exile in Avila.[93] The widespread sale of patents of nobility in order to bolster the government's finances, and the prodigality with which the favourite showered titles, of which the number more than doubled between 1788 and 1798, upon his protégés was equally offensive, for it clearly threatened to cheapen the status of the *hidalguía*.[94] Finally, the support which Godoy had given to the publication of Gaspar Melchor de Jovellanos' highly controversial *Informe sobre la ley agraria* was extremely alarming in view its bitter denunciation of such bastions of the nobility as the *mayorazgos*.[95] Godoy was therefore almost certain to incur the hostility of many senior generals, but the disadvantaged mass of subaltern officers might still have been expected to rally to his support as their natural representative. When their loyalties were put to the test, however, Godoy was seen to be totally isolated.

Ironically, Godoy's very reformism earned him many enemies in the army, especially in the Royal Guards. Godoy and his fellow reformers had always regarded the Guards as being both highly expensive and of limited military value, but the Junta de Generales y Ministros had refused to allow them to implement plans for their reform.[96] Only the poor performance of the household troops in the War of the Oranges allowed the issue to be resurrected: Godoy complained to María Luisa that the Guardias de Corps had been extremely dilatory in reaching the front, and that the officers of the Guardias de Infantería were the worst in the army.[97] His disgust with the Walloon regiment reached such a pitch that he advised Carlos and María Luisa to dismiss 'half the Guardias Walonas and all their officers', remarking that the regiment was 'not only useless but harmful'.[98] In 1803 Godoy accordingly issued new regulations for the two regiments of Guardias de Infantería. On the pretexts that both units had fallen well below strength and that the Walloons now contained very few men of that nationality, the number of battalions which each contained was reduced from six to three and their total strength reduced from 370 officers and 8,494 men to 196 officers and 6,026 men. Aside from the obvious blow that had been dealt to their pride, promotion prospects in the Guardias de Infantería were severely reduced by the attachment of the many surplus officers to their old units as *agregados*.[99] Such was the depth of the bitter hostility to the favourite that was engendered in their ranks that the Guardias Walonas are reported to have danced for joy on hearing the news of his downfall.[100] Godoy was equally unpopular with the Guardias de Corps: after the Motín de Aranjuez its members were only narrowly dissuaded from murdering him and, as his gaolers, treated him with extreme brutality.[101] This unit was initially saved from a similar fate to that meted out to the Guardias de Infantería by the personal opposition of the Queen, but it was highly jealous of the manner in which Godoy's personal guard of light cavalry, the Guardias de Honor del Generalísimo-Almirante, had succeeded in usurping its right to escort the royal family, a duty that brought with it considerable opportunities coming to the attention of the King or Queen.[102] In 1807 the unit's hostility was redoubled, for Godoy finally achieved his goal of reducing its strength by abolishing its fourth company.[103]

The burning hatred with which Godoy was regarded in the Guards was not shared with the same intensity by the rest of the army, but there was still little love lost for the favourite. Aside from the fact that both officers and men were as vulnerable to *fernandino* propaganda as any other section of Spanish society, conditions were hardly conducive to the encouragement of their loyalty. Far from building up a strong nucleus of support for the favourite, Godoy's lavish disbursement of patronage proved counter-productive. As a later historian pointed out, 'however numerous the legion of his ... clients, much greater was that of the discontented, the prejudiced and the envious'.[104] For the majority of regimental officers there was little chance of obtaining Godoy's patronage: indeed, their already slender hopes of promotion were reduced still further by the influx of new officers engendered by the formation of large numbers of new regiments, the encouragement given by Godoy to clientage and nepotism, and the increased premium that was being placed upon membership of the military estate. Aside from causing frequent disputes with regard to precedence, as even Godoy admitted, the general effect was to increase the number of *agregados*, much to the detriment of the hopes of many officers for advancement.[105]

The economic difficulties faced by the lower strata of the officer corps showed no signs of abating. Inadequate at the best of times, their pay was being steadily eroded by inflation, and was often badly in arrears. In 1796 conservative elements of the Junta de Generales y Ministros had suggested that the pay of the officer corps should be raised by an average of fifteen per cent from the savings that could be effected by abolishing the allegedly superfluous third battalions of the line infantry regiments.[106] It was not until 1802 that Godoy was able to introduce a pay rise of forty-three per cent, however. Since the cost of living had risen by fifty-nine per cent in the period 1780–98 alone, even this was a case of 'too little, too late'.[107] Nor did it do anything to alleviate the hardship experienced by retired and invalid officers without private incomes, whose meagre pensions, already devalued by inflation, were now paid in the rapidly depreciating *vales reales*. To make matters worse, many of the administrative posts on which they had depended for an adequate reward were now occupied by placemen of Godoy.[108]

The widespread financial distress offended the honour of the officer corps as much as it did its physical well-being. As the military ethos made the honour of an officer inseparable from the maintenance of his dignity and status, it followed that the first task of the régime must be to ensure that the army was 'full of ostentation and splendour'.[109] Godoy's rule fell manifestly short of this ideal. If many officers were suffering from a reduced standard of living and limited hopes of advancement, the rank and file were poorly dressed, ill housed and badly fed, sometimes to the extent that they were reduced to eating berries and roots in order to survive. Even the pampered Guardias de Corps did not escape the general air of penury, finding it difficult to provide adequate forage for their horses.[110] Against this background, Godoy's immoderation was certain to cause real offence to many officers: hence the fury that was aroused by his creation of the magnificently uniformed Guardias de Honor del Generalísimo-Almirante in 1801 as a sub-unit of the Carabinieros Reales.[111] The impression of frivolity to which his actions gave rise undermined Godoy's genuine claim to be a military reformer. Such suspicions were strengthened by his evident obsession with the army's uniforms, the dress of the line infantry being altered no fewer than four times between 1801 and 1806. In the face of such evidence, it was hardly surprising that many officers should have dismissed his reformism as the fruit of mere caprice.[112]

The simmering military discontent had serious effects on Godoy's programme of reform, for many officers chose to show their opposition to his rule by adopting the attitude of passive resistance exemplified by the refusal of certain generals to take part in the War of the Oranges on the grounds that the army was unfit to take the field. The favourite's correspondence with María Luisa provides further evidence of his isolation. In August 1803 he complained, 'The recruiting of the army is only going forward slowly and without the necessary energy. Everything, everything, is like this.'[113] Two years later, he gave further vent to his frustration, grumbling, 'I will attempt to ensure that the outstanding matters are resolved once and for all, but I have not yet been able to do this because of my inability to move men in the manner necessary; . . . men who obey humbly . . . are now unknown: everyone wishes to command and none to obey.'[114] The effect of this non-co-operation was to reinforce the favourite's dependence on Carlos and María Luisa, for he could only proceed in his reforms as far as they were prepared to back him against the military establishment. Thanks to the efforts of Godoy's enemies to persuade them to identify all reform with the onset of revolution, they simply would not furnish him with the support which he needed. One by one, the favourite was therefore forced to abandon or to curtail many of his most radical schemes. Any attempt to step outside the bounds of the permissible led to disaster: for example, in 1804 he was forced to dismiss Tomás de Morla, one of his most able subordinates, for proposing to reform the Guardias de Corps.[115]

For all Godoy's unpopularity, the army cannot be said to have been ready to overthrow his rule before 1808. The clique of conservative generals who had replaced his supporters in the military administration responded to Godoy's return to favour in 1800 by intriguing with Caballero to bring about the favourite's renewed disgrace.[116] The following year one of their number, Gregorio García de la Cuesta, attempted to use his position as president of the Council of Castile to block an attempt by María Luisa and Godoy to have themselves declared co-regents in the event of the death of Carlos IV.[117] Yet Godoy was able to overcome this challenge to his position without difficulty: the offending generals were either dismissed from office altogether or packed off to a decorous exile abroad.[118] The vast majority of the army remained quiescent, but subsequent events suggest that it was no more willing to come to Godoy's aid than it was actively to seek his destruction.

Military loyalties were finally to be put to the test as a result of the intrigues of the *fernandinos*. Ever since Godoy's attempted breach with France in 1806, they had believed that that the best way for Fernando to consolidate his position was to present himself as a loyal ally of Napoleon. To this end, secret negotiations were entered with the French ambassador for Fernando to be given a bride from the Bonaparte family. Once the Prince had attained this tangible demonstration of Napoleon's support, it was then intended that he should confront Carlos IV and demand Godoy's removal from power. However, the plot was betrayed to the favourite, and on the very night of the signature of the Treaty of Fontainebleau Fernando was arrested in his apartments at the palace of El Escorial and arraigned on a charge of high treason. Amongst the many incriminating documents found in his possession was the draft of a letter to Napoleon imploring his protection, and orders that were to be put into effect in the event of the death of Carlos IV, appointing the *fernandino* Duque del Infantado to be Generalísimo in place of the favourite.[119]

The actual details of the so-called 'Affair of El Escorial' are of considerably less importance than its consequences for Spain's increasingly precarious situation. Godoy's own position was immeasurably worsened, as his allegations were universally rejected as a devious plot to destroy Fernando; although the Prince was ultimately pardoned, the favourite was henceforth regarded as a tyrant. Not only was the régime now totally isolated at home, but for the first time Napoleon began seriously to consider the possibility of overthrowing the Bourbon monarchy. If his move against Portugal had had the useful side effect of allowing him to send troops into Spain, until now his policy had been directed towards ensuring the continued loyalty of his Spanish allies with the promise of Lusitanian acquisitions. The revelation of serious dynastic feuding in the Spanish court led him to re-evaluate his position. Ever suspicious of Great Britain, he was afraid that she might exploit the chaos with which Spain seemed threatened as a result of the Affair of El Escorial to wean her away from her alliance with France. Even if this did not occur, conflict within Spain would negate her value as an ally and severely compromise the position of the French forces that had been sent to Portugal. Aside from these military pressures, other factors were also encouraging the Emperor to intervene, including his interest in seizing control of the revenues of the Spanish empire and in annexing the area north of the river Ebro, and his desire to transform Spain into a reliable satellite state. Given the general detestation of Godoy and Spain's defenceless situation, the project seemed to offer every advantage.[120]

Though as yet undetermined as to the precise form his intervention should take, from November 1807 onwards Napoleon began to send large numbers of French troops into northern Spain. Although increasingly perturbed, Godoy had no option but to maintain the fiction that the new arrivals were on their way to Portugal or had come to defend Spain against a British attack. The Emperor had in the meantime been reviewing his options. Initially inclined to dethrone Carlos IV in favour of Fernando, he eventually came to the conclusion that the latter would be no more reliable as an ally than Godoy. The logical course of action therefore seemed to be to overthrow the Bourbons altogether and to replace them with a puppet monarch drawn from Napoleon's own family. After a short period of ever increasing tension, in February 1808 the French forces already in Spain duly seized the vital border fortresses of Pamplona and San Sebastián. Meanwhile, a new army marched into Catalonia, occupying Figueras and Barcelona. On 10 March Marshal Murat entered Spain as Napoleon's personal envoy and commander-in-chief of all the 100,000 French troops in the Peninsula. He brought with him yet another army corps at whose head he immediately set out for Madrid. Only a few days before the French went into action Godoy and Carlos IV had received a list of sweeping demands from Napoleon which included the cession of the left bank of the Ebro to France. As this demand could never have been met, it was clear that it was only being presented in order to furnish a pretext for Napoleon to enforce a change of government in Madrid.

Faced by the stark choice between war and surrender, Godoy decided to fight. He had already withdrawn the division of the Marqués del Socorro from southern Portugal, and he now ordered these troops to join all the other forces in central Spain behind the line of the river Tagus. Protected by this rearguard, the Spanish royal family could then retire to Seville from whence they could either preside over resistance to the French or join their Portuguese counterparts in fleeing to South America. Urgent messages were also dispatched to every military commander in the Peninsula, even in the occupied areas, to make ready for war.[121] Logical as this plan was, as Toreno noted, 'proposed by the Príncipe de la Paz, it did not have a single supporter'.[122] As it was universally believed that the French intended no more than 'the regency of Fernando and the ruin of Godoy', the latter's attempts at resistance were regarded as a desperate shift to evade the retribution that was about to come down upon his head.[123]

The *fernandinos* shared in this general conviction: believing that the arrival of Murat's army in Madrid would herald at the very least the downfall of Godoy, they had absolutely no interest in resisting the French. On the contrary, they now sought not only to prevent the outbreak of war, but to install a new regime in Madrid that would be looked upon with favour by the Emperor. In order to achieve these aims, a two-pronged strategy was adopted. Whilst Fernando and his adherents in the court sought to dissuade Carlos IV from the idea of resistance, Montijo and Infantado prepared an insurrection.[124] Their aims were in the meantime being facilitated by a number of officers and officials who on their own initiative had already taken action to sabotage Godoy's orders.[125] Never a man to relish decisive action, the King had been thoroughly confused by the fortuitous arrival of a number of flattering messages and gifts from Napoleon, and therefore agreed that the question should be referred to the Council of Castile. Having long since been won over to the *fernandino* cause, the Council ruled that there was no need to concentrate troops at Aranjuez because the court was in no danger. In a clear testimony to the aspirations of the disaffected magnates, it also stated that before taking a decision on any matter that affected 'the existing political and military system', the King should in future always consult the opinion of his leading subjects. In short, the governance of Spain should take full account of the views of the *grandeza*.[126]

Although he still ordered the Guards to concentrate at Aranjuez, on 16 March Carlos bowed before the mounting pressure and issued a proclamation renouncing the idea of flight and reiterating his confidence in Napoleon.[127] The conspirators nevertheless continued with their plans for an insurrection, a task in which they were aided by the excited state of public opinion. The wildest rumours were circulating to explain the crisis, with Godoy being variously accused of trying to evade the just deserts that were being prepared for him by Napoleon, and of betraying Spain to the Emperor in return for an endorsement of his personal power. There was also a strong belief that in an obvious moment of national danger, it was the duty of the King not to run away, but to protect his subjects.[128] When the Conde de Montijo and some of his confederates began to preach the need to go to Aranjuez to prevent the flight of the royal family in the villages around Madrid, they therefore met a ready response. Thousands of people began to pour into the *real sitio*, where they besieged the palace and set a watch on all the roads leading out of the town.[129] Aranjuez could produce its own mob even without their assistance, for the departure of the court would have represented economic disaster for its inhabitants as most of them were in some way dependant upon the royal palace. As Blanco White noted, 'Madrid and the *real sitios* would sink into insignificance were the court to be moved to a distance. The dissolution of the most wretched government fills its dependants with consternation.'[130]

Important though the popular aspect of the Motín de Aranjuez undoubtedly was, it should not be allowed to obscure the fact that the spearhead of the revolt was wholly military. But for the desertion of the armed forces to the rioters, there is no reason to suppose that the riots would have been any more dangerous than the Motín de

Esquilache of 1766. However, the Guard had been subverted by its hatred of Godoy, as had already been suggested at the time of the Affair of El Escorial: not only had Fernando's escort of Guardias de Corps attempted to prevent the removal of incriminating documents from his apartments, but elements of the garrison of Madrid had demonstrated in his favour.[131] As the Guards were well aware that the departure of the royal family would lead to their being 'levelled with the rest of the army', the numerous *fernandinos* amongst their officers, such as the three Palafox brothers, had no difficulty in persuading their men that the monarchy was in danger.[132] Their efforts soon bore fruit: all the Guard units already at Aranjuez 'engaged to support the people', and fraternised with the excited crowd, cheering Fernando to the echo whenever he appeared in public. Meanwhile, still further exciement was caused by the orders issued on 16 March for the battalions of the Guardias de Infantería that were still in Madrid to march immediately for Aranjuez.[133]

Although tempers were now at fever pitch, the necessary pretext for a rebellion – preparations for the immediate departure of the royal family – stubbornly refused to materialise. At the same time, it was known that the arrival of the troops of the Marqués del Socorro was imminent, and that their support could not be guaranteed. With Murat's army coming ever closer, the conspirators seem to have decided to precipitate a crisis. There is no evidence to suggest that the royal family was going anywhere, but on the afternoon of 17 March a rumour suddenly spread that Fernando had told an officer of his bodyguard, 'The journey is tonight and I do not want to go.'[134] What happened next is uncertain, but it seems likely that the conspirators laid plans to initiate the coup at midnight that same night.[135] In the event, however, the final spark was almost certainly accidental. Late in the evening of 17 March a group of Godoy's hated Guardias de Honor were confronted by an angry crowd of guardsmen and civilians outside the royal palace. In the ensuing quarrel a shot was fired, whereupon the mob immediately poured into the streets and made straight for Godoy's residence in search of the favourite. The few loyal sentries were swept aside and the building was ransacked, but Godoy himself escaped by hiding in a roll of carpet.[136]

Two days of intermittent rioting followed in which the Guards played a leading role. Of their officers, only Diego de Godoy attempted to restore order, and he was quickly arrested by Montijo. Throughout the disturbances events were orchestrated by the Count so as to bring growing pressure on the terrified Carlos and María Luisa, whilst reassuring and encouraging Fernando, who by all accounts was nearly as frightened as his parents.[137] The King and Queen were quickly persuaded firstly to dismiss Godoy, and then to have him imprisoned when thirst drove him out of his refuge. The disturbances continued, however, for the *fernandinos* were determined to show Carlos that his position had become untenable. The final blow was delivered on the morning of 19 March, when a delegation headed by the Príncipe de Castelfranco, the commander of the Guardias Walonas, warned the King that fresh violence was expected. Asked whether the troops could be relied upon, Castelfranco replied that only Fernando could answer for their loyalty. Weary and demoralised, Carlos IV could take no more, and finally abdicated his crown into the hands of the triumphant Fernando.[138]

In a development heavy with significance for the future, the fall of the favourite had been brought about by the first *pronunciamiento* in Spanish history. In order to achieve their ends, the *fernandinos* had had no option but to appeal to the discontent that had been occasioned by Godoy's rule in certain elements of the armed forces. In response, the Royal Guards had duly 'pronounced' against Godoy in favour of the alternative regime of Fernando VII. The rest of the army then went over to the rebellion *en masse*, soldiers being prominent in the rioting that broke out in Madrid and other cities following the arrival of news of the events at Aranjuez.[139] Deprived of their only means of actually enforcing their authority, Carlos and María Luisa were left with no choice but to surrender.

As far as Godoy is concerned, the total desertion of the army is suggestive of the failure of all his efforts at military reform: in the last resort the army was no better prepared for a major war in 1808 than it had been in 1792. Although Godoy had brought about many changes of detail, these paled into insignificance beside the fundamental problems that remained untouched. If the responsibility for this situation must in part be attributed to the favourite's own shortcomings, it is also clear that few statesmen could have overcome the obstacles to reform posed by Spain's financial problems, or the hostility to all forms of progress that had been engendered in the mind of Carlos IV by the French Revolution. Be that as it may, however, the army had been given no reason why it should reject the *fernandino* propaganda. By competing with Godoy for the loyalties of the military, the conspirators had reduced the *ancien régime* to tatters, as well as opening a veritable Pandora's Box. For the first time the army had assumed its classic role as the arbiter of Spanish politics. As one officer remarked to his *tertulia*, 'Gentlemen, we have cured a cold and caught tuberculosis.'[140]

Chapter 2 Notes

1. Toreno, *op. cit.*, I, p. 45.
2. Clonard, *Historia orgánica*, VI, 51–55, 297.
3. Bourgoing, *op. cit.*, II, p. 69; Priego López, *op. cit.*, I, p. 116.
4. Godoy, *op. cit.*, I, 112–13; M. Foy, *Histoire de la guerre de la péninsule sous Napoléon* (Paris, 1827), I, p. 340; L. Crusy de Marcillac, *Histoire de la guerre entre la France et l'Espagne pendant les années de la révolution française* (Paris, 1808), I, p. 12; Schepeler, *op. cit.*, I, p. 279.
5. Real Cédula, 4 February 1793, *cit.*, Sánchez, *Colección*, I, p. 307; Bourgoing, *op. cit.*, III, p. 243.
6. Real Cédula, 24 March 1794, *cit.*, Sánchez, *Colección*, II, 12–15; Bourgoing, *op. cit.*, III, p. 294.
7. 'Discurso o corección fraterna de un amigo al Sr. D. Antonio Despuig, Obispo de Orihuela' (MS), RAH. 9-31-7: 7021, 204–10; 'Papel anónimo al General Conde de la Unión' (MS), RAH. 9-31-7: 7025, 220–3; G. Anes Alvarez, *Economía e ilustración en la España del siglo XVIII* (Barcelona, 1972), 172–9 (hereafter Anes, *Economía e ilustración*).
8. Real Cédula, 28 February 1795, *cit.*, Sánchez, *Colección*, II, 102–4.
9. Real Cédula, 11 March 1793, *cit. ibid.*, I, 353–5; *Estado Militar*, 1801, 62–3; Crusy de Marcillac, *op. cit.*, II, p. 15.
10. Clonard, *Historia orgánica*, VI, 60–3, 298–9; *ibid.*, IX, p. 62; *ibid.*, XII, p. 130; *ibid.*, XIV, p. 6; *ibid.*, XVI, p.155; Bourgoing, *op. cit.*, II, 70–71; Vicens Vives, *op. cit.*, IV, p. 10.
11. J. Heredia to Archbishop of Toledo, 6 and 16 July 1793, SHM. ML.1793/7; Leith to Castlereagh, 6 June 1808, PRO. WO.1/229, 2–3; Marquesa de Lozoya to A. Chacón, 3 May and 10 October 1795, *cit. La campaña de Navarra en las cartas de la Señora Juana María de Escobar y de Silva Herrera, Marquesa de Lozoya*, ed. Marqués de Lozoya (Valencia, 1925), 3, 27; Godoy, *op. cit.*, I, p. 145; Crusy de Marcillac, *op. cit.*, iv.
12. Godoy, *op. cit.*, I, 353–6.
13. *Ibid.*, I, p. 387.
14. Toreno, *op. cit.*, I, p. 45.
15. Godoy to María Luisa, 8 June 1801, AHN. Estado, 2821/1.
16. Godoy to Carlos IV, 26 February 1796, RAH. 2-MS135, No. 7; 'Informe de la Comisión de Constitución Militar' (MS), RAH. 2-MS135, No. 16; 'Exposición de la plan que ha seguido y se propone seguir en sus tareas la Comisión de Constitución Militar' (MS), RAH. 2-MS135, No. 16; 'Prospecto de un plan de ejército y de una constitución militar' (MS), RAH. 2-MS135, No. 16; M. de Godoy, 'Dictamen

del Príncipe de la Paz a la Junta de Generales y Ministros' (MS), RAH. 2-MS135, No. 14 (hereafter Godoy (MS)).
17 Azanza to Colomera, 16 April 1796, RAH. 2-MS135, No. 12.
18 Godoy to Carlos IV, 26 February 1796, RAH. 2-MS135, No. 7.
19 Azanza to Colomera, 16 April 1796, RAH. 2-MS135, No. 12; Godoy (MS), RAH. 2-MS135, No. 14.
20 Reales Cédulas, 28 February and 17 March 1795, *cit*. Sánchez, *Colección*, II, 102–4, 112.
21 Godoy to Carlos IV, 26 February 1796, RAH. 2-MS135, No. 7.
22 Godoy to María Luisa, 3 June 1801, AHN. Estado, 2821/2.
23 L. Morales, 'Sobre un medio seguro de tener siempre un ejército numeroso y disciplinado para reemplazar al ejército de campaña sin recurrir a las quintas' (MS), RAH. 2-MS135, No. 4 (hereafter Morales (MS)); Godoy to Carlos IV, 26 February 1796, RAH. 2-MS135, No. 7.
24 Morales (MS), RAH. 2-MS135, No. 4; 'Informe de la Comisión de Constitución Militar' (MS), RAH. 2-MS135, No. 16.
25 Morales (MS), RAH. 2-MS135, No. 4; 'Prospecto de un plan de ejército y de una constitución militar' (MS), RAH. 2-MS135, No. 16.
26 'Prospecto de un plan de ejército y de una constitución militar' (MS), RAH. 2-MS135, No. 16; 'Informe de la Comisión de Constitución Militar' (MS), RAH. 2-MS135, No. 16; Pardo de Figueroa (MS), RAH. 2-MS135, No. 16.
27 Ustariz to Junta, 23 May and 4 July 1796, RAH. 2-MS135, No. 16; Barradas to Junta, n.d., RAH. 2-MS135, No. 16.
28 Barradas to Junta, n.d., RAH. 2-MS135, No. 16; 'Observaciones de la Comisión de Instrucción acerca del informe de la Comisión de Constitución Militar' (MS), RAH. 2-MS135, No. 16; Colomera to Junta, n.d., RAH. 2-MS135, No. 16.
29 Azanza to Colomera, 7 July and 2 September 1796, RAH. 2-MS135, No. 16.
30 Fischer, *Travels in Spain*, 265–6, 269.
31 Colomera to Junta, n.d., RAH. 2-MS135, No. 16.
32 Godoy, (MS), RAH. 2-MS135, No. 14; *Reglamento para la formación de un pie de ejército de voluntarios honrados en el Reino de Valencia con arreglo a Real Orden de 27 de mayo del presente año de 1794*, SHM. DG. 1794/7; P. Rodríguez de la Buria, *El Teniente General Pedro Rodríguez de la Buria a las Cortes Generales y Extraordinarias de España e Indias* (Cádiz, 1811), BS.038158; Godoy, *op. cit.*, II, p. 329.
33 Godoy, *op. cit.*, II, p. 331.
34 Laborde, *op. cit.*, IV, p. 274; Desdevises du Dézert,*op. cit.*, II, p. 255; Clonard, *Memorias*, 166–7; Salas, *op. cit.*, 43, 128.
35 Casa Cagigal (MS), RAH. 2-MS135, No. 6.
36 Godoy, *op. cit.*, II, 87–90, 120–1; Herr, *op. cit.*, p. 383; E. J. Hamilton, 'War and inflation in Spain, 1780–1800', *Quarterly Journal of Economics*, LIX, , 57, 65; Vicens Vives, *op. cit.*, IV, p. 38.
37 Priego López, *op. cit.*, I, 154–6; Godoy, *op. cit.*, II, 329–33.

38 Godoy, *op. cit.*, II, p. 358; *ibid.*, III, p. 166; Carrasco y Saíz, *op. cit.*, 843–69; Godoy to María Luisa, 9 September and 27 October 1800, AHN. Estado, 2821/1.
39 Blanco White, *op. cit.*, 313–14; 'Lettres d'un diplomate danois en Espagne (1798–1800)', ed. E. Gigas, *Revue Hispanique*, IX, 400–1.
40 Gigas, *op. cit.*, p. 420.
41 Godoy, *op. cit.*, III, 103–4.
42 Godoy to Carlos IV, 15 May 1801, AHN. Estado, 2821/1; Godoy to María Luisa, 27 May 1801, AHN. Estado, 2821/1.
43 *Reales Ordenanzas en que S.M. establece las reglas que inviolablemente deben observarse para el reemplazo del ejército*, 27 October 1800, BS. 039950.
44 Godoy, *op. cit.*, III, p. 174.
45 *Ibid.*, III, 175–6.
46 Godoy to María Luisa, 27 September 1801, AHN. Estado, 2821/2.
47 Godoy to María Luisa, 22 September 1801, AHN. Estado, 2821/2.
48 Schepeler, *op. cit.*, I, p. 119; Pardo González, *op. cit.*, 88–9.
49 *Reglamento de la nueva forma y constitución de los regimientos provinciales de la péninsula, su fuerza y medios de conservarla para el servicio que deben prestar en las urgencias del estado*, 19 July 1802, BS. 028672.
50 Godoy to Carlos IV, 14 September 1804, AHN. Estado, 2821/5; Godoy to María Luisa, 30 September 1806, AHN. Estado, 2821/7; Holland, *op. cit.*, 167–8, 171, 174.
51 Godoy to María Luisa, 5 January 1805, AHN. Estado, 2821/6.
52 *Reglamento en que han de establecerse los regimientos de infantería de linea y los batallones de tropas ligeras del ejército*, 26 August 1802, SHM. ML.1802/4.
53 Oman, *op. cit.*, I, p. 608.
54 Godoy to María Luisa, 29 October 1798, cit. *Cartas confidenciales de la Reina María Luisa y de Don Manuel Godoy*, ed. C. Peyreyra (Madrid, 1931), p. 191.
55 *Reglamento que S.M. manda observar en los colegios militares de Alcalá de Henares, Valladolid y Granada para la educación e instrucción de los cadetes del ejército*, SHM. ML.1802/5.
56 Desdevises du Dézert, *Ancien régime*, II, p. 226.
57 Casa Cagigal (MS), RAH. 2-MS135, No. 6.
58 Clonard, *Historia orgánica*, VI, 83, 85; Toreno, *op. cit.*, I, p. 31; Oman, *op. cit.*, I, p. 607.
59 Clonard, *Historia orgánica*, VI, 66–7.
60 *Instrucción para la igualdad de las maniobras de batallón y de linea en la división del Mariscal de Campo Don Xavier Castaños*, SHM. ML.1801/3; P. A. Girón, *Recuerdos de la vida de Don Pedro Agustín Girón*, ed. F. Suárez and A. Berazluce (Pamplona, 1978), I, p. 57; *Reglamento para el servicio y maniobras de la infantería*, (Madrid, 1807), SHM. ML.1808/4.
61 J. Gómez de Arteche, *Guerra de la Independencia: historia militar de España de 1808 a 1814* (Madrid, 1868–1903), I, p. 493.

The era of Godoy

62 E.g. Girón, *op. cit.*, I, p. 297.
63 Cf. Serrano Valdenebro, *op. cit.*; H. von Bulow, *Espiritu del sistema moderna de la guerra*, ed. J. X. de Lardizábal (Madrid, 1806).
64 Girón, *op. cit.*, I, p. 194; Clonard, *Memorias*, 178–80;
65 E.g. Schepeler, *op. cit.*, II, p. 38.
66 L. Baccigalupí, *Indicaciones acerca de las columnas volantes* (Badajoz, 1811), 11–12.
67 Clonard, *Historia orgánica*, VI, 300–1.
68 Oman, *op. cit.*, I, p. 610.
69 Godoy, *op. cit.*, II, 292–5; Schepeler, *op. cit.*, I, xlvii.
70 Godoy to María Luisa, 3 April 1805, AHN. Estado, 2821/6.
71 Proclamation of Godoy, 5 October 1806, *cit.* Oman, *op. cit.*, I, p. 603.
72 Samper to Navarro, 7 October 1807, BS. Colección de Arteche, carp. 341–2; Oman, *op. cit.*, I, p. 611.
73 Godoy to María Luisa, 3 April 1805, AHN. Estado, 2821/6; Clonard, *Historia orgánica*, VI, p. 301.
74 Godoy to María Luisa, 2 May 1804, AHN. Estado, 2821/5.
75 *Reglamento de S.M. para la creación y organización de un Cuerpo de Zapadores-Minadores en Alcalá de Henares*, 5 September 1802, SHM. ML.1802/8; *Ordenanza de Ingenieros*, 11 July 1803, SHM. ML.1803/5–6.
76 Salas, *op. cit.*, p. 155; *Ordenanza de artillería*, 22 July 1802, SHM. ML.1802/6–7; *Reglamento de la nueva constitución que S.M. manda observar para el Real Cuerpo de Artillería*, 18 March 1806, SHM. ML.1806/6; *Obligaciones de los capataces de brigadas de mulas del tren de artillería de campo*, SHM. ML.1807/1.
77 M. García y Loygorri, *Colección de ejercicios facultátivos aprobada por S.M. para la uniforme instrucción de la tropa del Real Cuerpo de Artillería* (Madrid, 1801).
78 Reding to Castaños, 22 July 1808, Servicio Histórico Militar, Archivo de la Guerra de la Independencia (hereafter SHM. AGI.) 1/2/2, No. 23; F. Guervos to his parents, 22 July 1808, RAH. 11-5-7:9003, No. 1.
79 E.g. Graham to Bunbury, 10 December 1810, PRO. WO.1/247, p. 739; Graham to Liverpool, 14 December 1810, PRO. WO.1/247, 744–5.
80 N. Benavides Moro and J. Yaque Laurel, *El Capitán General D. Joaquín Blake y Joyes, Regente del Reino, fundador del Cuerpo de Estado Mayor* (Madrid, 1960), 28–9; Pardo González, *op. cit.*, p. 81.
81 *Estado Militar*, 1792, 22–4; *ibid.*, 1807, 30–5.
82 *Real Cédula en que S.M. se sirve dar nueva planta a su Consejo Supremo de Guerra*, 16 May 1803, SHM. ML.1803/8.
83 Leith to Castlereagh, 16 October 1808, PRO. WO.1/229, 377–8; Castlereagh to Leith, 17 September 1808, PRO. WO.1/229, p. 331.
84 Godoy to Carlos IV, 15 May 1801, AHN. Estado, 2821/1; Girón, *op. cit.*, I, 190–1; Toreno, *op. cit.*, I, p. 20.
85 *Estado Militar*, 1792, 8–17; *ibid.*, 1801, 3, 11–13; *ibid.*, 1807, 8–20; Pardo González, *op. cit.*, 18–19.

86 Godoy to María Luisa, 21 May 1801, AHN. Estado, 2821/1; Godoy to Carlos IV, 23 December 1804, AHN. Estado, 2821/6.
87 Blanco White, *op. cit.*, 304, 324; Girón, *op. cit.*, I, 98–9.
88 Hamilton, *op. cit.*, 36–77; R.J. Harrison, *An Economic History of Modern Spain* (Manchester, 1978), 18–19.
89 Bourgoing, *op. cit.*, I, p. 198; *ibid.*, III, 185–7, 222, 266, 306; Anes, *Economía e ilustración*, 45–61.
90 Godoy to María Luisa, 29 April 1803, AHN. Estado, 2821/4; Godoy to Carlos IV, 7 April 1802, AHN. Estado, 2821/3.
91 H. Castro Bonell, 'Manejos de Fernando VII contra sus padres y contra Godoy', *Boletín de la Universidad de Madrid*, II, 397–408, 493–503; *ibid.*, III, 93–102.
92 Godoy to María Luisa, 23 November 1803, AHN. Estado, 2821/4; Godoy to María Luisa, 9 October 1804, AHN. Estado, 2821/5.
93 J. Pérez de Guzmán, 'El primer conato de rebelión precursor de la revolución de España', *España Moderna*, CCL, 105–24; *ibid.*, CCLI, 48–68.
94 Laborde, *op. cit.*, IV, p. 77; Vicens Vives, *op. cit.*, IV, 46, 49; Anes, *Antiguo régimen*, p. 46.
95 Godoy, *op. cit.*, II, p. 176; Herr, *op. cit.*, 376–80.
96 Cf. 'Observaciones de la Comisión de Instrucción acerca del informe de la Comisión de Constitución Militar' (MS), RAH. 2-MS135, No. 16.
97 Godoy to María Luisa, 15 and 18 May 1801, AHN. Estado, 2821/1.
98 Godoy to María Luisa, 30 May 1801, AHN. Estado, 2821/1.
99 *Reglamento del nuevo pie y fuerzas en que han de establecerse los regimientos de Reales Guardias de Infantería española y walona*, 8 April 1803, SHM. ML.1803/7; Laborde, *op. cit.*, IV, p. 463; Ordovas (MS), SHM. ML.1807/8.
100 *Diario exacto o relación circunstanciada de lo acaecido en el real sitio de Aranjuez y corte de Madrid de resultas de haber creido el pueblo que SS.MM. querían dejar la capital* (Córdoba, 1808), p. 18 (hereafter *Diario exacto*); Alcalá Galiano, *op. cit.*, I, p. 112; Guillaume, *op. cit.*, p. 237.
101 J. Palafox y Melcí, *Don José Palafox: autobiografía*, ed. J. García Mercadel (Madrid, 1966), p. 54; F. Marti Gilabert, *El Motín de Aranjuez* (Pamplona, 1972), p. 362.
102 Holland, *op. cit.*, p. 133.
103 Ordovas (MS), SHM. ML.1807/8.
104 Pardo González, *op. cit.*, p. 19.
105 Avalle to Campo Alange, 14 November 1795, RAH. 2-MS135, No. 16; Godoy to Carlos IV, 26 February 1796, RAH. 2-MS135, No. 7.
106 'Indice de los papeles que ha entregado la Comisión de Subsistencia y tenia formados para presentarlos a la Junta General lo que no pudo verificar por la suspensión de ésta' (MS), RAH. 2-MS135, No. 18; Colomera to Junta de Generales y Ministros, n.d., RAH. 2-MS135, No. 16.
107 Clonard, *Historia orgánica*, VI, p. 74; Vicens Vives, *op. cit.*, IV, p. 32;

Hamilton, *op. cit.*, 72–5.
108 Moya y Jiménez, *op. cit.*, p. 280; *Periódico Militar del Estado Mayor General*, 13 February 1812, p. 96, SHM. CDF.CXVI.
109 *Periódico Militar del Estado Mayor General*, 13 February 1812, p. 97, SHM. CDF.CXVI.
110 *Ibid.*, p. 96; Godoy to María Luisa, 13 May 1803, AHN. Estado, 2821/4; Godoy to María Luisa, 9 October 1804, AHN. Estado, 2821/5; Girón, *op. cit.*, I, 161–2.
111 Alcalá Galiano, *op. cit.*, I, p. 146.
112 Cf. L. Landaburu y Villanueva, 'Algunas ideas que presenta al Congreso Nacional el Segundo Ayudante de Estado Mayor Don Luis Landaburu y Villanueva', *El Redactor General*, 28 August 1811, 285–6, HMM. 6/3.
113 Godoy to María Luisa, 6 August 1803, AHN. Estado, 2821/4.
114 Godoy to María Luisa, 7 March 1805, AHN. Estado, 2821/6.
115 Gil Ossorio, *op. cit.*, p. 38; Holland, *op. cit.*, 154–5.
116 Godoy to María Luisa, 25 August, 9 September, and 27 October 1800, AHN. Estado, 2821/1; Muriel, *op. cit.*, II, 242–3; Schepeler, *op. cit.*, I, p. 10.
117 Muriel, *op. cit.*, II, 242–3; Schepeler, *op. cit.*, I, p. 10; Cuesta, *op. cit.*, p. 1.
118 Holland, *op. cit.*, p. 159; Toreno, *op. cit.*, II, p. 243;
119 J. de Escoiquiz, *Memorias de D. Juan de Escoiquiz* (Madrid, 1915), 83–98, 107–8, 111–12, 118–19.
120 Priego López, *op. cit.*, I, 333–5.
121 Godoy, *op. cit.*, V, 450–5.
122 *Manifiesto imparcial y exacto de lo más importante occurido en Aranjuez, Madrid y Bayona desde 17 de marzo hasta 15 de mayo de 1808* (Madrid, 1808), p. 8, (hereafter *Manifiesto imparcial*); Toreno, *op. cit.*, I, 39–40.
123 *Manifiesto imparcial*, p. 6.
124 *Manifiesto imparcial*, p. 9; J. Nellerto, *Mémoires pour servir à l'histoire de la révolution d'Espagne* (Paris, 1814–15), I, p. 13; *Diario exacto*, p. 1.
125 E.g. Rodríguez de la Buria, *op. cit.*, n.p.
126 Nellerto, *op. cit.*, I, p. 13; *Manifiesto de los procedimientos del Consejo Real en los gravísimos sucesos occuridos desde octubre del año próximo pasado* (Valencia, 1808), 2–4 (hereafter *Manifiesto del Consejo Real*); V. Martínez Colomer, *El filósofo en su quinta o relación de los principales hechos acontecidos desde la caída de Godoy hasta el ataque de Valencia* (Valencia, 1808), p. 9 (hereafter Martínez Colomer, *El filósofo*).
127 *Manifiesto imparcial*, p. 12; Nellerto, *op. cit.*, III, p. 262; Toreno, *op. cit.*, I, p. 42; *Diario exacto*, 2–3, 15.
128 *Manifiesto imparcial*, p. 10; *Conjuración de Bonaparte y Don Manuel Godoy contra la monarquía española* (Mexico, 1808), p. 5; P. Cevallos, *Exposición de los hechos que han preparado la usurpación de la corona de España* (Mexico, 1808), n.p.

129 *Manifiesto imparcial*, p. 10; Nellerto, *op. cit.*, III, p. 363;
130 Nellerto, *op. cit.*, III, p. 363; Blanco White, *op. cit.*, p. 354.
131 Escoíquiz, *op. cit.*, p. 119; *Semanario Patriótico*, 24 November 1808, HMM. AH1-6 (195).
132 Blanco White, *op. cit.*, p. 355; Palafox, *op. cit.*, 23–5; Martínez Colomer, *El filósofo*, p. 11; Marqués de Lazán, 'Resumen histórico del Marqués de Lazán' (MS), SHM. AGI. 3/4/32 (hereafter Lazán, 'Resumen histórico' (MS)).
133 Martínez Colomer, *El filósofo*, 9–10; Toreno, *op. cit.*, I, p. 41; *Diario exacto*, p. 3.
134 *Manifiesto imparcial*, p. 12; Toreno, *op. cit.*, I, p. 42.
135 Martínez Colomer, *El filósofo*, 10–11; P. J. de Gámez, *Exposición que hace a las Cortes Generales y Extraordinarias el Real Cuerpo de Guardias de Corps en contestación a la del Exmo. Sr. Secretario de Estado y del Despacho Universal de la Guerra* (Cádiz, 1811), BS. Colección de Arteche, 294–2.
136 Alcalá Galiano, *op. cit.*, I, p. 146; Martínez Colomer, *El filósofo*, 12–13; Nellerto, *op. cit.*, I, p. 17; *ibid.*, III, p. 262; *Manifesto imparcial*, p. 12; *Diario de Valencia*, 25 March 1808, p. 338, HMM. RVP.T46; Comte Murat, *Murat, Lieutenant de l'Empereur en Espagne 1808* (Paris,1897), 450–1; Schepeler, *op. cit.*, I, 23–4; *Diario exacto*, p. 4.
137 Alcalá Galiano, *op. cit.*, I, p. 146; Martínez Colomer, *El filósofo*, 13–18;
138 Toreno, *op. cit.*, I, p. 43; Nellerto, *op. cit.*, I, p. 19.
139 *Diario exacto*, 12–14; Blanco White, *op. cit.*, p. 358; Alcalá Galiano, *op. cit.*, I, 150–2.
140 Alcalá Galiano, *op. cit.*, I, p. 153.

Chapter 3

The army and the revolution, May–September 1808

The Spanish national uprising of May 1808 shook Napoleonic Europe to its foundations. For the first time since the French Revolution, it appeared that France was herself to be challenged by 'a people numerous and armed'. When the hitherto invincible French armies began to suffer serious setbacks in Spain, the effect was to encourage frustrated patriots everywhere to emulate what they saw as a 'people's war'. Both during and after the War of Independence, the view of the uprising as the spontaneous work of the Spanish people was reinforced by the Spaniards themselves. Such an explanation was convenient for both sides of the Spanish political divide. Just as conservatives could argue that the rising was a reaffirmation of fundamental Spanish values in defiance of the alien and subversive ideals of the French-inspired Enlightenment, so liberals could claim that it symbolised the determination of the Spanish people to regain their freedom after centuries of royal absolutism. The truth, alas, is far more opaque. Although the risings certainly enjoyed widespread popular support, they could not have been so successful had it not been for a series of conspiracies captained by members of the upper nobility, the army, the Church and the propertied classes. The military importance of popular resistance is also open to question, whilst it is clear that the traditionalist triptych of *Dios, Rey y Patria* was by no means the only inspiration for the insurrection.

The Spanish uprising drew its character from the decapitation of political authority brought about by Napoleon's sequestration of the Spanish monarchy in the so-called 'Ambuscade of Bayonne'. When the newly enthroned Fernando VII rode into Madrid to the tumultuous acclaim of the populace on 24 March 1808, he was actually riding to his downfall. Only the day before, the capital had been occupied by the army of Marshal Murat. Fernando and his suite had simply assumed that the French would welcome them with open arms, but in fact Murat refused to recognise his authority. On the contrary, he secretly persuaded Carlos and María Luisa to deny the validity of their abdication and to beg Napoleon for his protection. After an ever more abject display of devotion to the cause of France had failed to produce the imperial sanction which they so desperately desired, Fernando and his chief advisers allowed themselves to be lured to Bayonne for a conference with the Emperor. Having thereby placed themselves entirely at his mercy, they were stunned to be confronted with a demand that Fernando surrender his rights to the throne forthwith. Carlos, María Luisa and Godoy were also brought from Madrid and a long series of negotiations followed which culminated with the abdication by the rival monarchs of all claim to the Spanish throne. With the Bourbons removed from the scene, Napoleon replaced them with his elder brother, Joseph, whose task it would be to transform Spain into a reliable satellite state. By that time, however, Spain was already on the brink of war.

Alarm about Napoleon's intentions had been growing ever since the French occupation of Madrid, and several efforts had been made to prevent Fernando's journey to Bayonne. However, resistance did not become serious until definite news of the Emperor's treachery reached Madrid on the night of 29 April in the form of a secret message from Fernando to the Junta de Gobierno, the council of regency which he had left behind to govern Spain in his absence. The Junta was ordered to begin preparations for resistance, but in practice there was very little which it could do since Fernando had also stipulated that nothing should be done which should jeopardise his own safety.[1] Its relevance was in any case quickly to be destroyed by events in Madrid. Already enfuriated by the overbearing conduct of the French troops stationed in the capital, the *madrileños* had been excited to fever pitch by the news of Fernando's predicament. Wild rumours swept the city, demands began to be voiced that the French should be attacked immediately, and the Junta de Gobierno was generally condemned for its apparent pusillanimity.[2] In such an atmosphere, only the merest spark was needed to produce a conflagration. For this reason alone theories that the subsequent rebellion of the Dos de Mayo was premeditated seem unfounded. The rising was rather a genuinely spontaneous response to the news that the last members of the Spanish royal family remaining in Madrid were to be removed to Bayonne. On the morning of 2 May a large crowd gathered in front of the royal palace, scuffles broke out, and the French sentries opened fire. As the news spread, the population took to the streets armed with whatever weapons that they could find. A number of isolated Frenchmen were murdered, and the few troops actually posted within the city forced to withdraw. With 35,000 men at his disposal, Marshal Murat had no difficulty in restoring order, however. Powerful columns of French troops were soon fighting their way back into the city from their camps on the outskirts. Caught in the open streets and squares, the rioters were crushed without mercy. The only serious resistance came at the artillery park of Monteleón which had been seized by a small party of troops headed by the artillery officers, Daoiz and Velarde. These officers are traditionally supposed already to have been attempting to organise resistance to the French before the Dos de Mayo. Whether or not that was the case, they joined the *madrileños* with alacrity, and conducted a desperate last stand in the artillery park until finally overwhelmed by superior numbers.[3]

The Dos de Mayo totally discredited the Junta de Gobierno. Even after receiving the news of the Ambuscade of Bayonne, it had sought to maintain order in the capital. As tension mounted, the garrison had therefore been confined to barracks and the sentries posted in public places forbidden to carry ammunition. When fighting did break out, the Junta made repeated efforts to calm the populace, even lending Murat the services of the Guardias de Corps.[4] According to the claims of members of the Junta, their apparent collaboration was merely a device that was designed to win time for the preparation of resistance in the provinces, but in the general view it was ascribed to treason. Even had this not been the case, the Junta was no longer in a position to take effective action against the French, for its presidency had been assumed by Marshal Murat. The consequences were far reaching. With the way opened for extra-official resistance, all the disaffected or discontented groups in Spanish society were enabled to seize upon the organisation of an uprising as a means of realising their social and political aspirations. Furthermore, deprived of its only possible source of a central leadership, the patriotic movement was bound to be completely disunited.

Although many cities witnessed anti-French disturbances in the period following the Dos de Mayo, there was an appreciable delay before any other risings took place. The degree of preparation which this suggests is confirmed by the formation of conspiratorial cells in many cities in response to the news from Madrid and Bayonne. Examples include La Coruña, Oviedo, Valencia, Badajoz, Seville and Zaragoza.[5] The importance of these groups should not be overstated, however. Although they gave direction to the populace and orchestrated their demands, they did not create the popular sentiment which everywhere underlay the uprising. The crowd in the Spanish revolution is a subject that cries out for serious analysis, but it is clear that much of Spain was suffused with an intense wave of social and political unrest. Notoriously proud and xenophobic, the Spaniards were unlikely to have responded favourably to an attempt to impose regeneration upon them from the outside, and particularly not one which deprived them of the beloved Fernando VII. Their opposition was rendered all the more certain by the manner in which their religious sensibilities had been outraged by the excesses of the French Revolution, not to mention France's treatment of the Pope. Hostility to the French had also been stimulated by the war of 1793–95 and Spain's subsequent subordination to her powerful neighbour. In certain areas this had unleashed serious social tensions that were to find their outlet in the events of 1808. The clearest example is Valencia, where the important silk industry had experienced a severe depression in the course of the war. Furthermore, Hamnett has pointed out that seigneurial tensions in the province between the upper nobility and their tenants were particularly marked. It is therefore no surprise to find that the Valencian uprising was among the bloodiest in Spain, being marred by the massacre of over 300 French residents, most of whom were members of the commercial community. Another area where social tension is clearly apparent is Madrid, which had experienced a major growth in population in the latter years of the eighteenth century. As the newcomers could not be absorbed by the capital's economy, they tended to become classic victims of urban marginalisation. Hence the crowds of beggars complained of by Godoy. The extent to which the urban poor was affected by political considerations must be a matter of some doubt, but it is nevertheless clear that their hostility and resentment was always open to exploitation by agitators of the likes of the Conde de Montijo.[6]

A number of problems surround the question of popular participation in the uprising. It may justly be maintained that in a country as poor as Spain, where the vast majority of the population were illiterate, it is unwise to impart too strong a sense of national identity or political awareness to the common people. Furthermore, it is clear that the enthusiasm of May 1808 did not always produce wholehearted support for the war effort. Yet the fact remains that even in those cities where there was a conspiracy, the risings retained a strong popular content. In a few cases, as in Seville, where the conspirators were able to win over the garrison and launch a military coup, the crowd merely rallied to their leadership. However, other instances may be found, such as Valencia and Zaragoza where the conspirators had to seize the leadership of the revolt after the populace had taken to the streets. In Cartagena, too, the initial rising seems to have been a spontaneous response to the arrival of the definitive news of Fernando's abdication. Finally, the crowd undoubtedly took a leading role in the secondary insurrections that took place in response to the news of rebellion elsewhere: in town after town the arrival of emissaries from the nearest centre of revolt unleashed popular disturbances which led to the creation of fresh patriotic juntas.

As the conspiracies nevertheless played a vital role in fomenting resistance, they still deserve our attention. The French were later to allege that they were the work of English agents, or of fanatical members of the Spanish clergy. However, the presence of the former is ruled out by the astonishment with which the news from Spain was received in London. As for the Church, as many ecclesiastics preached submission to the French as placed themselves at the head of the patriots. Instead, the conspiracies drew their support from civilian notables, and subaltern officers of the army and navy. As the Duke of Wellington later wrote:

> It is my opinion that the officers of the Spanish army and the employés of the government ... are the principal ... supporters of the general sentiment which prevails among the people against the French. Excepting the grandees and a few men of large estate ... every person in Spain ... above the class of the cultivators of the soil was in the civil, military or naval service of the government. All these consider themselves to be deprived of their profession by the establishment of the government of Bonaparte, particularly the officers of the army ...[7]

The military was certainly in the forefront of many of the conspiracies. In Aragón the plot was headed by the dissident guards officer, José Palafox, amongst whose confederates were numbered the commanders of the local Resguardo. In Asturias, army officers distributed anti-French broadsheets and incited the populace to riot.[8] In

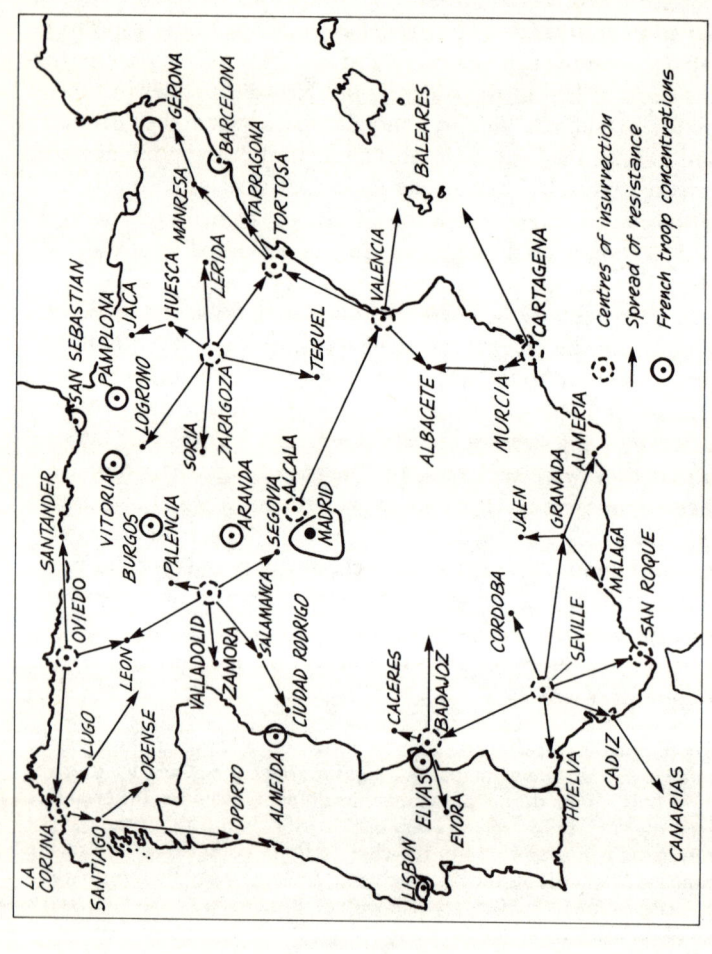

2 The Spanish national uprising, May 1808

Galicia the conspirators at La Coruña were largely drawn from the junior officers of the Navarra infantry regiment, whilst the rising at El Ferrol was led by retired naval officers, whose meagre pensions had not been paid for the last two months.[9] Subaltern officers were also important in Valencia and Cartagena, as well as in Andalucía where a plot was afoot to depose the Captain General, the Marqués del Socorro.[10]

The motivation for this activity was more complicated than Wellington supposed, however. For most army officers, the change of régime did not imply any threat to their commissions. What was far more alarming was the prospect of being forcibly incorporated into the Grande Armée and sent to serve in the 'frozen north' like the division of the Marqués de la Romana. Evidence that this was likely to be their fate was provided by the dispatch of the best troops of the Portuguese army to France early in 1808 as the Légion Portugaise. Such fears were clearly instrumental in sparking off the rising at La Coruña, where an attempt on the part of the Captain General to defuse the tension, by sending the Navarra regiment out of the city, was interpreted as the first stage of a supposed march into exile. Coupled with this hostility to entering the service of the Emperor, of course, was widespread devotion to the cause of Fernando VII, with which the army was just as strongly permeated as the rest of society. Less altruistic motives also encouraged the subaltern officers to work for a rising. Not only might an opportunity be provided to remove unpopular superiors, but a war would guarantee the promotion which so many of them had been denied.

A similar mixture of motives can be found amongst the civilian notables. For many of them, patriotic opposition to the French was linked to a sincere belief that the supposed evils of the régime of Carlos IV and Godoy had to be expurgated, as witness the wave of reformism that culminated in the famous Constitution of 1812. A considerable degree of opportunism is once again apparent, however. One of the chief preoccupations of the Cortes of Cádiz was to be the abolition of seigneurial jurisdiction as well as of all restrictions on the sale and ownership of land. In doing so it was to be acting in accordance with the interests of those who had already benefited from the considerable redistribution of property and sale of Church land that had taken place in the reign of Carlos IV – in other words the very urban professional, commercial and official groups that provided the personnel for many of the conspiracies.[11]

Finally, an uprising offered the notables the chance to settle many old scores with the army. Not only would it be possible to topple the generals from the exalted position which they had hitherto enjoyed, but the notables would be able to share freely in the coveted *fuero militar*. In addition, all those men who held some grievance against Godoy would now be able to revenge themselves upon his protegés: a considerable proportion of the various officers and officials murdered in the course of the rising were either related to the favourite or known to be his partisans.

The ability of both the subaltern officers and the civilian notables to further their sectional interests under the guise of an uprising rested upon the manner in which the French had taken over the Junta de Gobierno in the wake of the Dos de Mayo. Under Murat's presidency, this body was now ordering the military authorities to oppose all resistance to the French. It was therefore possible for the conspirators to shelter behind the suspicion that the generals could not be trusted to support an insurrection. In addition, it could also be argued that as 'almost all those who governed the provinces were the creatures of the Príncipe de la Paz ... they would sacrifice the people's happiness to the vile and sordid interest of the infamous source of their fortune'.[12] The conspirators could therefore find good reason for organising the rising in such a manner as to exclude the legitimate authorities. By fomenting popular risings in which the military hierarchy had no share, they could force the generals to choose between resisting the mob or surrendering to *force majeure*. Should they resist, they could legitimately be overthrown as traitors, but should they surrender they would still have abdicated their authority. In both cases, the way would then be open for the conspirators to achieve their aspirations.

Yet if many of those who were planning an insurrection had a vested interest in bringing down the established order, in most cases the conspiracies were genuine in their patriotism. So far as can be established none of the individual groups had any knowledge that their activities were being duplicated elsewhere in Spain. Instead, they were motivated by the hope that, by raising the standard of resistance in their own cities, they could inspire the rest of Spain to follow their example. Such was certainly the case in Aragón, where the driving force behind the revolt came from the *fernandinos*. Fernando's supporters had initially opposed resistance on the grounds that it would endanger the King, and were therefore seen attempting to calm the crowd during the Dos de Mayo.[13] However, the rising in Madrid left them with no option but to place themselves at the head of the popular outburst, which they sought to turn to their own advantage as a means of purging the numerous nominees of Godoy who still enjoyed high rank. If testimony is needed to the existence of such aims, it may be found in the activities of José Palafox, the charismatic leader of the revolt in Aragón. Palafox had been the commander of the party of Guardias de Corps which had escorted Godoy into exile in France, and at the time of the Dos de Mayo was still in Irun. According to his own account, he there received a secret message from Fernando to rescue the Infante Don Antonio from the French and to take him to Zaragoza, of which city Palafox happened to be a native. Antonio was then to be placed at the head of a council of regency which would captain a popular revolt against the French.[14]

Whether this story should be taken at face value is a moot point. All that can be said for certain is that the attempt to rescue the Infante never came to fruition, and that Palafox instead determined to place himself at the head of the insurrection as the self-appointed Lugarteniente del Rey. Travelling to Zaragoza in disguise, he arrived to find that the city already in turmoil as a result of the Dos de Mayo. Being well known in the city, he had no difficulty in forming a conspiratorial junta composed in part of friends and relatives of his family, and partly of representatives of the same groups who composed the backbone of the conspiracy elsewhere. Ordered by the Captain General, Jorge Juan Guillelmi, to return to Madrid, Palafox pretended to do so, but actually went into hiding in a country house just outside the city. In the meantime his followers stirred up unrest within the city, a task which was greatly facilitated by the obstinate refusal of the civil and military authorities to take any action in response to the ever more alarming reports that were arriving from Madrid and Bayonne.[15]

In his preparation of the uprising in Zaragoza, Palafox at least had the excuse that the Captain General was an avowed enemy of a popular revolt. Examples may also be found of conspiracies from which the legitimate authorities were excluded in the clear knowledge that the latter were actually in favour of resistance. Nowhere is this more apparent than in the chain of events surrounding the Captain General of Seville, the Marqués del Socorro. Socorro had been the commander of the Spanish division sent to invade

Portuguese Extremadura in October 1807, and was currently at Badajoz following his abortive march on Aranjuez. On 4 May 1808 in company with the acting Captain General of Extremadura, the Conde de Torre del Fresno, he received a copy of the famous *Bando de los Alcaldes de Móstoles*, a call to arms that had been penned in the village of Móstoles in the wake of the Dos de Mayo and then distributed throughout southwestern Spain.

A number of circumstances surrounding the Bando suggest that its authorities. Not only were all of its authors (an Intendant, an official of the Concejo Supremo del Almirantazgo and two village *alcaldes*) of the Concejo Supremo del Almirantazgo and two village alcaldes) quintessential civilian notables, but it was addressed not to the Captains General or their representatives, but to the local magistrates.[16] Socorro and Torre del Fresno proved themselves worthy of greater faith, however. On 5 May they issued a proclamation stating that all good Spaniards should arm themselves, and 'make ready to defend the fatherland'. In addition, messages were sent to many of their fellow military commanders, including the Captain General of the Campo del Gibraltar, Francisco Xavier Castaños, asking them for support.[17] The response to this appeal raises serious questions with regard to the nature of the uprising. It was only to be expected that most of the generals contacted by Socorro and Torre del Fresno should have rebuffed their appeals, for many of them had already chosen the path of collaboration. The only exception was Castaños, but for reasons best known to himself he chose to not to reveal his own plans for revolt. Yet the general turmoil should surely have produced an enthusiastic response from the civilian population and the various interest groups who were implicated in the anti-French conspiracies. Nothing of the sort occurred, however: the proclamation of 5 May was simply ignored. It would in consequence appear that the Spaniards were not prepared to accept the leadership of the military hierarchy, even when the latter were prepared to take action. For their part, Socorro and Torre del Fresno seem now to have despaired of all hopes of resistance. Leaving the Count at Badajoz, Socorro fled southwards to take refuge with the powerful garrison of Cádiz. Even as he did so, moves were already afoot to raise his Captain Generalcy in revolt against him. In Seville preparations for an uprising had been underway since the arrival in that city of one Nicolás Tap y Núñez, a successful entrepreneur who had been imprisoned by Godoy some years earlier on charges which Tap claimed to have been unjust. Motivated by a typical mixture of patriotism and revenge, he joined forces with a group of local patriots and discontented notables headed by the Conde de Tilly to subvert the garrison and and provoke an insurrection.[18]

The common theme that was shared by almost all the individual foci of revolt was a desire to overthrow the established military authorities. This goal proved attainable on account of the attitude adopted by most of the generals towards the uprising. Aside from Socorro and Torre del Fresno, the only senior officers prepared to do anything to instigate resistance to the French were Castaños and the Commandant General of Guipúzcoa, the Duque de Mahón. Even before the Dos de Mayo, Mahón had attempted to secure the border fortress of San Sebastián from the French, and then to raise the Basque provinces in revolt.[19] In Andalucía, meanwhile, Castaños had been negotiating with the governor of Gibraltar, Sir Hew Dalrymple, with a view to securing British intervention in Spain. Fortified by Dalrymple's promises of support, he eventually fixed upon Fernando's *santo* – 30 May – as the day he would declare war on the French.[20]

These were very much the exceptions to the rule. Far from instigating resistance to the French, most generals attempted to calm the excited population in accordance with the instructions which they had received from from the French-controlled Junta de Gobierno in Madrid. In Valencia, Zaragoza, Granada and La Coruña, the Captains General sought to suppress the conspiracies that emerged in their garrisons.[21] As for those generals caught in the French zone of occupation, they almost unanimously offered their services to the invaders.[22] When the uprising actually broke out, a few senior officers did rally wholeheartedly to the patriot cause, including the Captain General of Canarias, the Marqués de Casa Cagigal, and the commanders at Oporto, Segovia, and Alcalá de Henares.[23] Such officers were in a minority, however: most commanders either opposed the rising or sought some means of temporising, only to find themselves assailed by charges of treason and cowardice.[24]

In the eyes of many generals, there were powerful military and political reasons why a popular rising should be opposed. An illuminating example of their thinking is provided by a letter that was dispatched by Gregorio García de la Cuesta, the Captain General of Old Castile, to the Ayuntamiento of León on 29 May 1808:

My mode of thinking is, and always will be, to conform exactly with that of my government. It is to the government, and not to private citizens, that the task of deliberating on the affairs of state corresponds. Anything else would be opposed to the first duties of a vassal and a Catholic, and would produce anarchy, that is, the destruction of the monarchy and the state . . . All the members of the royal family have solemnly renounced their rights to the crown of Spain, absolving their vassals of their oaths of loyalty . . . We must therefore attempt nothing against their express determination, nor against the provisions of the Supreme Junta that governs us in the name of the Emperor of the French . . . The Emperor will give us a King in these circumstances in which we neither have one nor know who has the right to act in this capacity. Thus, prudence and the private . . . good demand that we await this choice with tranquility. The indications are that it will be favourable to us since 150 enlightened Spaniards of all classes have already been called to Bayonne to propose and discuss the reforms necessary for the defence of this Kingdom.

It is evident to me that all sensible and patriotic Spaniards think in the same manner, but as there are many among the masses who do not reason . . . they are unfortunately being swept towards an insurrection . . . by the sort of malevolent and rebellious men who always hope to prosper from disorder . . . In whose cause will they fight? Who will lead them? How will they be supplied with arms, munitions and supplies, supposing that all prudent and sensible men will be on the opposing side in order to defend their existence and property? What successes could an undisciplined mob be sure of against veteran armies? . . . if against all expectation they were to prevail, do they not consider that their own leaders would be bound to dispute the supreme command, and finish up by completely destroying their liberty and existence?[25]

That Cuesta was no coward is obvious from his later record in the War of Independence: until he was incapacitated by a stroke in August 1809, he fought a series of campaigns that showed him to be an implacable opponent of the French, albeit one without much military talent. Instead, he was bound by legitimist thinking, and convinced that a rising would lead not only to revolution, but also to military catastrophe: in his memoirs he specifically points out the defenceless nature of Old Castile, which was virtually devoid of regular troops and could easily be overrun by the French.[26] When revolt broke out in his capital of Valladolid on 1 June 1808 in response to the news of the risings elsewhere, he at first refused to grant the demands of the crowd that he take command of the insurrection, and is supposed eventually to have done so only when he was actually dragged out for execution. Self-preservation was undoubtedly the major reason for his capitulation, but it is still significant that he later chose to rationalise it by reference to the need

The army and the revolution

to bring the rebellious multitude to military and political order. As he wrote to the insurgent Junta of León:

> Since I am unable to resist the torrent of public opinion, it would appear necessary to give way before it and ... through the imposition of military discipline ... direct its impulse towards the best order possible.[27]

Cuesta had been extremely lucky. A noted opponent of Godoy, Fernando had rewarded him with the Captain Generalcy of Old Castile. As a result, he possessed sufficient prestige for the patriots to look upon him as the natural leader of the uprising, notwithstanding the fact that it had been the work of 'country gentlemen and various other persons of science and probity' – or, in short, the civilian notables.[28] Few other commanders shared his good fortune, as may be seen from the case of the Marqués del Socorro. Following the failure of the call to arms that he had issued in the immediate aftermath of the Dos de Mayo, Socorro had come to the conclusion that the only sensible option was to collaborate with the French. He was confirmed in this belief by the sudden appearance of a British fleet off Cádiz on 24 May. Unbeknown to Socorro, its presence was the work of General Castaños who had arranged for the Royal Navy to neutralise the French squadron that had been sheltering in Cádiz ever since the battle of Trafalgar. Completely unaware of Castaños' activities, Socorro immediately assumed that Cádiz was under attack. Rejecting the British admiral's protestations of friendship, he strengthened the town's seaward defences and appealed to Marshal Murat for help. Amusingly enough, Socorro actually sent a message to Castaños warning him of the impending British assault, but even when he was informed of the true state of affairs, the Marquess still refused to co-operate, apparently on the grounds that bringing in the British to eject the French would merely be to replace one foreign domination by another.[29] Unrest was growing in Cádiz, however, and on 28 May it exploded into revolt. Whilst a large crowd besieged Socorro's palace, the Conde de Montijo presented him with the demands of the Junta of Seville that he join the uprising forthwith. Seeing that he had no option but to comply, Socorro gave way, but in so unenthusiastic a manner as effectively to sign his own death warrant. As with Cuesta's letter to the Ayuntamiento of León, the proclamation issued by the council of war which Socorro summoned to decide on what to do provides valuable evidence of the proccupations of the *generalato*. After commencing by stating his pleasure at the patriotism of the inhabitants of Cádiz, Socorro went on to point out that an uprising would nevertheless amount to the height of folly. Cádiz would be left exposed to British treachery; the harvest would be lost for want of labour; the improvised levies who would constitute the bulk of Spain's forces would be certain of defeat; and the French would be justified in inflicting the most severe punishment upon the civilian population for having had the temerity to interfere in the conduct of war. In addition, Socorro maintained that resistance was not only futile but unnecessary, given that the Spanish royal family had abdicated their rights to the throne of their own free will, and had never ceased to proclaim their friendship with Napoleon. If the population nevertheless insisted on going to war, then Socorro would agree to lead them, but only if they would accept the need to accept military discipline and to form into regular units, for he would not be responsible for the masssacre that would otherwise be certain to ensue. Above all, the people must realise that they were on the brink of a long and bitter struggle that would require a major financial and economic, as well as military, effort.[30] Realistic though these words were, they were hardly calculated to reassure the increasingly angry crowd of Socorro's enthusiasm for the cause. After a night of growing tension, rioting broke out, almost certainly at the instigation of the Conde de Montijo, whose very presence suggests the existence of a *fernandino* plot to remove Socorro from power. The troops then went over to the mob, and the unfortunate Marquess was dragged out of his palace and murdered.[31]

Between them Cuesta and Socorro may stand as exemplars for the rest of the *generalato*. Their refusal to consider the idea of a people's war was mirrored by the Captain General of Aragón, who described the *zaragozanos*' desire to turn themselves into soldiers overnight as 'a ridiculous pretension'.[32] Their suspicions of the British were the reflection of a widespread distrust of 'perfidious Albion', which the outbreak of war did nothing to relieve. Even the staunchly patriotic Castaños had refused to accept Dalrymple's maladroit suggestions that British troops should garrison Cádiz, Ceuta and Menorca, and that Britain should be granted 'commercial advantages to enable her to sustain the contest in which she was engaged'.[33] In the same way, the Captain General of Mallorca at first would not send troops to the mainland for fear that the British would take advantage of their absence to seize the island, whilst the provincial juntas proved most unwilling to allow British troops to land at major ports such as Cádiz

The army and the revolution

and La Coruña.[34] Finally, their fear of popular disorder was not only shared by generals who had opposed the uprising or only joined it under pressure. If Socorro's successor, Tomás de Morla, who was one such officer, issued a series of proclamations that were expressly calculated to suppress popular enthusiasm, similar fears were also expressed by such supporters of the patriot cause as Blake and Palafox.[35]

Opposition to the rising proved unavailing. In the last resort the authority of the Captain General, like that of the absolute monarchy itself, rested on the bayonets of the standing army. That the rank and file and many junior officers were no longer to be trusted was clearly shown by events in the French zone, Portugal and Denmark. Napoleon had assumed that the 28,000 Spanish troops whose garrisons had actually been occupied, or who were serving with his forces outside Spain, could simply be incorporated into the imperial war machine. Nothing could have been further from the truth. The only units to accept their new masters with docility were the Swiss regiments of Reding *mayor* and Preux, but both of them went over to the patriots as soon as they were hazarded on the field of battle. As for the rest of the troops, many regiments chose either to disband themselves or to march to join the patriots *en masse*. Officers who refused to co-operate were attacked and deposed, or simply abandoned to their own devices. Those regiments which did not join the insurrection as a body experienced wholesale desertion and in some cases disintegrated altogether.[36] The unrest even spread to the 13,000 Spanish troops cantoned in distant Denmark. Although deeply unhappy at the turn which events had taken, their commander, the Marqués de la Romana, could see no means by which he could take action, and therefore sought to temporise with the French. Even when he was provided with the hope of rescue by the Royal Navy, the accounts of his subordinates suggest that his vacillations were only brought to an end by the threatening attitude adopted by the officers and men under his command.[37]

With their troops in this temper, the generals had no hope of restoring order; indeed, to attempt to do so was often literally suicidal. In the first few days of the rising, aside from the Marqués del Socorro, the Conde del Torre del Fresno, the Captain General of the Naval Department of Cartagena, and the military governors of Villafranca de Panades, Tortosa, Málaga and Ciudad Rodrigo were all murdered. Amongst the many officers who were deposed and imprisoned were the Captains General of Aragón and Catalonia, and the Commandant General of the Costa de Asturias y Santander.[38] Those who succeeded in escaping the purge only did so by throwing in their lot with the insurgents, albeit with varying degrees of enthusiasm. If some, like Cuesta, were to serve the patriot cause without reserve, others remained opposed to the rising, sending secret appeals to the French for help and attempting to sabotage the insurgents' operations. In a few cases, like that of Tomás de Morla, they merely bided their time until a suitable opportunity came for them to escape.[39]

The established order having thus been swept away, the way was open for the creation of new organs of political authority. In most areas of Spain, these took the form of a network of local and provincial juntas. The membership of these committees generally consisted of the original leaders of the insurrection, to whom was added an admixture of notables who were elected or co-opted from the local community. Often presided over by leading churchmen or even those generals who had survived the initial turmoil, these bodies may nevertheless be said to have been dominated by the civilian notables. The spectre of military authority was still not laid to rest, however, for few generals followed the example of Francisco Xavier Castaños who had immediately placed his troops at the disposition of the Junta of Seville.[40] So strong was the habit of giving way to the claims of the army that the civilians found themselves unable to press home their advantage. In Catalonia the provincial junta had deposed the existing Captain General, the Conde de Espeleta, in favour of the Marqués del Palacio. However, it first allowed itself to be beguiled into transferring itself from Lérida to Palacio's headquarters at Tarragona, and was then overawed into offering him not only the presidency of the Junta, but also supreme executive authority.[41] Elsewhere, rather than seeking to insinuate themselve into the confidence of the juntas as in the case of Palacio, the generals instead chose the path of open confrontation through the formation of personal dictatorships.

These attempts may be classified as having either been 'legitimist', in that they justified themselves by reference to the viceregal status enjoyed by the Captains General before 1808, or 'populist', in that they based themselves upon an appeal to the crowd. Of the former, the best example is the régime established by García de la Cuesta in Old Castile. Despite the fact that he had almost no regular troops with which to back up his authority, Cuesta was able to browbeat his civilian rivals into accepting him as their master. A provincial junta was established at Valladolid, but its function was simply to maintain order, enlist recruits and amass the sinews of war.[42] Cuesta's political survival was in part a tribute to the strength of his character, which by all accounts was particularly obdurate, but a number of other factors also reinforced his position. Unlike Catalonia or Valencia, for example, Old Castile did not have a recent tradition of resistance to the Bourbon monarchy or its representatives. In addition, unlike most of his fellows, Cuesta carried with him the seal of Fernando VII's personal approval. For the time being, therefore, no one sought openly to challenge his position. Yet as soon as this was done, the Captain General was found to be a 'paper tiger': in an era where power in the last resort rested upon an appeal to the populace, the forms of the *ancien régime* could not survive unless backed up by the sort of military force that was no longer available to Cuesta or any of his fellows. The fragility of his position is demonstrated by the fate of the Conde de Conquista when he attempted to establish a similar régime in Valencia. Having initially agreed to accept the presidency of the provincial junta, he suddenly assumed supreme political and military authority and ordered the arrest of all those who refused to obey him. Supported by the crowd, his civilian subordinates promptly threatened to put him on trial for treason. With his bluff having thus been called, Conquista had no option but to relinquish his ambitions.[43]

The weakness of the legitimist position is underlined by the survival of the dictatorship established by José Palafox in Zaragoza. A similar example of populist militarism may be found in Córdoba where the commander of the local Resguardo, Pedro Agustín Echávarri, briefly set himself up as dictator of the city. However, defeated by the French at Alcolea on 7 June 1808, Echávarri was soon forced to flee.[44] Palafox proved far more durable. Whereas Cuesta had essentially ruled in opposition to the notables and the mob, Palafox was from the very start careful to co-opt the former and to shelter behind the latter: as one, admittedly hostile, observer put it, 'Palafox governed Zaragoza in the midst of confusion; the agitators who acted as the instruments of his power made speeches in front of his lodging ... demanding in the name of the people that which he wished to be done.'[45] An examination of the manner in which he gained power certainly reveals both a high degree of stage management, and total reliance upon popular pressure. When the growing discontent spilled over into an uprising on 24 May 1808, Palafox was still in hiding outside the city. Guillelmi having been deposed following his refusal to arm the people, the conspirators incited the crowds to call for his replacement by Palafox. As soon as the cry had been taken up, one of their members was immediately on hand to lead a delegation to fetch that officer from his hiding place. Palafox affected surprise and even terror at their appearance, and then adopted an attitude of the most exaggerated reticence, refusing to accept the command unless it was offered him with proper form by the Audiencia. By the time that body had been assembled two days later, the mob had worked itself into a frenzy and was threatening the unfortunate councillors with death. Yet Palafox still refused to give way and the ensuing delay gave rise to rumours that he was being detained against his will. The Audiencia's palace was promptly invaded, and its terrified occupants had to beg Palafox on bended knee to save them. Having thus created the impression of being a selfless patriot pushed to the fore by forces beyond his control, he at last agreed to accept the Captain Generalcy, though not without a further display of reluctance.[46]

On taking power, the new Captain General's first action was to rid himself of the *godoyista* Intendant, Ignacio Garciny. The rising had caught Garciny in Madrid where he had gone in an apparent attempt to ingratiate himself with Fernando VII. As soon as he heard of events in Zaragoza, he wrote to Palafox to offer his services, but all his approaches were ignored and he was not even permitted to return. Instead, Palafox replaced him with one of his chief confederates, a wealthy merchant named Lorenzo Calvo de Rozas.[47] His dictatorship was now secure, but Palafox nevertheless felt the necessity of providing it with a greater measure of legitimacy. To this end he convoked the long-since defunct Cortes of Aragón. When it assembled on 9 June, Calvo de Rozas demanded that it should appoint the Captain General Jefe Político y Militar – or, in other words, Dictator – of Aragón, but the Cortes refused to agree to this proposal. Instead, although quite prepared to confirm Palafox in the Captain Generalcy, it voted that a junta should be elected to exercise the sovereign power. Somewhat taken aback by this unexpected display of independence, Palafox responded by postponing further discussion of the issue until the next session. There was no other session, however: before it could be held, the French had attacked the city, and thus put an end to all political discussion. In the meantime, Palafox's appointment as Jefe Político y Militar of Aragón was brazenly published as fact, a lie that was thereafter consistently to be maintained by all his numerous partisans.[48]

No civilian junta was ever formed in Zaragoza, Palafox remaining in power until the city finally succumbed to a second French siege in February 1809. His success was due in part to the prestige which accrued to him from the French failure to take Zaragoza in the siege of June–August 1808. At the same time, however, he was himself a part of the revolutionary movement. Ruling as a popular demagogue, he was careful to retain the support of local society by showering his patronage upon all and sundry, abolishing unpopular measures of taxation, fraternising with the crowds, and appealing to the vanity of the population, not only by issuing a series of bombastic proclamations, but also by rewarding the popular heroes of the siege.[49] In this manner, Palafox was able to escape from the onslaught experienced by many of his fellow officers even after they had joined the uprising. Had the purge of the high command solely been restricted to those generals who had refused to join the insurrection, then its traditional explanation would have continued to be acceptable. The very fact that the killings and arrests continued stands testimony to the presence of other explanations for the violence besides that of simple patriotism. In the Canaries, for example, the Captain General declared for the rising as soon as news of its outbreak had been received from the mainland, only to be overthrown by a group of his subordinates headed by Colonel Carlos O'Donnell.[50] Nor was joining the patriots sufficient to save the Captain General of Galicia firstly from being replaced by the more malleable Joaquín Blake, and then from being murdered by a mob of his own soldiers.[51] More junior officers also found themselves under attack: in Ronda, for example, a mob stormed the house of Pedro Agustín Girón after being persuaded by a friar that a guillotine was hidden there.[52] It is difficult to pinpoint the responsibility for such attacks on particular individuals, but it is nevertheless apparent that the mood of anger and suspicion from which they sprang was in part the work of the army's enemies. The clearest example of this process comes from Asturias where the ardent liberal Alvaro Flórez Estrada forged a letter purporting to come from Fernando, in which he made the most unfavourable comparisons between the heroism of the Spanish people and the pusillanimity shown by *los Castaños, Morlas* *y otros generales.*⁵³

The generals were also fettered by the provincial juntas' efforts to ensure that the army would remain firmly under their control. Many of them placed their armed forces in the hands of new commanders who owed their advancement entirely to the revolution, as in Murcia and Asturias where the command was given to retired officers of the provincial militia.⁵⁴ Another example is Joaquín Blake whom the Junta of Galicia promoted from the rank of Brigadier to that of Lieutenant General. Civilian commissioners were often sent to the various headquarters in the style of the *représentatives-en-mission* of the French Revolution.⁵⁵ The juntas could also rely upon their control of the sinews of war: as each provincial army was 'dependent on its own junta for bread', the commanders could simply be blackmailed into submission.⁵⁶ The Junta of Seville provides an excellent example of how this control could be exerted. After the victory of Bailén (19 July 1808), in which the Spaniards forced an entire French army to surrender, the logical course would have been for General Castaños to have followed up his success as fast as possible. Instead, he was forced to return to Seville and prevented from marching on Madrid until it was clear that only in this fashion could the Junta 'settle the government of the country according to their will and pleasure'. Despite the fact that the military situation demanded that he should now advance to the Ebro, he was not allowed to proceed a step further on pain of the pay and supply of his army being entirely cut off.⁵⁷

The inability of the generals to resist such pressures did not bode well for the success of the war which the uprising had brought in its train. At this stage, however, their greatest problem was not so much their freedom of operation as the quality of the forces which they had at their disposal. The bulk of the old regular army had been deployed around the coast of Spain or in its maritime possessions so as to ward off potential British raids. A large part of it had therefore remained in Spanish hands, for the French zone of control was still limited to a corridor connecting the area around Madrid with the frontier fortresses of San Sebastián and Pamplona. Outside this axis the invaders only held Figueras and Barcelona. In all the patriots could reckon upon a little over 100,000 men, but, dispersed as they were, these troops were everywhere in need of reinforcement. Practically the first act of all the new authorities had therefore been to declare all men to be eligible for military service, although the number of volunteers

The army and the revolution

was at first great enough to allow them to leave such measures in abeyance.[58] As far as the generals were concerned, the ideal course would have been to channel the new levies into the units of the old army, as was actually done to some extent in both Galicia and Andalucía. In their eyes, any unit in which the proportion of raw recruits amounted to more than one third of the whole was not to be trusted in the slightest.[59] In some cases, of course, such a policy was rendered impossible by the total absence of regular troops, as in both Old Castile and Aragón where Cuesta and Palafox were forced to form their levies into new regiments *faut de mieux*.[60] The civilian notables had other ideas, however. Preferring to form 'as many corps and companies as there were men of a certain influence desirous of a command', they broke up such regular units as they had, or at least contrived to starve them of recruits.[61] Their motives were simple. The patronage engendered by the creation of large numbers of new regiments would allow the provincial juntas both to gratify their own supporters, and to build up a substantial party in the officer corps whose interests would be bound up with the survival of the revolution. Should the juntas be so inclined, they would also be free to throw the military estate open to a far wider spectrum of society than had been the case before 1808. Whether this was actually done is a moot point, however: in an edict of 14 June 1808 the Junta of Seville stipulated that aspirants to the post of officer cadet would have to produce exactly the same documentation as they would have done before the revolution.[62]

At least two hundred new infantry regiments appeared in the course of 1808.[63] Their organisation and strength varied enormously, but the majority consisted of no more than a single battalion – as each regiment had its own headquarters, the more regiments that were created, the greater the patronage. Of negligible fighting value at the best of times, many of the new regiments did not even represent a notional addition to the army's ranks. A number of them only existed on paper, notwithstanding the appointment of a full quota of officers. In Catalonia, for example, the provincial junta decreed the formation of forty Tercios de Miqueletes, each of one thousand men, only to find that the population would not enlist, preferring to serve in their traditional capacity as *somatenes*.[64] Several other units, such as the Voluntarios Distinguidos de Cádiz, served no other purpose than to allow the notables to indulge in patriotic martial posturing and enjoy the *fuero militar* whilst yet avoiding service in the field. Generally limited to those men who could afford to pay for their own uniforms and equipment, the members of these units were not expected to serve outside their own cities. At best, they could be regarded as a civic militia, whose job was as much to protect the notables from the mob as to protect Spain from the enemy.[65]

Spanish mobilisation in 1808 was also affected by the ingrained hostility to the army in general, and to military service in particular. Several officers who were engaged upon the organisation of resistance found themselves under attack by mobs who were convinced that they were actually French agents.[66] In Vizcaya, for example, the provincial junta refused to form any regular units at all, and chose instead to rely entirely upon bands of irregulars in the style of the Catalan *somatenes*.[67] As for the general populace, they clearly preferred the picturesque and the novel to service in the ranks of the old army. When General Castaños' victorious troops finally entered Madrid after the battle of Bailén, the inhabitants showed no interest in the regular soldiers who had actually borne the brunt of the fighting, and instead flocked to see the Lanceros de Jérez, a troop of Andalucían horsemen dressed in bull fighting costume.[68] An added inducement to enlist in the ranks of the new regiments was their high pay: whereas private soldiers in the regular army earned a meagre half a *real* per day, their counterparts in the new regiments received from three to six.[69] The result was that the regulars often found it impossible to gain the recruits which they needed; still worse, they also lost many deserters to their rivals.[70]

The mere creation of masses of new regiments was not enough to prepare Spain for war against the French. As a later analysis put it:

Victories are not won by large armies, but by those which are well organized and well constituted . . . Experience has shown . . . that the reunion of considerable forces, far from being useful, is harmful and disadvantageous unless they are disciplined . . . Such masses of men, which are improperly given the name of divisions and armies, do not provide more than an apparent strength that, taken for real in moments of excitement and illusion, leads only to the most unfortunate disasters . . . To create soldiers, it is not enough to issue uniforms to men whose individual courage is not matched by knowledge of military service . . . a truth which is all the more apparent in arms like the cavalry and horse artillery where at least four months is needed to make a soldier.[71]

The rising, in short, had given Spain not an army, but the raw material of an army. Means had to be found by which the new levies could be armed and maintained, they had to provided with an adequate proportion of cavalry and artillery, and, above all, they had to be given the solidity and reliability of regular troops through the imposition of military discipline. Otherwise patriot Spain could expect only to be over-run. The central problem which she faced was how this was to be achieved in the midst of war and revolution.

Aided by the financial and material assistance that began to pour in from Great Britain, the contents of Spain's own arsenals, and the contributions of the population, the new authorities were at first able to dominate the logistical question, albeit in a somewhat haphazard fashion: General Castaños' Army of Andalucía was already going hungry as early as the battle of Bailén.[72] A more immediate problem was posed by the question of discipline. Many of the levies immediately deserted or simply dispersed to their homes, whilst others perpetrated serious disorders in the pursuit of rabid witch-hunts against suspected traitors. Attempts to curb their exhorbitant pay were met by riots, and they often proved a greater terror to the civilian population than the French.[73] It was therefore not long before even the provincial juntas began to see the value of military discipline as means of controlling the popular disorder which they had themselves unleashed.[74] Yet the levies often refused to be disciplined. In Jaca, Santander and Oviedo officers who attempted to bring their troops to order were immediately accused by them of trying to stifle their patriotic spirit.[75] However, for all their refusal to allow themselves to be militarised, the patriot levies were as vociferous in demanding that they be led against the French as they were prone to accuse their generals of treason if they proved unwilling to do so.[76]

Given time there was no reason why the levies should not have been turned into soldiers, but time was not a commodity that was possessed by the insurgents. As the French responded to the uprising by sending out punitive expeditions in all directions, fighting actually began almost immediately. The result was predictable. As a British liaison officer wrote in 1809:

Crowds flocked to arms, but while untaught to bear them were from time to time hazarded all at once in the field, creating confusion from the want of military knowledge of their leaders as well as their unsteadiness . . .
Though in some instances I have observed that the . . . peasantry have acted against the enemy with peculiar resolution and resistance, it has always been in very particular actions, in strong passes, in woods, or where

the knowledge of the country has peculiarly favoured them. Almost in every instance where reliance has been placed upon the favourable results of a general action in which the Spanish troops were employed, combined with the new militia and peasantry, a failure has been the consequence.[77]

Nobody could deny the courage of the Spanish levies. Placed in a situation where they were not required to manoeuvre and where they were safe from the French cavalry, they displayed a ferocity that astonished even their own leaders. Hence the failure of the French assaults on the cities of Valencia, Zaragoza and Gerona. In the open, however, they were absolutely helpless. The very men who put up such a desperate resistance at Zaragoza had only days before been scattered by the French with almost no loss to themselves at Tudela, Mallén and Alagón. Moreover, however long it would have taken, even Zaragoza must ultimately have fallen had not the French abandoned the siege in the wake of the battle of Bailén. The civilian defenders might have fought the French to a standstill in the streets of the city, but they could not forever have remained impervious to the establishment of a proper blockade: the most exalted patriotism is not proof against starvation.

The real salvation of Zaragoza may be regarded as the victory of Bailén. So influential were the myths generated by this battle that for once it is worth examining its campaign history in some detail. On 24 May a French column commanded by General Dupont had set out from Madrid with orders to crush the Andalucían insurgents and secure the vital port of Cádiz. On 7 June Dunpont defeated Echávarri at Alcolea, and went on to sack the defenceless city of Córdoba. Alarmed at his own isolation, he had then drawn back to Andujar to await reinforcements. His inactivity continued for some weeks, during which time Castaños was able to prepare his army for action. Eventually forced to move against Dupont by popular pressure, at least he was able to do so with the cohesion of his forces still intact: having been badly shaken by the fate of Echávarri's levies at Alcolea, the Junta of Seville had permitted Castaños to fill up the ranks of the old regiments and even to send home a mass of unwanted recruits.[78]

Profiting from Dupont's continued inactivity, Castaños had decided to envelop his opponent. Pinning him down with a demonstration in his front, he dispatched the divisions of Reding and Coupigny along the south bank of the Guadalquivir with orders to cross the river further east and then to strike northwards to cut the main road to Madrid. Unknown to the Spanish commander,

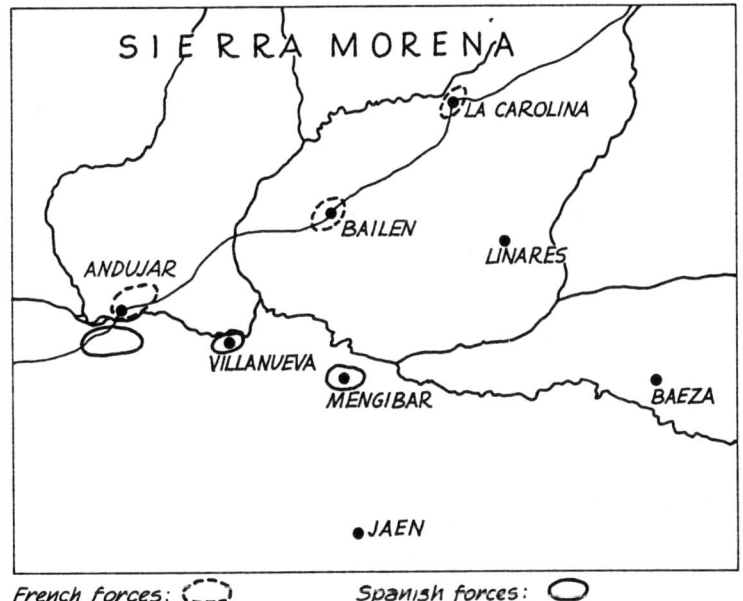

3 The campaign of Bailén

however, Dupont had received the divisions of Gobert and Vedel from Madrid as reinforcements. Gobert's troops were mostly echeloned along the high road to protect communications with Madrid, but Vedel was stationed at the town of Bailén, sixteen miles to the east of Andujar, where he was well positioned to repel any thrust on the part of Reding and Coupigny: indeed, the mere news of his presence proved sufficient to deter the former from attempting to cross the Guadalquivir on 15 July. Matters would now have remained at a stalemate, but for the fact that on the same day Castaños had demonstrated against Dupont's position at Andujar with such determination that the Frenchman had concluded that he was heavily outnumbered and had sent to General Vedel asking him for reinforcements. Vedel had in the meantime concluded that Reding, whose performance on 15 July can only be described as lacklustre, was no threat to his position. Receiving Dupont's message, he marched to join his chief with his entire command, except for a small detachment that was left to watch the Guadalquivir. He arrived at Andujar on the afternoon of 16 July, only to discover that Castaños had never pressed his attack. Moreover, in Vedel's absence from Bailén, on the morning of 16 July Reding had fallen upon his rearguard at Mengibar. Although they were supported by a detachment of Gobert's division, the French were routed and forced to flee north-eastwards along the road to Madrid.

Vexatious as this was, the French position was still very strong. With 21,000 men concentrated at Andujar, Dupont could launch a sudden strike on either Castaños or Reding, and defeat them before they could come to each other's aid. Instead of doing so, however, he chose to send Vedel back to Bailén with orders to chase Reding back over the Guadalquivir. Meanwhile, Dupont himself would continue to watch Castaños at Andujar. On the morning of 17 July Vedel duly marched back to Bailén, but when he got there he could find no trace of Reding. Hearing rumours that a Spanish force had seized the passes by which the road to Madrid crossed the Sierra Morena, Vedel immediately assumed that they must belong to Reding and set off in pursuit, continuing his march as far as La Carolina where he picked up the troops who had been defeated at Mengibar.

In reality, however, Reding had merely fallen back across the river in order to rest his troops. It was only after being joined by the division of General Coupigny (which had spent the previous few days demonstrating against the ford of Villanueva midway between Andujar and Mengibar) on 18 July that Reding bestirred himself and marched to occupy Bailén. Bivouacking there that evening, he planned to move on Andujar the next morning. To his astonishment, however, at dawn on 19 July he was himself attacked by Dupont. Although he had had no idea that Bailén was in danger, Dupont had still become alarmed at the gap which had opened between himself and Vedel, especially as it had become clear that only a part of the Spanish army was facing him at Andujar. On the morning of 18 July the French general had therefore resolved to retreat. Had this decision been implemented immediately, there seems little doubt that Dupont could have got away, but a number of factors led him to delay his march until nightfall, thereby enabling Reding and Coupigny to get across his line of march. Even though the French army had been split in two and a part of it trapped, all was not yet lost. On the one hand, Dupont had sufficient forces with him to stand a reasonable chance of breaking through had he launched them

The army and the revolution

against the Spaniards in a concentrated mass. On the other, it was open to Vedel, who had now decided to return to Bailén, to take Reding and Coupigny in the rear. Yet neither occurred: whilst Dupont squandered his forces in a series of piecemeal assaults that the Spaniards were easily able to beat off, Vedel was so dilatory in his return that he only arrived when the battle was already lost. With his artillery silenced, every unit in his army defeated, his troops exhausted by the effects of a night march and then a day of battle without water in the full heat of an Andalucían summer, and Castaños' main body rapidly coming up in his rear, Dupont was forced to surrender. Even then, Vedel might still have got away, for his troops were still intact and possessed a safe line of retreat to Madrid. However, the Spaniards secured his capitulation as well by promising that all the French forces would be returned to France by sea. As a result, some 19,000 men fell into Spanish hands.

In view of its immense repurcussions, it is important that the battle of Bailén should be placed in perspective. The troops of Reding and Coupigny had fought extremely well, but they had only had to face around half the forces available to the French, Dupont having been accompanied by only 11,000 men. Dupont's troops had been as mediocre as his conduct of the battle, whilst those of Castaños had largely consisted of disciplined veterans. Disastrous though Bailén was, there was also no reason why the mass of French troops still in central and northern Spain could not have maintained their positions until such time as reinforcements had been sent by Napoleon. Rather than standing their ground, however, on 1 August the French evacuated Madrid, and retired behind the river Ebro. Not only had the campaign been lost by the French rather than won by the Spaniards, but the contribution of the Spanish people was by no means so great as was later to be claimed by proponents of the Nation-in-Arms. Popular resistance had certainly helped demoralise the French, whilst armed civilians had fought with great courage in the defence of beleaguered Spanish cities. In the field, however, the raw levies had proved to be a liability. Problems even occurred when they were employed in guerrilla operations. In Catalonia, for example, although the *somatenes* proved adept at harassing the French columns, they could never be relied upon to appear at a given place and time, and were notoriously unwilling to serve outside their home districts.[79] If the French were soon bottled up in Figueras and Barcelona, the situation would undoubtedly have been different had the invaders had more troops at their disposal, or the *somatenes* not been supported by regular troops brought from the Balearic islands.

Patriot Spain was blind to such nuances, however. Thanks in large part to the powerful undercurrent of anti-militarism which had accompanied the uprising, both the provincial juntas and the press represented the Spanish successes as the fruit of popular heroism and magnified them beyond all reason. Just as Dupont's half-trained conscripts were described as 'the conquerors of the world', so minor Spanish victories were compared to those of Jena and Auerstadt.[80] The press, in particular, became ever more euphoric, inventing victories were none had taken place, playing down the significance of Spain's frequent defeats and giving credence to foolish rumours, of which perhaps the most absurd was that the Spanish uprising had inspired the people of France to overthrow Napoleon.[81] Whilst it could be argued that such propaganda was necessary to encourage popular resistance, its effects were to some extent counter-productive, for patriot Spain became filled with increasing over-confidence and complacency.[82] A further obstacle to the effective prosecution of military operations existed in the political struggle that now broke out over the establishment of a new central government. At the beginning of the uprising, the fragmentation of Spain into its constituent regions had been a positive blessing, for the French had been denied the chance to decapitate the uprising at its very inception.[83] A consolidation of authority was now essential, however, for, as one British liaison officer wrote:

No regular or combined system of action is to be expected from any of the armies, whose movements and operations have nothing to depend upon but the caprices of the respective juntas, who are solely activated by narrow-minded, short-sighted policy, never extending their views beyond the precincts of their respective districts.[84]

According to the general report, the administration of the juntas left much to be desired owing to the incompetence, ambition and inexperience of many of their members.[85] If such charges are perhaps too sweeping, their attitude to the common cause certainly left much to be desired. For example, having first declared itself to be the supreme government of Spain and the Indies, the Junta of Seville embarked upon a blatant programme of empire building, sending out emissaries to take control of Cádiz, Granada and Badajoz. Socorro's murder brought Cádiz within its orbit almost immediately, but Badajoz and Granada both refused to accept its tutelage. A move on the part of the Conde de Tilly to bring the latter to heel by the dispatch of an army was only scotched by General Castaños. Unable to overcome the resistance of its Spanish rivals, the Junta then switched its attention to the annexation of southern Portugal.[86] In the meantime, it also sought to make an alliance with the Juntas of Galicia and Catalonia by suggesting that the three of them should divide Spain between them, and rule in conjunction with one another.[87] Similar aspirations were displayed elsewhere. The Junta of Galicia attempted to establish its preponderance in the northwest through the establishment of a Cortes del Norte which would bring the Juntas of Asturias and Old Castile under its influence.[88] The Junta of Extremadura attempted to seize the Portuguese fortress of Elvas.[89] In Aragón, José Palafox had been extending his power base by sending out officers, arms and supplies to many towns within a wide radius of his capital.[90] From the very beginning of the uprising, he and his supporters made repeated calls for the election of a single regent – who would presumably be none other than Palafox himself – to rule Spain in the absence of the monarch.[91]

These ambitions and jealousies inevitably had a severe impact on the war effort. Often threatened by rival factions in their own districts, the various authorities attempted to retain as many troops under their direct control as possible. When the Junta of Seville refused to permit Castaños to march on Madrid, the Juntas of Granada and Jaén demanded the return of the troops they had 'lent' him for the campaign of Bailén.[92] The Junta of Asturias consistently refused to send more than a token force of troops beyond its borders on the grounds that it needed the bulk of its forces to maintain order at home.[93] Because they were the only regular troops that he had, Cuesta refused to send his cavalry to join the Army of Galicia, even though they were of no use to him on their own and could greatly have facilitated the operations of General Blake.[94] Thanks to the Junta of Extremadura's designs on Elvas, a large part of its forces had still not reached the front when the French finally launched their counterattack in November.[95]

With their British allies becoming increasingly restive, it was clear even to the most obstreperous of the new authorities that they would have to agree to the formation of a central government. Under what auspices this should be done was unclear, however. The institutions of the *ancien régime* were both unrepresentative and politically suspect. Nor were the provincial juntas prepared to tolerate a military dictatorship camouflaged as a regency. As the Junta of Seville argued in a proclamation of 3 August 1808:

... the moment has arrived to establish a civil government of the entire nation ... to which the military will be subordinated. The confidence of the nation – and by implication its resources and wealth – will necessarily be given to the civil government. Without the civil government, the army would find itself in the indispensable necessity of having to use violence to obtain support. It could never win the confidence of the public by such means, however, any more than it would be able to make use of the nation's resources, so that it would end by destroying the general good ... which is the sole aim of all government. Do not let us vainly flatter ourselves with talk of the dictators of Rome ... Very wise restrictions were placed upon them and ... their powers limited to a very brief period. The risk of despotism ... forced the adoption of very strict precautions which the customs of our times no longer permit. Spain has learnt wisely from past centuries. She has never established a military dictator. Her military commanders ... have been the first to embrace this state of affairs, which is as old as the monarchy itself.[96]

An interim solution to the problem was eventually found in a plan that had originally been put forward by the Junta of Murcia. Each provincial junta was to send two representatives to a national congress known as the Junta Central that would elect a new government.[97] The Junta of Seville jibbed at these proposals, but threats from the British, popular unrest and its own fear of the military soon convinced it of the need to give way. After some negotiation it was duly agreed that the congress should meet at the neutral site of Aranjuez.[98] The revolutionary authorities were not alone in their contemplation of the formation of a new government. In Madrid a legitimist faction had coalesced around the Council of Castile which had been attempting to promote its own claims in this area ever since the French had evacuated Madrid.[99] Its president, the Duque del Infantado, had accompanied Fernando to Bayonne, but had then joined the suite of Joseph Bonaparte. Returning to Madrid with *el rey intruso*, he had changed sides again on the arrival of the news of Bailén. Yet this display of opportunism had not been sufficient to deter the British liaison officer, Charles Doyle, from encouraging him to 'crush private piques ... and pour the energies of the different provinces into one stream'.[100] Why Doyle should have placed such confidence in the Duke is unclear: not only had he been totally discredited by his defection to King Joseph, but the accounts of his vapidity are legion.[101] At the same time, the Council of

Castile's unpopularity was shown by the contemptuous reception given to its attempts to seize the leadership of patriot Spain.[102] Doyle's flattery was nevertheless sufficient to encourage Infantado to approach his fellow generals for support. Hardly surprisingly, Blake would not co-operate, but Cuesta was delighted to join the plot.[103] The dictator of Old Castile had never reconciled himself to the revolution, and had quickly become embroiled in a series of disputes with the civilian authorities. His relations were especially poor with the Junta of Galicia, which had been pressing him to send his handful of regular cavalry to join Blake's army. His anger was exacerbated by the defeat of Medina de Río Seco (14 July 1808), which Cuesta attributed to Blake's failure to give him adequate support (Blake, in contrast, blamed the defeat on Cuesta).[104] The conflict was fuelled by the political situation in Old Castile. The president of Cuesta's puppet junta, Antonio Valdés, had soon tired of the Captain General's pretensions. After Medina de Río Seco, he had therefore fled to join the Cortes del Norte, whose authority he was now ordering Cuesta to recognise.[105]

Even with Cuesta's support, Infantado still needed the help of General Castaños. Not only did Castaños command the largest army in Spain, but he had acquired immense prestige from his victory at Bailén. In return for his assistance in crushing the provincial juntas, he was offered a place in a triumverate composed of himself, Cuesta and Infantado, which would govern Spain with the aid of the Council of Castile. However, unlike most of his fellows, Castaños was realistic enough to realise that the revolution had to be accepted as a *fait accompli*, and would therefore only agree to the convocation of a council of war that would elect a commander-in-chief.[106] Within a very few days his common sense had been vindicated, first of all by the result of the council of war of 5 September, and then by the downfall of General Cuesta. As the council of war could not even agree on a common candidate for the post of supreme commander, it is hard to see how the *generalato* could have found the unity necessary to bring about a successful military coup.[107]

The impotence of the generals was underlined by the collapse of Cuesta's dictatorship as soon as he attempted to challenge the new government. At the Cortes del Norte, the fugitive Junta of Old Castile had selected Valdés and the Marqués de Quintanilla to be its representatives to the proposed congress at Aranjuez. To reach their destination, however, they had to cross Cuesta's domain. Furious at what he regarded as a fresh act of defiance, the Captain General arrested them at Segovia on charges of treason and rebellion.[108] This action naturally excited a great deal of alarm, but the nascent Junta Central refused to be over-awed. Its president-designate, the Conde de Floridablanca, wrote to Cuesta ordering him to release his prisoners immediately, relinquish the command of his army, and come to Aranjuez to stand trial. Moreover, the two deputies who had been sent to act in place of Valdés and Quintanilla were refused recognition.[109] Cuesta's first reaction was to claim that the Junta Central had no authority other than to elect a regency.[110] His defiance met with no support, however. Castaños wrote to him condemning his actions out of hand, and warning that they could provoke civil war.[111] Even the Council of Castile disowned his rebellion and advised him to submit.[112] Sensing the direction in which events were moving, the officer whom Cuesta had placed in charge of the captives decided to release them. Deserted by his own subordinates and deprived of his hostages, Cuesta had no option but to surrender and come to Aranjuez as ordered. It was to little avail that the Supreme Council of War later determined that he had acted within his rights: by that time, the Army of Castile had been disbanded and amalgamated with the forces of General Castaños.[113]

Cuesta's humiliation left the way clear for the establishment of the Junta Central. Most of the provincial juntas had intended that this body should either elect a new government or function as a mere co-ordinating committee that would direct their efforts towards a common goal.[114] In the event, however, on 26 September 1808 their representatives proclaimed the Junta Suprema Central de Gobierno to be the sovereign government of Spain and the Indies.[115] Dramatic though this development was, it did little to alter the essential political realities of patriot Spain: whether she was ruled by a collection of provincial juntas or the Junta Central, the principle of civilian power stood supreme. If the fall of General Cuesta had not been enough to persuade them of this lesson, within days the generals had received another reminder in the treatment meted out by the Junta Central to José Palafox. Ignoring his protests at its assumption of the sovereignty, the Junta refused to admit the delegates which he had sent to Aranjuez on the grounds that they had not been chosen by a proper provincial junta. Forced to return to Zaragoza, they had formally to be 'elected' by a hastily-convened meeting of the city's church wardens.[116]

More seriously, the Junta Central refused to appoint a commander-in-chief. Although Castaños was an obvious candidate for this post, the Junta had been imbued with a deep suspicion of the military by Cuesta's rebellion, and therefore refused to contemplate such an appointment. According to Castaños himself, it was particularly unwilling to appoint him because of his great popularity.[117] Despite much pressure from the British, the supreme command was placed, not in the hands of a single general, but in those of a six-man sub-committee of the Junta Central presided over by the War Minister, General Cornel. This body was assisted by an advisory committee of generals known as the Junta General de Guerra, of which Castaños was given the chair.[118] Strategy was thus to be the preserve of the civilian government, to which the field commanders were to be responsible for their operations.

The arrangements made by the Junta Central with regard to the army did no more than institutionalise the transformation in its position which had been brought about by the uprising of 1808. From being the most dominant figures in the Spanish administration, the Captains General and military governors were reduced to being the mere tools of a revolutionary government, though not before many of the men who had held office in May 1808 had been killed or imprisoned. Even when they chose wholeheartedly to place themselves at the head of the insurrection, they still found that they had no option but to submit to the rule of the civilian juntas. The only viable alternative was to adopt a populist stance and appeal directly to the crowd, though in reality this was merely to exchange one master for another. The downfall of the generals, as with that of Manuel de Godoy, was once more the result of a political choice on the part of their subordinates. Professional and patriotic motives alike dictated that the officers and men of the Bourbon army should rally to the uprising. By the time the former had realised that by doing so they were jeopardising their own privileges, resistance had already become futile. The notables were triumphant, but it remained to be seen whether they could consolidate their victory.

Chapter 3 Notes

1 *Manifiesto del Consejo Real*, p. 34; M. Azanza and G. O'Farrill, 'Memoria de D. Miguel de Azanza y D. Gonzalo O'Farrill sobre los hechos que justifican su conducta política desde marzo de 1808 hasta abril de 1814', *Memorias de tiempos de Fernando VII*, ed. M. Artola

Gallego (Madrid, 1957), p. 289.
2. Blanco White, *op. cit.*, 361–2; *Manifesto imparcial*, 23–4.
3. *Manifesto imparcial*, p. 28; Schepeler, *op. cit.*, I, 50–1.
4. Schepeler, *op. cit.*, I, p. 49; *Manifesto imparcial*, p. 28; Alcalá Galiano, *op. cit.*, I, 165–8; Toreno, *op. cit.*, I, p. 78; Nellerto, *op. cit.*, I, p. 55; Gámez, *op. cit.*, n.p.; for a modern, if somewhat uncritical, view of the Dos de Mayo, see J. C. Montón, *La revolución armada del Dos de Mayo en Madrid* (Madrid, 1983).
5. Priego López, *op. cit.*, II, p. 22; Schepeler, *op. cit.*, I, 117, 259; Alvarez Valdés, *op. cit.*, p. 26; Toreno, *op. cit.*, I, p. 126.
6. B. Hamnett, *La política española en una época revolucionaria, 1790–1820* (Mexico City, 1985), 65–6.
7. Wellington to H. Wellesley, 3 May 1812, US. WP.12/1/5.
8. Alvarez Valdés, *op. cit.*, 11–13; Toreno, *op. cit.*, I, p. 102.
9. Toreno, *op. cit.*, I, p. 106; Schepeler, *op. cit.*, I, p. 406.
10. Schepeler, *op. cit.*, I, p. 117; Girón, *op. cit.*, I, 201–2; Toreno, *op. cit.*, I, p. 132.
11. Cf. Hamnett, *op. cit.*, 57–8.
12. V. Martínez Colomer, *Sucesos de Valencia desde el dia 23 de mayo hasta el 28 de junio del año de 1808* (Valencia, 1810), p. 1 (hereafter, Martínez Colomer, *Sucesos de Valencia*).
13. R. Mesonero Romanos, *Memorias de un setentón* (Madrid, 1880), p. 9.
14. Palafox, *op. cit.*, 55–8.
15. *Gazeta de Valencia*, 7 June 1808, HMM. AH2-6(408); A. Alcaide Ibieca, *Historia de los dos sitios que pusieron a Zaragoza en los años de 1808 y 1809 las tropas de Napoleón* (Madrid, 1830–31), I, 4–5.
16. Priego López, *op. cit.*, II, 1–5.
17. Schepeler, *op. cit.*, I, 320–3; Priego López, *op. cit.*, II, p. 4.
18. Schepeler, *op. cit.*, I, p. 259.
19. Nellerto, *op. cit.*, III, 425–34.
20. J. Bouligny, 'Memorias sobre la guerra de España' (MS), p. 2, SHM. AGI.1/2/8, No. 6 (hereafter Bouligni, MS); H. Dalrymple, *Memoir written by Sir Hew Dalrymple, Bart., of his Proceedings as connected with the Affairs of Spain and the Commencement of the Peninsular War* (London, 1830), 8–18.
21. *Gazeta Ministerial de Sevilla*, 1 June 1808, 6–7, HMM. AH2-5(373); *Gazeta de Valencia*, 17 June 1808, HMM. AH2-6(408); Palafox, *op. cit.*, p. 59; Schepeler, *op. cit.*, I, 117–8.
22. *Correo de Sevilla*, 14 May 1808, p. 238, HMM. AH3-5(343); M. Muñoz Maldonado, *Historia política y militar de la guerra de la independencia de España contra Napoleón Bonaparte desde 1808 a 1814*, I, 183–4; Schepeler, *op. cit.*, I, 167–8;
23. *Suplemento a la Gazeta de Valencia*, 7 June 1808, HMM. AH2-6(408); *Gazeta Ministerial de Sevilla*, 29 June 1808, HMM. AH2-5(373); Schepeler, *op. cit.*, I, 348–9;
24. Spencer to Castlereagh, 29 May 1808, PRO. WO.1/226, p. 320; Schepeler, *op. cit.*, I, p. 77; Blanco White, *op. cit.*, p. 374.

25 Cuesta to Ayuntamiento of León, 29 May 1808, PRO. WO.1/234, 259–60.
26 Cuesta, *op. cit.*, p. 3.
27 Cuesta to Junta of León, 2 June 1808, PRO. WO.1/234, 261–2.
28 Cox to Dalrymple, 17 September 1808, PRO. WO.1/234, p. 223.
29 Socorro to Gore, 24 May 1808, PRO. WO.1/226, p. 349; Jacob, *op. cit.*, p. 27; Schepeler, *op. cit.*, I, p. 289.
30 Proclamation of Socorro, 28 May 1808, SHM. CDF.DCCCLXIV, p. 40.
31 Toreno, *op. cit.*, I, 121–2; Schepeler, *op. cit.*, I, 273–5.
32 V. Pina Ferrer, *Paginas de 1808: memorias de un patriota* (Zaragoza, 1889), 302–3.
33 H. Dalrymple, *op. cit.*, 14–17.
34 Spencer to Castlereagh, 10 June 1808, PRO. WO.1/226, 443–8; A. Wellesley to Castlereagh, 21 July 1808, PRO. WO.1/228, 70–1; Oman, *op. cit.*, I, p. 323.
35 Proclamations of Morla, 30 May and 14 June 1808, PRO. WO.1/226, p. 421, SHM. CDF.DCCCLXIV, p. 58; Blake to Mahy, 2 June 1808, SHM. AGI.3/4/24, No. 2; Palafox, *op. cit.*, p. 69.
36 Anonymous letter from Madrid, 27 May 1808, PRO. WO.1/226, p. 417; Roche to Castlereagh, 1 August 1808, PRO. WO.1/233, p. 364; *Diario de Badajoz*, 1 July 1808, HMM. RVP.T46; *Diario de Granada*, 1 July 1808, HMM. AH14-2(2452); Lazán, 'Resumen histórico' (MS), p. 1, SHM. AGI.3/4/32; Toreno, *op. cit.*, I, 101–2, 131, 144; Schepeler, *op. cit.*, I, 163, 348–9, 352, Alvarez Valdés, *op. cit.*, 55–6.
37 MSS of J. O'Donnell, Barón de Armendariz and E. Salvador, SHM. AGI. 3/2/4, Nos. 2, 4, 5; Nellerto, *op. cit.*, I, p. 112.
38 Toreno, *op. cit.*, I, 109, 115, 120–2, 126, 129, 143, 145; Schepeler, *op. cit.*, I, 398–405; Alvarez Valdés, *op. cit.*, p. 35; Muñoz Maldonado, *op. cit.*, I, p. 210.
39 Bouligni (MS), *op. cit.*, p. 4, SHM. AGI.1/2/8, No. 6; Toreno, *op. cit.*, I, p. 135; Schepeler, *op. cit.*, I, 141–2; Oman, *op. cit.*, II, 174–5.
40 Girón, *op. cit.*, I, 202–3.
41 Schepeler, *op. cit.*, I, 450–1; F.X. de Cabanes, *Historia de las operaciones del Ejército de Cataluña en la primera campaña de la guerra de la usurpación o sea de la independencia de España* (Tarragona, 1809), II, 34–7 (hereafter Cabanes, *Ejército de Cataluña*).
42 Cox to Dalrymple, 17 September 1808, PRO. WO.1/234, p. 223; *Gazeta de Valencia*, 10 June 1808, HMM. AH2-6(408); Cuesta to Floridablanca, 17 September 1808, *cit.* 'Documentos que justifican la respuesta al manifiesto de Don Gregorio García de la Cuesta', 3–5 (hereafter JSC, Documentos), in *Impugnación que hacen los individuos que compusieron la Suprema Junta Central al manifiesto del Capitán General Gregorio de la Cuesta* (Cádiz, 1812), SHM. CDF.DCCLXXVII.
43 Schepeler, *op. cit.*, I, 450–1.
44 *Ibid.*, I, p. 280; *El Español*, 30 April 1812, p. 12, HMM. AH4-2(710);

Gazeta de Valencia, 28 June and 5 July 1808, 96, 102–3, HMM. AH2-6(408).
45   I. Garciny, *Cuadro de la España desde el reinado de Carlos IV* (Valencia, 1811), p. 24.
46   Palafox, *op. cit.*, 60–3, 65–7; Marqués de Lazán, 'Exposición del Teniente General Marqués de Lazán en justa defensa de su hermano el Capitán General de Aragón, D. Josef Palafox y Melcí' (MS), 4–5, RAH. 14-9-6:6925 (hereafter Lazán, 'Exposición'); Alcaide Ibieca, *op. cit.*, I, 6–10; Toreno, *op. cit.*, I, p. 141.
47   Garciny, *op. cit.*, 20–3, 29; Schepeler, *op. cit.*, II, p. 162.
48   *Gazeta de Valencia*, 21 June 1808, HMM. AH2-6(408); Garciny, *op. cit.*, 23–6; L. Calvo de Rozas, 'Representación de Don Lorenzo Calvo de Rozas en defensa del Exmo. Sr. D. José de Palafox y Melcí y paralelo entre este y el General Castaños' (MS), 6–9, BS. Col. de Arteche, 292–2 (hereafter Calvo de Rozas, 'Defensa de Palafox').
49   Proclamations of J. Palafox, 11 and 26 October 1808, *cit. Gazeta de Valencia*, 21 October and 11 November 1808, 492, 563, HMM. AH2-6(408); L. de Villalva, *Zaragoza en su segundo sitio* (Palma de Mallorca, 1811), 18–20; Schepeler, *op. cit.*, II, 159–62.
50   Schepeler, *op. cit.*, I, p. 316.
51   *Gazeta de Valencia*, 17 June 1808, HMM. AH2-6(408); Schepeler, *op. cit.*, I, 410–11; Toreno, *op. cit.*, I, 118, 122–3, 186.
52   Girón, *op. cit.*, I, p. 217.
53   Alvarez Valdés, *op. cit.*, p. 41.
54   *Ibid.*, p. 21; Toreno, *op. cit.*, I, p. 133.
55   Patrick to Castlereagh, 8 August 1808, PRO. WO.1/233, p. 566; *Gazeta Ministerial de Sevilla*, 6 July and 30 August 1808, 87, 215, HMM. AH2-5(373); *Diario de Granada*, 24 July 1808, HMM. AH14-5(2452); Toreno, *op. cit.*, I, 122–3, 186.
56   Doyle to Castlereagh, 28 August 1808, PRO. WO.1/227, p. 218.
57   Doyle to Castlereagh, 28 and 29 August 1808, PRO. WO.1/227, 213, 238; Holland, *op. cit.*, p. 404.
58   Decree of Junta of Valencia, 23 May 1808, PRO. WO.1/226, p. 423; decrees of Junta of Seville, 28, 29 and 31 May 1808, SHM. CDF.DCCCLXIV, 39, 41–2, 44; decrees of Junta of Granada, 31 May and 4 June 1808, SHM. CDF.DCCCLXIV, 45–60; Palafox, *op. cit.*, p. 71.
59   Conde de Bacon, *Manual de un joven oficial o ensayo sobre la teoría militar* (Madrid, 1813), viii–xi; Morla to Castaños, 11 August 1808, RAH. 11-2-2:8154, 11–21; P. Ramírez y Vandama, *Táctica general de la infantería* (Palma de Mallorca, 1811), 22–4; Girón, *op. cit.*, I, p. 220.
60   Whittingham to Bentinck, 28 October 1808, PRO. WO.1/230, 140–1; Schepeler, *op. cit.*, I, p. 163.
61   Leith to Castlereagh, 13 September 1808, PRO. WO.1/229, 207–9; Doyle to Infantado, 31 August 1808, PRO. WO.1/227, p. 209; Pusterla to Junta Central, 30 September 1808, RAH. 11-2-2:8154, IX, 24-B; Schepeler, *op. cit.*, II, p. 310;

The army and the revolution

62 Bando of Junta of Seville, 14 June 1808, SHM. CDF.DCCLXI, p. 120.
63 Clonard, *Historia orgánica*, VI, 284–94.
64 Doyle to Cooke, 18 December 1808, PRO. WO.1/227, p. 601; *Manifiesto de la Junta Superior del Principado de Cataluña* (Tarragona, 1809), p. 5 (hereafter Junta de Cataluña); Cabanes, *Ejército de Cataluña*, I, p. 47; Oman, *op. cit.*, I, p. 373; Schepeler, *op. cit.*, II, 216–20, 276; Toreno, *op. cit.*, II, 125, 180.
65 Decree of Junta of Cádiz, 12 June 1808, SHM. CDF.DCCCLXIV, p. 53; *Diario de Málaga*, 17–18 November 1808, 654–8, SHM. CDF.XL; Alcalá Galiano, *op. cit.*, I, 227–8; Schepeler, *op. cit.*, II, p. 522.
66 M. García del Barrio, *Sucesos militares de Galicia en 1809 y operaciones en la presente guerra del Coronel D. Manuel García del Barrio, comisionado del gobierno para la restauración de aquel reino, y electo Comandante General por los patriotas gallegos* (Cádiz, 1811), 8–12; Schepeler, *op. cit.*, I, p. 117.
67 Lefevre to Leith, 25 October 1808, PRO. WO.1/229, p. 451.
68 Mesonero Romanos, *op. cit.*, 53–5; Alcalá Galiano, *op. cit.*, I, 202–3.
69 Proclamation of Junta of Seville, 28 May 1808, SHM. CDF.DCCCL-XIV, p. 38; Spencer to Castlereagh, 21 June 1808, PRO. WO.1/226, p. 478; Schepeler, *op. cit.*, I, 127, 232; Alvarez Valdés, *op. cit.*, p. 106.
70 'Diario de operaciones del Ejército de la Izquierda al mando del Tnte. General D. Joaquín Blacke [sic]' (MS), p. 25, SHM. AGI.3/4/28, No. 1 (hereafter *Ejército de la Izquierda* (MS)).
71 *Periódico Militar del Estado Mayor General*, 9 January 1812, SHM. CDF.CXVI.
72 F. Guervos to his parents, 22 July 1808, RAH. 11-5-7:9003, No. 1.
73 Proclamation of Junta of Seville, 4 July 1808, SHM.CDF.DCCLXI, p. 127; Toreno, *op. cit.*, I, p. 273; Schepeler, *op. cit.*, I, 127, 183; Blanco White, *op. cit.*, p. 386; Alvarez Valdés, *op. cit.*, 79–80, 83, 105; Alcalá Galiano, *op. cit.*, I, p. 202.
74 Doyle to Stewart, 30 and 31 July 1808, PRO. WO.1/227, 43, 60–1;
75 Spencer to Castlereagh, 17 June 1808, PRO. WO.1/226, p. 464; F. García Marín, *Memorias para la historia militar de la guerra de la revolución española* (Madrid, 1817), 26–7; Toreno, *op. cit.*, I, p. 112; Alvarez Valdés, *op. cit.*, 55–6.
76 Bouligny (MS), 6–8, SHM. AGI.1/2/8, No. 6; Toreno, *op. cit.*, I, p. 205.
77 Green to Cooke, 1 September 1809, PRO. WO.1/237, 555–7.
78 Spencer to Castlereagh, 21 June 1808, PRO. WO.1/226, p. 478; Girón, *op. cit.*, I, p. 220.
79 F. Guervos to his parents, 20 January 1809, RAH. 11-5-7:9003, No. 13; Schepeler, *op. cit.*, II, p. 98.
80 Girón, *op. cit.*, I, p. 205; proclamation of Ayuntamiento of Manresa, 6 July 1808, *cit. Guerra de la Independencia: proclamas, bandos y*

combatientes, ed. S. Delgado (Madrid, 1979), 152–9.
81 *Diario de Badajoz*, 1 July 1808, HMM. RVP.T46; *Gazeta Ministerial de Sevilla*, 9 and 13 July 1808, 90, 99, HMM. AH2-5(373); *Gazeta de Valencia*, 2 August 1808, p. 205, HMM. AH2-6(408).
82 Cox to Castlereagh, 3 August 1808, PRO. WO.1/231, p. 320; Blanco White, *op. cit.*, 344–5; Schepeler, *op. cit.*, II, p. 309.
83 Wellington to Castlereagh, 21 July 1808, PRO. WO.1/228, p. 72; Toreno, *op. cit.*, I, p. 124.
84 Carroll to Leith, 8 September 1808, PRO. WO.1/229, p. 240.
85 Cox to Dalrymple, 27 August 1808, PRO. WO.1/231, p. 343; A. Pillado to Garay, 6 December 1808, AHN. Estado, 17/1–2, p. 38; Leith to Castlereagh, 8 and 13 September 1808, PRO. WO.1/229, 91–2, 208; Garciny, *op. cit.*, p. 28; Schepeler, *op. cit.*, I, p. 126.
86 Dalrymple to Castlereagh, 16 September 1808, PRO. WO.1/234, 181–2; Whittingham, *op. cit.*, 43–4; *Gazeta de Valencia*, 19 July 1808, p. 155, HMM. AH2-6(408).
87 Schepeler, *op. cit.*, I, 455–8.
88 *Ibid.*, I, 435–7; Toreno, *op. cit.*, I, 197–8.
89 Dalrymple to Castlereagh, 27 September 1808, PRO. WO.1/234, p. 219.
90 Garciny, *op. cit.*, p. 157; Schepeler, *op. cit.*, I, 163–4; García Marín, *op. cit.*, p. 27; Calvo de Rozas, 'Defensa de Palafox' (MS), 9–11.
91 Proclamation of J. Palafox, 31 May 1808, *cit.* Toreno, *op. cit.*, I, p. 143; Palafox to Council of Castile, 14 August 1808, *cit. Gazeta Extraordinaria de Madrid*, 18 August 1808, PRO. WO.1/233, p. 597; Palafox to Junta of Valencia, 13 August 1808, *cit. Gazeta de Valencia*, 19 August 1808, p. 271, HMM. AH2-6(408); proclamation of Conde de Montijo, 4 August 1808, SHM. CDF.DCCCLXIV, p. 22; Schepeler, *op. cit.*, I, p. 166.
92 Dalrymple to Welllington, 9 September 1808, PRO. WO.1/228, 233–4; Junta of Jaén to Castaños, 7 July 1808, RAH. 11-2-2:8154, IX-34.
93 Bishop of Santander to Leith, 2 September 1808, PRO. WO.1/229, 137–8; Junta of Asturias to Leith, 6 September 1808, PRO. WO.1/229, p. 123.
94 Doyle to Stewart, 12 August 1808, PRO. WO.1/227, p. 131; Birch to Leith, 8 September 1808, PRO. WO.1/229, p. 226; Carroll to Leith, 8 September 1808, PRO. WO.1/229, p. 234.
95 Oman, *op. cit.*, I, p. 420.
96 Proclamation of Junta of Seville, 3 August 1808, PRO. WO.1/231, p. 309.
97 *Circular de la Junta de Murcia*, 22 June 1808, SHM. CDF.XXVII, p. 27.
98 Cox to Castlereagh, 6 August 1808, PRO. WO.1/231, p. 295; Cox to Dalrymple, 17 September 1808, PRO. WO.1/234, 223–4; Toreno, *op. cit.*, I, p. 270.
99 Toreno, *op. cit.*, I, p. 266.

The army and the revolution

100 Doyle to Infantado, 31 August 1808, PRO. WO.1/227, 251–2; Doyle to Castlereagh, 16 August 1808, PRO. WO.1/227, p. 190.
101 Moore to Castlereagh, 24 November 1808, PRO. WO.1/236, p. 79; J. García de León y Pizarro, *Memorias* (Madrid, 1953), I, p. 107; W. Beckford, *The Journal of William Beckford in Portugal and Spain 1787–88*, ed. B. Alexander (London, 1954), 311, 313; Alcalá Galiano, *op. cit.*, I, p. 297; S. Whittingham, *A Memoir of the Services of Sir Samuel Ford Whittingham*, ed. F. Whittingham (London, 1868), p. 64; G. Jackson, *The Diaries and Letters of Sir George Jackson*, ed. Lady Jackson (London, 1872), II, p. 322; Girón, *op. cit.*, I, p. 239.
102 Palafox to Council of Castile, 14 August 1808, *cit. Gazeta Extraordinaria de Madrid*, 18 August 1808, PRO. WO.1/233, p. 597; Patrick to Castlereagh, 15 August 1808, PRO. WO.1/233, p. 579; Leith to Castlereagh, 13 September 1808, PRO. WO.1/229, p. 114.
103 Doyle to Stewart, 12 August 1808, PRO. WO.1/227, p. 131; Doyle to Castlereagh, 20 August 1808, PRO. WO.1/227, 189–91.
104 Birch to Leith, 8 September 1808, PRO. WO.1/229, p. 226; Carroll to Leith, 8 September 1808, PRO. WO.1/229, p. 234; Holland, *op. cit.*, p. 404; Cuesta, *op. cit.*, p. 10.
105 Doyle to Stewart, 12 August 1809, PRO. WO.1/227, p. 131; Toreno, *op. cit.*, I, p. 263; *ibid.*, II, p. 5.
106 Castaños to Dalrymple, 13 August 1808, PRO. WO.1/224, p. 89; Toreno, *op. cit.*, I, 267–8.
107 Doyle to Castlereagh, 26 August 1808, PRO. WO.1/227, 211–13; Toreno, *op. cit.*, I, p. 268.
108 Toreno, *op. cit.*, I, p. 268; Cuesta, *op. cit.*, p. 12.
109 Cox to Dalrymple, 24 September 1808, PRO. WO.1/234, 249–50; Floridablanca to Cuesta, 16 September 1808, *cit*. JSC. *Documentos*, 13–14; Cuesta, *op. cit.*, p. 13.
110 Cuesta to Floridablanca, 17 September 1808, *cit*. JSC. *Documentos*, 3–5.
111 Castaños to Cuesta, 26 September 1808, PRO. WO.1/227, 395–9.
112 Council of Castile to Cuesta, 21 September 1808, *cit*. JSC. *Documentos*, 8–9.
113 Cuesta, *op. cit.*, 21, 24; Toreno, *op. cit.*, I, p. 279; Garciny, *op. cit.*, p. 90.
114 *Semanario Patriótico*, 22 September 1808, 65–9, HMM. AH1-6(195); Cox to Dalrymple, 10 September 1808, PRO. WO.1/231, 327–8; Jackson, *op. cit.*, II, p. 300; Toreno, *op. cit.*, I, 273–4.
115 Toreno, *op. cit.*, I, 275–6.
116 Garciny, *op. cit.*, 31–3; Palafox, *op. cit.*, p. 81.
117 Doyle to Castlereagh, 9 October 1808, PRO. WO.1/227, p. 418; F.X. de Castaños, *Reales Ordenes de la Junta Central Suprema de Gobierno del Reino y representaciones de la de Sevilla y del General Castaños acerca de su separación del mando del Ejército del Centro* (Seville, 1809), p. 182.
118 Bentinck to Floridablanca, 30 September 1808, PRO. WO.1/230,

46–50; Bentinck to Burrard, 2 October 1808, PRO. WO.1/231, 117–8; proclamation of the Junta Central, 2 October 1808, *cit. Gazeta de la Coruña*, 5 November 1808, p. 432, HMM. A592; *Gazeta Ministerial de Sevilla*, 14 October 1808, HMM. AH.2-5(373bis); Bentinck to Moore, 15 October 1808, PRO. WO.1/230, p. 93.

Chapter 4

The war of the Junta Central

The establishment of the Junta Central in September 1808 was greeted with the highest hopes even by members of the Bourbon *generalato*.[1] If they had been denied the political power to which they had been accustomed, they could at least hope for some amelioration in the military situation. With political and geographical unity restored to the Spanish nation, it would be possible to reunite the various provincial forces into a single national army, to implement a common strategy, and to make full use of Spain's resources in the struggle against Napoleon. Yet these hopes were never realised, the record of the Junta Central being one of unbroken defeat. Indeed, by the time of its downfall in January 1810, Spain had been reduced to such a state of prostration that she could hope to do no more than to survive until such time as she could be liberated by the Anglo–Portuguese army of the Duke of Wellington. Spanish resistance did not come to an end, and was to play a major part in the defeat of the French, but it is nevertheless true to say that from 1810 onwards the Spaniards were increasingly forced to take a secondary role in their own liberation.

Contemporary observers had no hesitation in attributing the blame for Spain's misfortunes to the shortcomings of the Junta Central, whose members were widely accused of corruption, incompetence and megalomania. In April 1810, for example, *El Español* published a seering critique of its rule, remarking:

It was not necessary to have had very close dealings with the Junta Central to know that it was a collection of men for the most part intent on obtaining personal advantages, and that the few times that it was obliged to attend to public business, it did not take decisions, but rather shifts to avoid having to do so.[2]

The Junta Central was certainly not without its faults. As the Conde de Toreno recognised, its leading members, Jovellanos and Floridablanca, were both 'stricken with years and ills'; furthermore, 'accustomed to the regularity and pause of our government, they could not overcome the customs and habits in which they had been brought up and grown old'. As for the other deputies, Toreno remarked that they were mostly 'men of probity, but lacking in outstanding and noble attainment'.[3] Their inexperience was also commented on by the British diplomat, Sir George Jackson, who described them as 'men who, although probably for the most part persons of the first prominence in their respective provinces, have been as little accustomed to deal with the great affairs of state as to see themselves invested with the means of patronage which they now enjoy'.[4] Exactly as had been the case with the Bourbon court, the Junta became surrounded with a crowd of place seekers who were eager to secure its patronage.[5] Their activities not only brought the government into considerable disrepute, but also had a serious effect upon the conduct of the war, for plans of campaign inevitably became one more weapon in the struggle for influence.[6]

The Junta also suffered from the inherent weaknesses of its own constitution. As the Marquess of Wellesley complained in September 1809:

> The... constitution of the Supreme Central Junta is not founded on any well understood system of union among the provinces, and still less on any just or wise distribution of the elements or powers of government; the confederacy of the provinces yet exists; the executive power is weakened and dispersed in the hands of an assembly too numerous for unity of council or promptitude of action, and too contracted for the purpose of representing the body of the Spanish nation. The Supreme Central Junta is neither an adequate representative of the Crown, nor of the aristocracy, nor of the people; nor does it comprise any useful quality either of an executive council or of a deliberative assembly, while it combines many objects which tend to disturb both deliberation and action ... It is not an instrument of sufficient power to accomplish the purposes for which it was formed...[7]

The Junta Central also received some plaudits, however, such as that penned by A. Cochrane Johnston in April 1809:

> I must do ... the Supreme Junta the justice to state that I never saw more activity, vigilance, and attention to business than exists in their administration of the government ... At nine o'clock every morning ... the Supreme Junta assemble to transact business, and they remain until two o'clock ... They again assemble in the evening at seven o'clock and remain until eleven

The war of the Junta Central

or twelve o'clock, agreeable to the business on hand. All the Secretaries of State and other public officers are always ready to give audience even to the lowest peasant if he wishes it . . . and they dispatch business with a promptitude and regularity which does them infinite honour. There are no holidays on the different days, *not even on Sundays* . . . You hear of no turtle feasts, haunches of venison or country seats, no expense for messengers carrying the red box at an enormous expense as in England from one watering place to another.[8]

The root of the problem was not so much the misdeeds of the Junta Central as the politico–military situation with which it was faced. As Spain's fortunes continued to deteriorate, so the pressure, and, indeed, the necessity for reform, became ever greater. Yet the Junta simply had no means of meeting the demands that were placed upon it and of translating its undoubted goodwill into effect. Every branch of the bureaucracy had been thrown into complete confusion by the revolution. As with the officer corps, the Intendance had become filled with the placemen of the provincial juntas, many of whom were not only totally incompetent but also inclined to treat their posts primarily as a source of personal gain.[9] As for the Ministry of War, it was swamped under the immense amount of work that had been generated by the creation of large numbers of new regiments and the appointment of equally large numbers of new officers.[10] In addition, although the Junta Central had proclaimed itself to be the supreme government of Spain, the authority of the provincial juntas effectively remained untouched, especially as they continued to control almost all the national revenue.[11]

An excellent illustration of the impotence of the Junta Central may be found in the situation relating to the supply of the Spanish armies on the Ebro in the autumn of 1808. Even before the campaign had actually begun, the Spaniards found themselves in serious difficulties: food was short, the men's clothing was in rags, and, despite the wintry weather, there were hardly any tents, blankets or greatcoats.[12] As usual, British observers were quick to blame this situation on the inactivity of the government, of which Lord William Bentinck wrote, 'The Central Junta have certainly not done and are not doing their duty. They have sacrificed the public interest to their own private views of ambition and advantage.'[13] Yet only twenty-four hours before Bentinck had written this letter the Junta had issued a decree in which it noted the sufferings of the troops and ordered the provincial juntas to open a public subscription for the supply of clothing to the army, and to reward those citizens who would make voluntary donations of clothing themselves. In addition, the juntas were authorised to place orders for uniforms with civilian contractors.[14] In the same way, it had authorised the Junta of Valencia to raise a loan of 2,000,000 *reales* from the propertied classes, as well as issuing orders to increase the production of saddles and muskets.[15] However, the practical effect of these orders was almost non-existent, either because of the disruption caused by the French offensive of November–December 1808 or because of the neglect and incompetence of the provincial juntas. The only remedy was for the Junta Central to have made its authority effective, but, in view of the widespread opposition to its rule, the only means of doing so would have been to achieve a dramatic military victory. Given the numerous defects of the forces which it had been bequeathed by the revolution of 1808, such a policy was not only unlikely to bring success, but also liable to increase Spain's difficulties.

The Spanish armies which took the field in the autumn of 1808 had by now begun to assume the aspect which they were essentially to retain for the rest of the war. On the one hand, the Bourbon veterans had been subsumed into the forces of the revolution, whilst on the other the raw levies of May 1808 had had sufficient time to acquire some of the rudiments of drill and military discipline. Between a half and two thirds of the troops were still composed of men who were little better than armed civilians.[16] Yet in theory there was no reason why these men should not have been turned into good soldiers: during the campaign that followed British observers frequently found occasion to praise 'the patience and ... the cheerfulness of the Spanish soldier under the greatest privations'.[17] The problem was not so much the men as the officers. As the Duke of Wellington remarked long after the war had ended, 'The Spaniards make excellent soldiers. What spoils them is that they have no confidence in their officers – this would ruin any soldiers – and how should the Spaniards have confidence in such officers as theirs?'[18] In much the same vein in May 1812 he had written to Henry Wellesley, 'Subordination and habits of obedience ... can be acquired by soldiers only in proportion as they have confidence in their officers: and they cannot have confidence in officers who have no knowledge of their profession, ... have no subordination among themselves, and never obey an order'.[19]

Wellington's opinion of the Spanish officer corps was shared by many other British observers.[20] It would be tempting to attribute the blame for this situation entirely to the influx of new officers who had entered the army in 1808. Many of the insurgent authorities had certainly showered commissions upon their supporters without any regard for their suitability. When the Supreme Council of War was charged with the task of examining the reasons for Spain's defeats, it concluded that this rash of appointments had been amongst the most serious and proposed that every commission issued since 1808 should be annulled.[21] By then, however, the damage had been done: because dismissing the new officers was clearly a political impossibility, Spain was left encumbered with a mass of officers who were so incompetent that they attracted the ridicule even of their own men.[22] Yet this is too simplistic an explanation of the problem. There is considerable evidence to suggest that many of the men appointed to command the new regiments were actually drawn from the mass of retired and supernumerary officers that had existed before 1808. In some units between one third and one half the officers had actually seen service before 1808, whilst, of the thirty infantry captains in the Fourth Army who were eligible for promotion to the rank of *sargento mayor* in February 1813, only four had been civilians at the beginning of the war.[23] To maintain that the revolution was solely responsible for the poor quality of the patriot officer corps would therefore appear to be wishful thinking.

Reports of misconduct among the officer corps are in any case so common that it is impossible to believe that the problem was confined to any one group within its ranks. Aside from the question of incompetence, absenteeism was widespread.[24] Rather than enduring the miseries of active service, many officers seized any available pretext to travel to such cities as Cádiz, Seville and La Coruña, in which sanctuaries they lived in the best style they could afford and served only 'to make a military appearance in the streets and gaming houses'.[25] The problem of absenteeism was compounded by the cavalier fashion in which many generals appointed serving officers rather than supernumeraries to be their *aides-de-camp*.[26] On the battlefield many officers proved to be worse than useless, British observers accusing them of placing themselves in the rear of their regiments, so as to be 'foremost in the front when running away'.[27] So serious did the problem become that in 1809 the Junta Central attempted to deprive all infantry officers of their horses in order to prevent them from absconding so easily.[28] The fact that they had horses at all is symptomatic of the indiscipline prevailing in the officer corps, for the Ordenanzas did not permit officers below the rank of captain to be mounted. In a similar breach of regulations, large numbers of common soldiers were employed as servants, a practice that removed large numbers of troops from the fighting line (by 1811 it was estimated that at least ten per cent of the Cádiz garrison were so employed).[29] Gambling and whoring were widespread, whilst fanciful non-regulation uniforms and extravagant moustaches were very much *de rigeur*.[30] Equally essential were vast quantities of baggage that served merely to encumber the movements of the Spanish armies.[31] Far from attempting to set a good example to their subordinates, many senior officers were instead inclined to look upon their posts as 'a recompense for the bad times they had endured in the lower ranks'.[32] Corruption was common. On the one hand, generals commandeered much-needed military transport for the use of their large personal entourages, which often included their mistresses as well as numerous servants, barbers, cooks and valets.[33] On the other, regimental commanders exaggerated their returns of strength, permitted their men to go sick on the slightest excuse, and connived at desertion so as 'to receive to their own emolument the pay of those who shall fall short of the number'.[34]

With officers of this nature, it was impossible to expect that the Spanish levies could possibly have been transformed into an adequate fighting force in the few months of respite bought by the victory of Bailén. Sapped not only by their lack of training, but by material wants of every description, the Spanish armies presented a sorry picture. Writing of the Army of Castile, for example, Whittingham described it as 'a complete mass of miserable peasantry, without clothing, without organization, and with few officers worthy of the name. The . . . principal officers have not the least confidence in their troops, and, what is yet worse, the men have no confidence in themselves'.[35] His pessimism was shared by Lord William Bentinck who informed Lord Castlereagh that in the event of a French attack, '. . . the Spaniards could not much be counted upon. The ignorance and inexperience of their officers and men scarcely entitles them . . . to the appellation of good and regular troops. In case of necessity . . . it would not be reasonable to place much dependence on the steadiness and support of a Spanish army constituted as they are at present'.[36]

Such worries were only too well founded. The history of the Spanish War of Independence is replete with examples of the fragility

The war of the Junta Central

of armies such as those which faced the French along the Ebro in the autumn of 1808. In the first place, the reaction of raw troops to combat was quite unpredictable. Though sometimes capable of the utmost heroism, particularly in the defence of fortified positions, they were also liable to sudden outbreaks of panic, of which the routs that took place on the eve of the battle of Talavera (28 July 1809), and at the battle of Belchite (18 June 1809), provide excellent examples.[37] Even when the Spaniards stood their ground, throughout the war the state of their drill was generally so poor that they were incapable of performing anything other than the simplest manoeuvres on the battlefield. As the Duke of Wellington complained to Henry Wellesley after the battle of Albuera (16 May 1811):

The Spanish troops, I understand, behaved admirably. They stood like stocks, both parties at times firing upon them, but they were quite immoveable, and this is the great cause of all our losses. After they had lost their position, the natural thing to do would have been to attack it with the nearest Spanish troops, but they could not be moved. The ... Spaniards can do nothing but stand still, and we consider ourselves fortunate if they do not run away.[38]

In view of the vital role played by the Spaniards at Albuera, these words must be considered somewhat churlish. Yet the fact remains that as late as 1812, Wellington was still being forced to complain that the Spaniards could 'neither advance nor retreat in order', all their movements being carried out '*à la débandade*'.[39] In practical terms, therefore, the Spanish armies could at best be expected either to march directly upon the enemy or to defend a position against attack. As long as no crisis intervened, they could generally be relied upon to to carry out either role with considerable determination. Although both battles were ultimately lost, the attacks delivered by the Spaniards at the battles of Valls and Medellín (25 February and 29 March 1809) stand witness to the courage with which they were capable of pressing home their assaults; indeed, at Medellín, a counter charge by two regiments of French dragoons was actually repulsed by Spanish infantry formed in line.[40] As shown by the example of Albuera and their victories at Bailén, Alcañiz, Tamames and San Marcial, the Spaniards could often show equal courage when on the defensive.

Yet the Spanish infantry were always vulnerable to their opponents. Particular problems were caused in the early days of the war by their shortage of skirmishers. The heavy screen of *tirailleurs* who preceded the advance of the French columns were always able to drive back their Spanish counterparts, and then to direct a destructive fire upon the immobile battle line behind them. As their casualties mounted, particularly among their officers, and their own volleys proved ineffective, so the Spaniards would sooner or later begin to waver, at which point the waiting French columns would charge home to administer the *coup de grace*.[41] The vulnerability of the Spanish infantry was accentuated by the weakness of their cavalry. Because of their complete inability to manoeuvre in the face of the enemy, it was essential for the Spaniards to protect the flanks of their defensive line with a powerful force of mounted troops, particularly in the perfect cavalry country constituted by the open plains of the Castiles. Throughout the war, however, the Spanish cavalry was execrable. In the first place, suitable horses and trained horsemen were few and far between: hence the frequent appeals that were made in 1808 for substantial numbers of British cavalry to be attached to the Spanish armies.[42] Furthermore, the punishing conditions of warfare in the Peninsula, which Wellington referred to as 'the grave of horses', made such cavalry as could be collected the subject of constant erosion. Inferior saddlery and deliberate neglect (occasioned by the 'infamous practice of purposely giving the horse a sore back that the dragoon may be sent with the horse to Seville') only accentuated the wastage.[43]

Even so, the Spaniards managed to field a substantial number of cavalry during the campaigns of 1809, and on occasion had more mounted troops than did their opponents. The problem was therefore ultimately one of quality rather than quantity. As the Duke of Wellington had complained after the battle of Talavera:

The Spanish cavalry are . . . in general well clothed, armed and accoutred, and remarkably well mounted, and their horses are in good condition . . . But I have never heard anybody pretend that in any one instance they have behaved as soldiers ought to do in the face of the enemy. They make no scruple of running off, and after an action are to be found in every village and every shady bottom within fifty miles of the field of battle.[44]

Although the Spanish cavalry did score a few successes, many Spaniards would have agreed that on the whole the remark was fair comment.[45] The cavalry had been thrown into even greater disorder by the uprising than the infantry, it being that much more difficult to improvise a scratch force of mounted troops. Such new regiments as were formed lacked the training to do anything other than, at best, to gallop upon the enemy in wild, and extremely vulnerable, disorder.[46] With time, of course, the training of the cavalry did improve, but, despite Wellington's comments, it seems certain that their horses were smaller than those of their opponents, as well as being severely undernourished, with the result that they could neither deliver a successful charge of their own nor withstand one delivered by the enemy.[47]

The inferiority of their cavalry placed the Spaniards at a serious disadvantage in any action that took place where the terrain was at all open. In battle after battle the course of the fighting would tend to assume a common pattern. Drawn up in linear order, the patriot armies would await the onslaught of their opponents, or alternatively march against them in a frontal attack. If they were on the defensive, the infantry would generally stand their ground, and on the offensive they might sometimes even drive back their opponents. On the flanks, however, the Spanish cavalry would be put to flight with monotonous regularity, thereby opening the way for a torrent of French horsemen to burst in upon the flanks and rear of the unfortunate infantry. Caught entirely by surprise, the infantry would not have the time to form square, and could only flee for their lives, to be ridden down or captured in their thousands. The collapse would frequently be so rapid that there would be no time to evacuate either the baggage or the artillery; indeed, when the moment came for the gunners to hitch up their pieces, they would frequently discover that their civilian drivers had absconded with the draught animals at the first sign of danger.[48]

The tactical inferiority of the Spanish armies was exacerbated by the poor quality of their commanders. A few generals won renown for the skillful and determined defence of the fortresses entrusted to their charge, whilst others showed themselves to be competent subordinates when placed in command of a division. With a number of exceptions, their courage and devotion was beyond question. For the most part, however, their personal bravery was not matched by their capacity to take command of a complete army. To be fair to the Spaniards, it should be stressed that their generals were really not so very different in their quality from those of any other nation, even Wellington frequently being driven to distraction by the failings of his subordinates. The difference was that the political and logistical conditions of warfare in Spain were much more complicated than elsewhere in Europe. Furthermore, Spain did not possess a native Wellington or Napoleon who could have led a collection of well-meaning mediocrities to victory. Nor were the Spanish generals well served by their headquarters. In the absence of a permanent general staff, which was not formed until 1810, each general appointed his own staff officers. The result was that the headquarters of the Spanish armies became filled with an ever-changing collection of well-connected young noblemen with little idea of how to fulfil their responsibilities.[49]

It was therefore hardly surprising that the Spanish army which took the field in the autumn of 1808 should have been poorly trained, organised, equipped and commanded. It is less apparent why there should have been so little improvement during the course of the long struggle which followed. As the Duke of Wellington complained in 1809:

> ... it is extraordinary that when a nation has devoted itself to war ... for the last two years, so little progress has been made in any one branch of the military profession by any individual, and that the business of an army should be so little understood. They really are children in the art of war, and I cannot say that they do anything as it ought to be done, with the exception of running away and assembling again in a state of nature.[50]

The explanation for this paradox may be found in the relentless nature of the war in which the Spaniards were engaged. Only in the autumn of 1808 between the retreat of the French armies to the river Ebro and the subsequent counterattack that was launched by a furious Napoleon was there a lull in the fighting of the sort that the Junta Central needed to restore order to its armies. Whether enough could ever have been achieved to forestall the Emperor's revenge is a moot point, but contemporary observers were convinced that the Junta was not making the best use of its opportunities. As Lord William Bentinck alleged, 'they are more preoccupied with trifles and nonsense about their own rank and state than with great national measures'.[51] The Junta's concern with its own status was far from being entirely frivolous, however. Although it was essential that it should impose its authority on patriot Spain, its rule was under attack from the very earliest days of its existence; indeed even some of its own members continued to demand that it form a regency and proceed to the election of a Cortes.[52] Convinced that a regency would inevitably produce a military dictatorship, the dominant faction within the Junta instead attempted to defuse the unrest by issuing an ambitious manifesto of social and political reform, only for this to attract renewed criticism of its priorities.[53]

The Junta's reformism was far from being irrelevant, for the pressure for reform generated in reaction to the rule of Godoy, María Luisa and Carlos IV had been redoubled by a growing belief that Spain could only emerge victorious from the struggle against Napoleon if she was prepared to put an end to the abuses that had brought about her downfall in 1808. However, unless the government could amass sufficient troops on the Ebro to hold off the counter-stroke that at that very moment was being made ready by Napoleon, there would be no time to implement the most apposite programme of reform. In this respect, all the patriot authorities must be held to be gravely at fault. After the battle of Bailén, Spain had fallen into a paralysing 'vertigo of triumph', thanks to the general exaltation of the supposed victory of the heroic Spanish people over 'the strongest and most warlike *tercios* of the north'.[54] Although not entirely proof against such excesses, the Junta Central did at least proclaim the need to raise a huge new army of 550,000 men.[55] Its means of putting such declarations into effect were extremely limited, however. All that it could do was to decree a reduction in the number of exemptions from the *sorteo* and the formation of an urban guard known as the Milicias Honradas.[56] The actual process of recruitment had to be left to the provincial juntas. At the beginning of the war many of these bodies had decreed the introduction of universal conscription, but fear of popular unrest and lack of resources ensured that this never became a reality. The precise situation varied from province to province, but most of the Spanish armies were initially composed of volunteers rather than conscripts. In May 1808, for example, the Junta of Seville had declared all male inhabitants ultimately to be liable for military service, with the proviso that unmarried men would be taken before men with families. However, it also decided that conscription should not actually be enforced until the supply of volunteers had been exhausted. Although fifty thousand men came forward, this was still well short of the Junta's stated target of 200,000. Yet rather than resorting to impressment, the authorities instead attempted to make good the shortfall by offering free pardons to bandits, smugglers and deserters who would agree to enlist.[57]

Reliance on the voluntary principle may have been politically necessary, but it could not provide the army with an adequate supply of manpower, for the patriotic fervour of 1808 seems to have been insufficient to outweigh ingrained popular hostility to military service.⁵⁸ Indeed, some British observers gained the impression that the Spanish people were not interested in fighting the French at all: as Sir George Jackson put it, that there was 'much froth, but little substance'.⁵⁹ Events such as the defence of Zaragoza demonstrate that these remarks were over-harsh, but it is hard to escape from the impression that the general desire to fight the French did not produce more than a limited number of recruits for the regular army: between May and November 1808 its strength only rose from 131,000 to 215,000 men.⁶⁰ Even these forces could not be deployed to the best possible advantage. Because the new government had been unable to wrest *de facto* control of the armed forces from the provincial juntas, it could not prevent them from keeping a part of their troops at home, or at the very least from delaying their dispatch to the front.⁶¹ Not that the Junta Central was much better, however: the large numbers of troops belonging to the Army of Andalucía who were still in Madrid at the time of the French attack make it difficult to contest the allegations later made by General Castaños that the Junta had attempted to reinforce its domestic position with the aid of troops purloined from his army.⁶² As many other units were still not ready to take the field, the result was that only 150,000 men actually reached the front in time to meet the French counterattack.⁶³

As Napoleon had amassed an army of over 230,000 men, the Spaniards were heavily outnumbered. They were also qualitatively inferior: unlike its predecessor, the new French Army of Spain was largely composed of the disciplined veterans of the Grande Armée. Nor were the Spanish forces on the Ebro concentrated to receive the impending blow. The council of war of 5 September 1808 had agreed to a joint plan of campaign which called for the bulk of the Spanish forces to mass in Old Castile. In the meantime, José Palafox was to attempt to turn the eastern flank of the French army which was then concentrated in the area between Miranda de Ebro, Vitoria and Pamplona.⁶⁴ However, in the absence of a commander-in-chief, the plan had little chance of being carried into effect, and was soon ruined by the actions of General Blake. Blake had been extremely perturbed at the prospect of bringing the Army of Galicia, or, as it had now been renamed, of the Left, into the Castillian plains on account of his want of cavalry.⁶⁵ Ignoring the agreed plan, he therefore advanced along the skirts of the Cantabrian mountains and

The war of the Junta Central 127

then struck northeastwards towards Bilbao. Since Palafox had simultaneously advanced on the right flank, the outnumbered and inferior Spanish armies were now strung out along a very wide arc around their opponents, and were thus exposed to defeat in detail. As if that was not serious enough, there was a yawning gap in the centre of their line between Blake's Army of the Left and Castaños' Army of the Centre – a clumsy amalgam of the Armies of Andalucía, Castile, and Valencia and Murcia – which had moved forward to the line of the Ebro between Logroño and Tudela. The gap should have been filled by the Army of Extremadura, but this force had been badly delayed in reaching the front, and had only just begun to come up when the French offensive began in November. As a result, the main road to Madrid was almost undefended.[66]

Rather than concentrating their armies whilst there was still time in the favourable defensive positions offered by the line of the river Ebro, the Spaniards instead chose to compound their errors. At a second council of war held on 20 October Castaños and Palafox agreed that whilst they launched an offensive towards Pamplona, Blake should be requested to press eastwards along the coast towards Irun. The French would thereby be surrounded and forced to surrender in a gigantic repetition of the battle of Bailén.[67] Foolhardy though this plan may have been, it is but fair to point out that the generals were no longer free agents. Thanks to the bombastic outpourings of the patriotic press and the pernicious influence of the battle of Bailén, the civilian population had no conception either of the miserable state of the Spanish armies or of their dangerous strategic situation: not only were the people 'exhibiting most happily the most perfect contempt for French courage', but it was widely believed that 300,000 Spaniards faced perhaps 80,000 starving and disease ridden Frenchmen.[68]

The chances of disaster were now increased still further by a renewed outbreak of political intrigue. The advent of the Junta Central had not put an end to the political ambitions of José Palafox, who was still determined to purge all the partisans of Godoy who had survived the turmoil of May 1808. It was therefore inevitable that both Castaños and Blake should have attracted his particular enmity. Not only were both of them potential regents, but Castaños was one of the last of the commanders appointed by Godoy and Carlos IV still to retain his position. Moreover, his obvious patriotism gave the lie to much of the black propaganda that had been

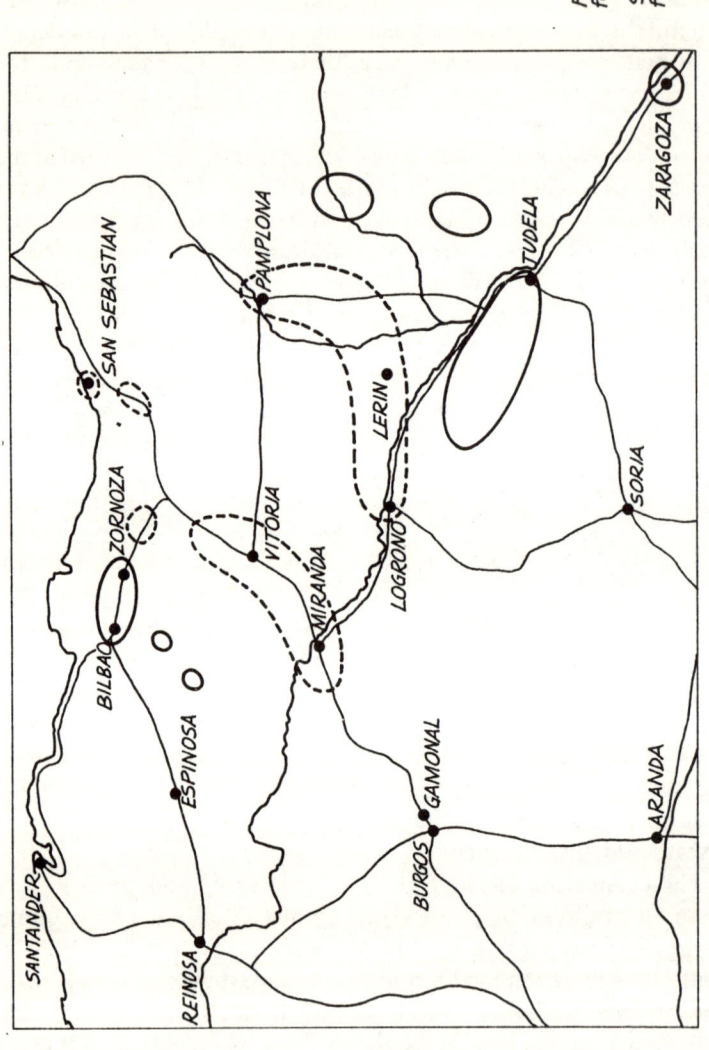

4 The military situation in northern Spain, October 1808

heaped upon the previous régime. In his own eyes Palafox therefore had good reason to remove both generals, and he was now provided with what seemed to be an excellent opportunity for doing so. The wild excitement generated by the battle of Bailén and the retreat of the French had created an expectation of further successes, but the expected victory had stubbornly failed to materialise. As the population was completely unaware of the lack of men and supplies that had effectively paralysed the operations of the Spanish armies, it was an easy task for the *palafoxistas* to portray Castaños and Blake as being at the best lukewarm in their support for the patriot cause.

Trading on the renown José Palafox had won from his successful defence of Zaragoza in the first campaign of 1808, his representatives in the Junta Central, Francisco Palafox and Lorenzo Calvo de Rozas, began to poison the minds of their fellow deputies against the two generals. These intrigues soon bore fruit: Blake was sent a series of peremptory orders to advance immediately, and a military commission dispatched to Castaños' headquarters with the task of speeding up his operations.[69] The composition of this body, which consisted of Francisco Palafox, the Conde de Montijo, and the Marqués de Coupigny, is significant. The vested interest of Francisco Palafox does not require further dilation, but it should be noted that both he and Montijo shared a common reputation as foolish and persistant troublemakers who were ever given to intrigue for its own sake. Montijo, moreover, was related to the Palafox family, and had been one of the leaders of the aristocratic clique who had engineered the coup at Aranjuez. As far as this group was concerned, a *palafoxista* dictatorship was now the only means of achieving their ends. As for the Marqués de Coupigny, he had commanded one of the two Spanish divisions that had borne the brunt of the fighting at Bailén, and had ever since been bitterly jealous of the fame which it had brought to Castaños.[70]

The disastrous effects of injecting political intrigue into the conduct of war soon made themselves apparent. During the second half of October substantial French forces had begun to press in upon Blake's isolated position in Vizcaya, and had forced him to evacuate Bilbao. Blake should have retreated immediately, especially as the French were already threatening his line of retreat, but at the crucial moment a letter arrived from Francisco Palafox ordering him to attack the French.[71] Paralysed by indecision, Blake wavered between the two alternatives, and was eventually defeated by the French at

Espinosa de los Monteros on 10–11 November. Finally compelled to retreat, he then discovered that the invaders had blocked the road at Reinosa, leaving him with no option but to abandon all his guns and baggage, and to flee northwards into the wilds of the Cantabrian mountains from where the survivors of his army eventually reached safety in León.

By then, however, Blake was no longer at their head. Back at Aranjuez, as Lord William Bentinck reported, 'the Junta here are very impatient for the attack of [i.e. upon] the French, and are very angry both with Castaños and Blake for their apparent inactivity'.[72] Even before the defeat of Espinosa it had therefore decided to replace the latter general with the Marqués de la Romana, who was newly arrived from Denmark.[73] His disgrace was soon shared by Castaños who since the end of October had been locked in conflict with the commission sent to his headquarters by the Junta Central. Far from aiding his operations, this body had been stirring up discontent among his subordinates and collaborating with José Palafox to make his task impossible.[74] At the same time, mysterious rumours began to spread that Castaños was under the influence of creatures of Godoy and even that he was in the pay of the French.[75] As Sir George Jackson noted, the result was that:

Castaños is at present very unpopular at Madrid, and such is the state of the public mind ... that I would not answer for his life should he prove unsuccessful. Indeed, it appears to me that that he has no alternative but to conquer or fall gloriously on the field.[76]

With his erstwhile popularity reduced almost to nothing, the victor of Bailén was unlikely to survive the growing discontent. On 14 November the Junta 'yielded to the popular demand which has generally and loudly condemned the inactivity and supineness of General Castaños' and agreed to his replacement by the Marqués de la Romana.[77] However, as La Romana was at that moment about to take the command of the Army of the Left in distant Cantabria, it was decided not to tell Castaños, but to leave him *in situ* until such time as his replacement could actually take up his new appointment (how La Romana was actually to take command of two armies at once was never made clear: there was no suggestion that he should ever be appointed as a central commander-in-chief).[78]

The chaos that beset the Spanish command could not have come at a worse time, for on 10 November the great offensive of the French

The war of the Junta Central

army had finally begun under the command of Napoleon himself. Pouring through the gap in the Spanish centre, the invaders had overwhelmed the newly arrived Army of Extremadura outside Burgos at Gamonal (10 November 1808), and had then fanned out across the plains of Old Castile. Whilst the Emperor led one column southwards towards the capital, other forces struck out northwards and eastwards so as to surround the Armies of the Left and the Centre. Thanks to Blake's break-neck flight across the Cantabrian mountains, the former managed to escape, but the paralysis which reigned in the headquarters of the latter prevented it from either escaping the trap that had been set for it, or from launching an offensive that might have diverted the attention of the enemy from a march on Madrid. After a fortnight of inconsequential manoeuvring, quarrelling, confusion and intrigue, the combined forces of the Armies of the Centre and Aragón were beaten at Tudela on 23 November. Total disaster was only averted by the fact that the turning column sent by Napoleon from Old Castile to block the Spanish retreat had not been able to reach its designated position in time.[79]

In consequence, the way was still clear for Castaños to adopt the only logical course of action left open to him, which was to withdraw the Army of the Centre into central Spain, leaving José Palafox to defend Zaragoza as best he could. The Junta Central had belatedly sent orders for Castaños to do just that, taking with him two divisions of the Army of Aragón, but the Palafoxes could not contemplate such a move. Loudly proclaiming Zaragoza to be the 'citadel of Spain', they proposed that both armies should retreat within its walls. After every effort had failed to persuade Castaños to accede to this futile plan, Francisco Palafox retaliated by instructing all the Army of the Centre's stragglers to rally on Zaragoza, inciting its troops to desert, and seizing its military chest, which had been sent to the city for safety. As for the order placing two Aragonese divisions under the command of General Castaños, who was by now in full flight with the French in hot pursuit, it was simply ignored.[80]

On reaching Sigüenza, Castaños received orders to return to the capital to take up his position as the head of the Junta General de Guerra. On his journey, he was on several occasions attacked by angry mobs, and then was arrested as soon as he arrived in Seville, remaining in prison until November of the following year. His downfall was the work of the *palafoxistas*, who were alleging that

Castaños had betrayed the Army of Aragón at Tudela and was now proposing to abandon Zaragoza to its fate – or, in short, that he was a traitor.[81] Desperate for a scapegoat who could be blamed for Spain's misfortunes, the Junta Central was only too happy to give credence to their insinuations, leaving the hero of Bailén to become the villain of Tudela. Yet much of the responsibility for that defeat belonged to the *palafoxistas*, who showed a total lack of concern for the interests of the nation. Whilst they had been intrigueing against their rivals, Spain had been beaten to her knees. As soon as he had heard the news of Tudela, Napoleon had launched an offensive against Madrid. Sweeping aside the few Spanish troops that were left to oppose him at the battle of Somosierra, the Emperor arrived before the capital on 2 December. For a brief moment the population attempted to defend themselves, but their resistance was as ineffectual as it was disorderly, and the city surrendered two days later. The troops who had fought at Somosierra in the meantime fled southwestwards in a state of total mutiny, murdering their commander, General San Juan, and pillaging all the towns on route in the process.[82] Nor were the Armies of the Left and the Centre in much better condition. The former was described as having 'the appearance of a large body of peasants, driven from their homes, famished and in want of everything'.[83] As for the Army of the Centre, the Duque del Infantado, who had taken it over following the departure of Castaños, wrote:

> I saw a ruined army, and troops who presented a most distressing appearance. Some were entirely barefoot, others almost naked, and all disfigured ... by the most ravenous hunger (there were many who had had no bread for eight days, and misery and hunger had reached such a pitch that ... many had died of hunger along the roads and in the mountains). They appeared more like walking corpses than men ready to defend their fatherland ... Battalions had been formed from fractions of different regiments; the strength of the largest was less than 600 men, and some had only 100 ... The cavalry were in the same state ... the greater part of the horses could hardly bear the weight of their riders.[84]

The Army of Catalonia also having been badly beaten at Cardedeu and Molíns de Rey (16 and 21 December 1808), the only force left in any semblance of order was José Palafox's Army of Aragón. However, on 20 December it had once more been besieged in Zaragoza and was therefore incapable of doing anything to prevent the French from over-running the rest of Spain. Exactly two months later it was forced to surrender after a defence that was marked as much by the ineptitude of José Palafox as the heroism of its defenders. Spain therefore lay prostrate before Napoleon, and would doubtless have been overrun altogether had it not been for the British army under Sir John Moore. This force had been assembling in the area of Salamanca and by sheer good fortune had escaped attack by the French. Striking eastwards against the French communications in Old Castile, Moore stung the Emperor into sending almost the whole of his disposable field force against him. There followed the famous 'Retreat to Corunna' in which Moore was forced to run for the sea with an overwhelmingly superior French army in hot pursuit. After a successful rearguard action at La Coruña, the British were evacuated (though Moore himself was killed), leaving the French in fruitless possession of the strategic cul-de-sac of Galicia. The effect of this campaign was to win a vital respite for the Junta Central and its shattered armies, for it was impossible for the French to follow up their successes in central Spain whilst their armies were embroiled in the far north west. Furthermore, once conquered, Galicia could not be abandoned, and instead had to be used as a base for fresh offensive operations. As a result, for months afterwards two whole army corps were tied down in a futile campaign in Galicia and northern Portugal that had no relevance whatsoever to the real French objectives.

Napoleon had left Spain early in January 1809 under the impression that the war in the Peninsula had been reduced to the status of a mere mopping up operation that could safely be left to his lieutenants. However, he could not have been more wrong. Moore's offensive had given the Junta Central a chance to reconstitute its battered armies south of the Tagus and to establish a new capital at Seville, from where it was to continue to defy the invaders for the whole of the next year. Far from attacking the Spaniards, the French forces in central Spain were for a long period actually forced to surrender the initiative to their opponents. Yet the strategic outlook had immeasurably worsened for the patriot cause. With the French once more in control of Madrid, the Spanish armies were condemned to fight a long series of operations on external lines in the wide plains of the Castiles. At the same time, the Junta Central had suffered a shattering blow to its already tarnished reputation, with the result that the Spanish war effort was certain to be subjected to the same tensions that had sabotaged it in the campaign of November–December 1808.

Forced by the French offensive to flee to Seville, the Junta Central had responded to the shock of defeat by making a determined effort to restore its authority. Not only could this be seen to be essential with respect to the war effort, but its political opponents had been seeking to capitalise upon its temporary eclipse: indeed, the irrepressible Junta of Seville had even declared itself to be a new provisional government.[85] The Junta Central had already enlisted the aid of the Marqués de la Romana to enforce its rule in the north west by appointing him Jefe Político, or Viceroy, of Old Castile, León, Asturias and Galicia.[86] On leaving Madrid it had also sent out twelve of its members to act as its representatives to the provincial juntas, whose authority it proceeded strictly to limit by a decree of 1 January 1809.[87] Measures were also taken to end the disorder which had raged in the army ever since the national uprising. Correctly identifying one of the chief problems as the haphazard creation of large numbers of new regiments, it prohibited the formation of any more until all existing units had been brought up to strength.[88] An attempt was also made to bring spontaneous popular resistance under the control of the government by the establishment of rules for the organisation of guerrilla bands.[89] Finally, an investigation was begun of the officers' commissions issued by the new authorities, which eventually ruled that many of them should be annulled.[90]

These decrees were by no means the end to the Junta's efforts to reform the army. In May 1809, for example, the office of Inspector General was re-established in both the infantry and the cavalry, whilst the strictest obedience to the Ordenanzas was enjoined at all times. A number of new military academies were also created in the hope that they might do something to improve the quality of the officer corps.[91] Yet these efforts were unavailing. Powerful vested interests had been thrown up by the rising of 1808 which the Junta Central simply lacked the strength to overcome: for example, any attempt to disband even a single one of the new regiments caused a storm of protest that sometimes ended in mutiny.[92] Against such opposition, the government could only have made headway had it possessed the support of the provincial juntas. However, the latter were convinced that the Junta Central's only object was to perpetuate its rule, whilst they had also been enfuriated by the decree of 1 January 1809, which they regarded as a stratagem to deprive them of all the perquisites of office. They were therefore less than co-operative, and actively sought to prevent any attempt to interfere with regiments which they identified as their own.[93] In some cases, they also refused to accept the authority of the commissioners sent out by the Junta Central, those sent to Valencia and Cádiz both being driven out by outbreaks of rioting.[94]

The numerous aristocratic generals who were opposed to the Spanish revolution on principle, or who desired to see a resurrection in the power of the nobility, constituted a further source of resistance. It was, for example, suspected that the Conde de Montijo's presence in Cádiz at the time of the rioting there was anything but a coincidence.[95] The chief members of the legitimist faction were Infantado, Cuesta and La Romana. Infantado was currently in Seville as President of the Council of Castile, but was very resentful of having been relieved of the command of the Army of the Centre after it had been defeated at Uclés (13 January 1809). Cuesta, on the other hand, had been appointed to the command of the Army of Extremadura by the junta of that province, an appointment which the Junta Central felt it had no option but to confirm. However, he was still furious at his removal from the command of the Army of Castile, and his anger had in no wise been assuaged when that force had been incorporated into the Army of the Centre in October 1808. As a result he was only too happy to renew his intrigues of the previous summer with Infantado.[96]

The other wing of the military opposition to the Junta Central consisted of the clique of noblemen who had been behind the Motín de Aranjuez, and who still hoped to translate its benefits into reality through the creation of a regency. Until the fall of Zaragoza the leading figure of this group had been José Palafox, whereupon his place was taken by his younger brother, Francisco, aided and abetted as usual by the Conde de Montijo. It was axiomatic to these officers that the reputation of José Palafox should be defended as the foundation of their appeal to the public, for which reason they devoted much energy to claiming that his downfall was the result of treason.[97] At the same time, they sought actively to overthrow the Junta Central, to which end Montijo organised a revolt in Granada in April 1809. Francisco Palafox travelled to join him from Aragón, but the rising had collapsed before he got there, leaving him unable to do more than make lame denunciations of the provincial authorities. Montijo, in the meantime, was arrested and sent into internal exile in Badajoz.[98] Nor was this the limit to the intrigues directed against the Junta Central in the early part of 1809, for the Junta of Seville had become involved in a scheme known as the 'grand plot of the grandees', whereby the Junta was supposed to seize power in the capital whilst a number of disaffected generals, including the Duque de Alburquerque and Francisco Palafox, simultaneously took control of the armies in the provinces.[99]

The existence of these intrigues placed the Junta Central in an impossible position: it could not surrender to the demands of its opponents for fear of a military dictatorship, but resisting their demands laid it open to charges that it merely wished to hang onto power for its own sake. After much deliberation, its members agreed that the only possible political solution was for the convocation of an entirely new Cortes. On 22 May 1809 it accordingly issued a decree promising that such a body would meet within one year, and asking that all interested citizens should submit their ideas as to how it should be organized and the sort of reforms that it should undertake. The task of producing a plan of action was placed in the charge of a special commission of the Junta, headed by the universally respected Jovellanos.[100] In the meantime it sought to defuse the situation by by playing one general off against another, and ensuring that armies that were commanded by men known to be hostile to the Junta were always counter-balanced by others which were commanded by its friends.[101] In order to restore its battered credibility, it also sought to achieve military victory, launching a series of offensives against the French positions in central and northern Spain.

Although politically indispensable, such a strategy took little account of the military situation. After their traumatic experiences in the autumn and winter of 1808, the Spanish armies were in desperate need of a period of rest and reorganization. As the decisive battles of the ensuing campaigns could not but be fought out in the open terrain of the *meseta*, their glaring inadequacies were certain to be more exposed than ever. Finally, the French enjoyed a central position, whilst the Spaniards would be operating on external lines. The continued parochialism of the provincial juntas also constituted a serious obstacle to an offensive strategy, for in many cases they were still inclined to hoard their troops and military supplies within their own borders.[102] In view of these difficulties, it would have been far more appropriate to adopt a defensive strategy of the type later envisaged by the *Memorial Militar y Patriótico del Ejército de la Izquierda* whereby the regular armies would limit themselves to holding their positions in the mountains surrounding the French

The war of the Junta Central

zone. In the meantime, the French would be worn down by the guerrillas of the interior, supported if necessary by small bodies of regular troops, leaving the generals free to train their forces for an eventual counter offensive.[103] An embryonic form of this strategy was already being implemented in Galicia where the Marqués de la Romana had succeeded in stirring up a considerable outbreak of guerrilla warfare. Whilst the French wore themselves out chasing the partisans, the Marquess kept his army hidden in the shelter of the mountains that ran along the northern frontier of Portugal, emerging only to launch the occasional raid on isolated French positions. However, the mere presence of his army prevented the invaders from applying all their forces against the insurgents, just as the activities of the latter prevented a decisive blow from being launched against La Romana. In this manner, the struggle might have been continued indefinitely.

However, there was little chance that this strategy could have been adopted. Aside from the political need for a dramatic victory, few of the Spanish generals shared La Romana's caution, their ambitions having been greatly excited by the victory of Bailén.[104] Furthermore, generals and government alike were limited in their freedom of action by the pressure of public opinion. Responsibility for this situation ultimately lay with the civil and military authorities themselves. Rather than being honest about their defeats, many generals preferred to dress them up in their dispatches with exaggeration and half truths.[105] Nor was the Junta Central much better: desperate to retain the support of public opinion and to maintain popular enthusiasm for the war, its statements and proclamations often bore little resemblance to the actual military situation.[106] The *Gazeta de Valencia*'s coverage of the campaign of November–December 1808 may be taken as a good example of the sort of distortion that could result. On 22 November, eleven days after Blake's defeat at Espinosa de los Monteros, it reported that he had beaten the French. On 16 December, twelve days after the fall of Madrid, it announced that the capital was defending itself heroically and added news of a wholly fictitious Spanish victory in Old Castile. On 30 December Madrid was still holding out, and a non-existent army marching to its relief from Talavera. The loss of the capital was finally acknowledged on 3 January 1809, but two weeks later it was reported that Napoleon was now besieged there by a huge Anglo–Spanish army.[107] The outcome of this bombast, which unfortunately continued throughout the war, was that 'the minds of the people were filled ...with the most determined belief of the superiority of the Spanish army, which now in the public opinion neither admits of nor requires improvement, being already perfect'.[108] So great was the general confidence in victory that any show of caution was ascribed to cowardice or to a want of patriotic fervour, the Marqués de la Romana winning the scornful nickname 'Marqués de las Romerías' (Marquess of the Pilgrimages) on account of his constant marching and counter-marching in the mountains of Galicia.[109] Many generals, who might otherwise have inclined to caution, were therefore forced into giving battle in the most unfavourable circumstances for fear of being lynched as traitors.[110]

If an offensive strategy was to be adopted, then it was essential that the Spanish armies should strike hard and fast, for their only hope was to make use of the advantage of surprise conferred on them by the guerrillas to catch the French off balance. Yet speed and decision were precisely the factors that were most often absent from the conduct of the Spanish generals. Not only did the armies tend to be encumbered by unnecessary quantities of baggage and swarms of non-combatants, but the half-trained soldiers rarely kept their ranks and straggled along without any semblance of order.[111] Even when they did manage to make reasonable time, they frequently had also to contend with the vacillation of their commanders. Realising that they were likely to be dismissed or even accused of treason if they were defeated, many generals lost their nerve at moments of crisis. Paralysed by indecision, they procrastinated until it was too late either to strike a telling blow or to save their armies by a timely retreat. Alternatively, they would attempt to evade their responsibilities by convening a council of war, a procedure that invariably tended only to increase the confusion.[112]

A further problem which beset the generals was the possibility of intervention on the part of the Junta Central, which regarded its armies as much as pawns in the political game as instruments of military victory. At certain moments, it therefore became more important that they should be conserved intact than that they should be committed against the enemy. Perhaps the most significant example of such a situation occurred during the crucial Talavera campaign of the summer of 1809. The success of this venture – a concentric advance on the French forces occupying Madrid – depended on the actions of the Army of La Mancha, which was then commanded by a placeman of the Junta named Venegas. Whilst the British army of the then Sir Arthur Wellesley and the Spanish Army of Extremadura under General Cuesta advanced against Madrid from the west, Venegas was supposed to push forward form the south. By pinning down the forces facing him, it was hoped that Venegas would enable Wellesley and Cuesta to march on Madrid with overwhelming numbers. However, on 18 June 1809, the Army of the Levante had been destroyed at Belchite in Aragón. As its commander, Joaquín Blake, had been a loyal supporter of the Junta Central, it became essential that the Army of La Mancha should remain in good order so as to provide a counterweight to Cuesta's Army of Extremadura. Secret orders were therefore sent to Venegas ordering him on no account to allow any risk to befall his army. Provided with an excellent pretext to pander to his natural caution, Venegas therefore stayed his hand and allowed the French to escape the trap that had been set for them.[113]

The tactical inferiority of the Spanish army was thus compounded by the fumbling and hesitant manner in which it was committed to battle. Nor could its deficiencies ever be remedied, for every time that a Spanish force was beaten, which was generally every time that it took the field, it had to be remade virtually from nothing. Not only were casualties frequently enormous, but the Spanish levies lacked the discipline and cohesion necessary to retreat in good order from the battlefield. Every defeat therefore entailed the complete disintegration of the army that had been involved, with the consequent loss of much of its equipment.[114] Moreover, scattering all over the countryside, many of the survivors took the opportunity to slip away to their homes or to join the guerrillas.[115] In the light of the loss of so many men who might otherwise have gone on to form a cadre of veterans, it was to no avail that the Spanish armies should have sprung back to life again as quickly as they were defeated. Each reincarnation merely duplicated the deficiencies of its predecessors, and inevitably went on to share their experiences.

It is possible that something might have been done to arrest this cycle of defeat and reconstruction had the Spanish army been placed under the command of British officers, as had been done with the Portuguese. However, even had this been politically possible, such a plan would have made little difference unless the Spaniards were also properly maintained, a task that was quite beyond the capabilities of the Junta Central.[116] Substantial aid was received from Great

Britain, including 155 artillery pieces, 42,800 rounds of artillery ammuntion, 200,277 muskets, 39,000 sets of belts, 6,660,000 musket balls, 15,400 barrels of powder, 23,477,955 cartridges, 61,391 swords, 79,000 pikes, 40,000 tents, 50,000 canteens, 54,000 packs, 92,100 uniforms, 343,900 pairs of shoes and boots, 39,100 shirts, 1,600 shakos and hats, 472,212 yards of linen, calico and wool, and £1,412,354 in cash and bills of exchange in the period May 1808–May 1809 alone.[117] In addition, the end of the war between Britain and Spain had reopened communications with the Spanish empire. As the Americans had initially responded to the war with a great upsurge of patriotic enthusiasm, the Junta Central had been bolstered by the arrival of large consignments of bullion.[118] Yet so great were the resources had been lost to the French that Toreno estimates that without the support it received from Britain and America the Junta would have been totally bankrupt.[119]

The logistical problem was compounded by the the revolution of 1808, which had greatly increased the cost of Spain's mobilisation whilst simultaneously disrupting the efficient utilisation of her resources.[120] The defects of the army's supply system were also cruelly exposed. Much of the food and equipment that reached the unfortunate soldiery was rotten, or so badly made as to be completely useless.[121] Although the armies were in effect expected to live off the country, much of the interior of Spain was simply too poor to support them.[122] Furthermore, when food was available the civilian population were frequently able to charge exhorbitant prices for their produce.[123] Nor did the army possess an adequate system of transport: aside from the difficulty and expense of hiring sufficient animals and carts, the drivers often went unpaid, and therefore displayed an understandable tendency to abscond with their charges at the first opportunity.[124] Hence the misery that was the perpetual lot of the Spanish armies throughout the Peninsular War. Its effect upon them could not have been more serious. It was clear, for example, that men who were starving and dressed in rags could hardly be expected to bear themselves as disciplined veterans upon the battlefield.[125] Furthermore, privation brought the death of thousands of soldiers, whilst many others deserted to avoid a similar fate. With its cadres of veterans subjected to further erosion, the army was never able to reduce the proportion of raw recruits that filled its ranks.

One of the reasons why the incidence of desertion was so high was that it was an easy option. The lack of marching discipline off the battlefield and the frequent routs upon it made it simple for a soldier to slip away from the ranks. Once the deserter had gone, he was very often almost impossible to apprehend because the troops were generally dressed in clothing that resembled that of the Spanish peasantry.[126] Even if he was caught, he knew that he was unlikely to be shot, for there was a marked reluctance to execute men who had only run away to avoid starvation.[127] It should be stressed that a great many deserters and *dispersos* simply returned to their homes, where they were generally allowed to remain in peace by the French.[128] However, an indeterminable proportion of them chose instead to join one of the numerous bands of guerrillas that had sprung up all over Spain in the wake of French occupation. Nor was this an end to the drain on the strength of the regular army which the guerrillas represented, for they were joined by many young men who might otherwise have become soldiers, whilst some of their leaders went so far as to impose conscription themselves or to impress detachments of regular troops which fell into their hands.[129]

It was inevitable that service with the guerrillas should have been more popular than service with the regular army, especially in view of the anti-militarism which had characterised Spanish society before 1808. They offered 'more freedom and less discipline'; they did not require men to leave their home districts; they had a reputation for success whereas the regular army could only offer defeat and starvation; and, above all, they offered substantial material benefits, the Junta Central having decreed that all money and other personal effects seized from the French became the property of whoever had taken it.[130] Whilst it would be a gross exaggeration to suggest that all of the guerrillas were mere bandits, they were often the subject of bitter complaints and became firmly associated with the idea of personal gain; as a popular epigram had it: '¡*Viva Fernando y vamos robando!*'[131]

The men who joined the guerrillas were not entirely lost to the patriot cause, for the *partidas* undoubtedly involved the French in enormous difficulties. Yet by sapping the strength of the regular army, they exacerbated the military crisis facing the Junta Central. The constant haemorrhage of trained troops could only be borne if an equivalent number of recruits was sent to replace them. However, there were too few volunteers, and the provincial juntas were for the most part unwilling to enforce the decrees of conscription which they had promulgated in 1808. As for the few recruits that could be obtained, many of them had to be rejected on account of their poor physique, whilst others either deserted at once or had to be dismissed to their homes because there was no means by which they could be paid or fed.[132] As a result, the Spanish armies were very much a finite resource, which should have been husbanded with the utmost care. By the summer of 1809, this ought to have been fully apparent to the Junta Central, but circumstances constrained it to ignore what was miltarily advisable and instead, as Wellington put it, to allow the conduct of operations to become determined by 'political intrigue and the attainment of trifling political objectives'.[133]

Despite, and in part because of, its efforts to consolidate its domestic situation through the achievement of military victory, the position of the Junta Central had continued to deteriorate. Although the various conspiracies against its rule in the early part of 1809 had been quashed, its failures had kept alive a demand for political reform that the promise of a new Cortes had done nothing to ameliorate. This pressure was seconded by the British government, which naturally expected the Spaniards to make a productive contribution to the common cause. Matters came to a head following the campaign of Talavera of July 1809. Blaming its failure on Spanish bad faith and incompetence, the Duke of Wellington withdrew the co-operation of his army from the Spaniards, advising the Junta Central henceforward to adopt a defensive strategy.[134] To comply with such advice was impossible, however, for the Talavera fiasco engendered a new wave of discontent.[135] Furthermore, the opposition now had a new and potent leader in the person of the Marqués de la Romana. The quintessence of the military aristocracy, La Romana had been horrified by the situation that he found on his return from Denmark in December 1808, confiding to Sir John Moore 'that had he known how things were, he neither would have accepted the command nor have returned to Spain'.[136] Appointed by the Junta to act as its viceroy in the northwest, he had immediately shown his enmity by refusing to recognize the authority of the commissioner whom it had dispatched to his headquarters.[137] Nor was he prepared to tolerate the pretensions of the provincial juntas. On 2 May 1809 he accordingly descended on Oviedo and dissolved the Junta of Asturias, which he replaced by a new council dependent upon himself.[138] He would have gone on to deal with the Junta of Galicia in similar fashion, had not the Junta Central forestalled him by recalling him to Seville to take up a position as one of its members.[139]

Bringing La Romana to the capital brought him into contact with a natural ally, for Francisco Palafox was still a member of the Junta despite his participation in numerous plots against its rule. Following the battle of Talavera, Palafox had joined with Infantado and the Junta of Seville in yet another conspiracy to overthrow the government by means of a military coup. However, the plan had been ruined by the British ambassador, the Marquess of Wellesley, who had warned the Junta Central of its existence when the conspirators had approached him for support. Wellesley had refused to disclose any of the names of those involved, but the government had nevertheless been able to end the immediate danger by transferring all the regiments stationed in Seville.[140] Yet no sooner had they dealt with this threat than they were challenged by La Romana, who was by now being billed as the saviour of Spain.[141] In October 1809 the commission that had been established to examine the question of political reform issued its report. This called for a rotating five-man *comisión ejecútiva* drawn from the ranks of the Junta Central to exercise the sovereignty until such time as the Cortes could meet. La Romana responded by issuing a manifesto of his own in which he denied the legitimacy of the Junta Central, made numerous accusations against its probity, and demanded the immediate establishment of a regency.[142] The Junta ordered the suppression of this document, but it was published by La Romana's brother, who was the Captain General of Valencia, with a postscript calling for the Marquess to be made sole regent.[143] The Junta went ahead with the plan for the *comisión ejecútiva*, and even appointed La Romana to be its first president, but it had been badly shaken and therefore resumed its quest for military victory with even greater intensity.

Predictably enough, the only result was the double defeat of Ocaña and Alba de Tormes (19 and 29 November 1809) in which the Armies of La Mancha and the Left were shattered with the loss of 40,000 men and 59 guns. Their defeat represented the end of the road for the Junta Central. Thanks to the staunch support of the new British ambassador, Henry Wellesley, the Junta was able to overcome the fresh intrigues sparked off by the catastrophe, and even to imprison the Conde de Montijo and Francisco Palafox, but it was now so discredited that it had no option but to promise to convoke the Cortes by 1 March 1810.[144] However, the military situation was now so bleak that there seemed little chance of the patriot cause surviving till that date. With the conclusion of the war against Austria in October 1809, Napoleon was now pouring fresh troops into the Peninsula with a view to the invasion of Portugal. A large proportion of the forces already in Spain were thus relieved for service against the patriot stronghold of Andalucía. To face the impending offensive, the Spaniards had only the relics of the Army of La Mancha – some 30,000 men – to defend the entire length of the Sierra Morena, for the British had withdrawn into Portugal and the Armies of the Left and of Extremadura were simply too far away to be able to offer much assistance. Nor was there any means of making up the huge losses that had been suffered at Ocaña: having been drawn upon incessantly for almost a year, the finite military resources available to the Junta Central were all but exhausted. When the French offensive against Andalucía began on 19 January 1810, it therefore swept all before it.

With the French bearing down on Seville, the Junta Central fled for the relative safety of Cádiz, only for revolution to break out in their wake. During the interval following the battle of Ocaña, a large amount of black propaganda had been circulating with regard to the government, alleging that its members were mere 'creatures of Godoy . . . promoted by the intrigue of whores, pimps and cuckolds'.[145] On 24 January the resultant discontent erupted in open revolt. Having previously ignored several orders that should have taken him out of Seville, the Marqués de la Romana released the imprisoned Montijo and Palafox, who had allegedly been behind much of the unrest. The original intention of the conspirators seems to have been to constitute themselves as a regency, but they were soon dissuaded from their pretensions by the rapid approach of the French. Realising that Seville was defenceless, La Romana hastily abandoned the city after once again securing the command of the Army of the Left. He was followed by Palafox and Montijo, and the Junta of Seville was therefore left to proclaim itself to be the supreme government of Spain. Its rule proved short-lived, for Seville surrendered to the French on 31 January 1810. Meanwhile, on reaching Cádiz the fugitive Junta Central had immediately established a regency headed by General Castaños.[146]

The French triumph was by no means total. Not only had some relics of the Army of La Mancha succeeeded in evading their assailants, but Cádiz had been saved from certain enemy occupation by the Duque de Alburquerque's Army of Extremadura, which had at the last moment succeeded in throwing itself within its walls. Furthermore, the new régime that now ruled patriot Spain seemed certain to be far more effective than the despised Junta Central. Although that would not have been difficult, it is only fair to point out the immense obstacles that had rendered the Junta's task virtually impossible. It had no means of enforcing its power over the wayward provincial juntas, its hands were tied by public opinion, its generals were quarrelsome and mediocre, its opponents were more numerous than its supporters, and it was constantly challenged by a clique of disaffected aristocrats who were eager to establish a military dictatorship that would overturn the revolution of 1808. Realising that it could only function as an effective government if it enjoyed a wider measure of support, it had embarked on a desperate search for military victory that had achieved nothing except to increase its own discredit, to alienate the British, to exacerbate the disorder in the Spanish army, and to squander Spain's limited military resources. Hence the *débâcle* of January 1810.

The army's part in this sorry story had, of course, been particularly unhappy, and there can be few officers who did not look to the new régime for some redress of their many professional grievances. So far most of them had remained loyal to the civilian authorities, if only because so many of the various military malcontents were notorious for their frivolity. La Romana, Francisco Palafox and their fellow conspirators had been neutralised by the formation of a regency, but the danger of military intervention was by no means at an end. It was therefore essential that the new administration should pay close attention to military affairs. When it became clear that it was no more capable of meeting the professional aspirations of the officer corps than the Junta Central, and considerably less willing to do so, the army fell into the grip of a swelling wave of discontent that was eventually to make a military coup a virtual certainty.

Notes

1 E.g. Mahy to Malespina, 11 October 1808, SHM.AGI.3/4/24, No. 22.
2 *El Español*, 30 April 1810, 20–3, HMM. AH4-2(710); cf. also Garciny, *op. cit.*, p. 166.
3 Toreno, *op. cit.*, I, p. 273.
4 Jackson, *op. cit.*, II, 294–5.
5 Schepeler, *op. cit.*, II, 387–8.

6 *Memorial Militar y Patriótico del Ejército de la Izquierda*, 10 April 1810, 15–16, HMM. AH3-3(536).
7 R. Wellesley to Canning, 15 September 1809, *The Dispatches and Correspondence of the Marquess Wellesley during his Mission to Spain as Ambassador Extraordinary to the Supreme Junta in 1809*, ed. M. Martin (London, 1838), 119–35.
8 Memorandum of A. Cochrane Johnstone, 26 April 1809, *Supplementary Despatches, Correspondence, and Memoranda of Field Marshal Arthur, Duke of Wellington*, ed. Second Duke of Wellington (London, 1858–72), VI, 239–40.
9 *Diario de las sesiones y actas de las Cortes* (Cádiz, 1810–13), VI, p. 344 (hereafter, *Diario de las Cortes*); Garciny, *op. cit.*, p. 153; González Carvajal, *Intendente del ejército*, 161–2.
10 Report of War Minister to Cortes, 15 September 1813, SHM. CDF.CCCXLVIII.
11 Schepeler, *op. cit.*, II, 11; Villalva, *op. cit.*, 38–40.
12 Broderick to Castlereagh, 10 September 1808, PRO. WO.1/233, 18–19; Doyle to Castlereagh, 22 September 1808, PRO. WO.1/227, p. 377; Stuart to Dalrymple, 23 September 1808, PRO. WO.1/235, 129–30; Narciso de Pedro to La Peña, 4 November 1808, RAH. 11-2-2:8154, VI–13; Blake to Leith, 9 November 1808, PRO. WO.1/229, p. 527.
13 Bentinck to Castlereagh, 14 November 1808, PRO. WO.1/230, 160–1.
14 Real Orden, 13 November 1808, cit. *Diario de Granada*, 20 November 1808, HMM. AH14-5(2543).
15 *Gazeta de Valencia*, 25 October 1808, HMM. AH2-6(408); Real Orden, 17 November 1808, SHM. CDF.DCCCLXIV.
16 Doyle to Castlereagh, 11 September 1808, PRO. WO.1/227, p. 322; Birch to Leith, 8 September 1808, PRO. WO.1/229, 225–6.
17 Carroll to Castlereagh, 5 November 1808, PRO. WO.1/229, 514–15.
18 Earl of Stanhope, *Notes of Conversations with the Duke of Wellington, 1831–1851* (London, 1889), p. 9.
19 Wellington to H. Wellesley, 14 May 1812, US. WP.12/1/5.
20 E.g. J. Leach, *Rough Sketches in the Life of an Old Soldier* (London, 1831), p. 33; Holland, *op. cit.*, p. 17.
21 Report of Supreme Council of War to Cortes, 25 September 1810, cit. *Memorial Militar y Patriótico del Ejército de la Izquierda*, 22 October 1810, 396–404, HMM. AH3-3(536).
22 *El Redactor General*, 11 August 1811, 217–8, HMM. 6/3; A. J. M. de Rocca, *Memoirs of the War of the French in Spain* (London, 1815), p. 270; Ramírez y Vandama, *op. cit.*, 33–4.
23 Proclamation of Junta of Seville, 14 June 1808, SHM. CDF.DCCCLXIV, p. 55; Alvarez Valdés, *op. cit.*, 222–4; returns of regiments of Illiberia and Cazadores de Bailén, February and March 1809, RAH. 9-31-6:6964, 6965; 'Subinspección de Infantería del Cuarto Ejército: relación de los capitanes que no han sido promovidos a jefes' (MS), 1 February 1812, US. WP.1/382, f. 2.

24 'Ejército de la Izquierda' (MS), 33–4, 37–8, SHM. AGI.3/4/28, No. 1; Porlier to Mahy, 25 March 1811, SHM. AGI.25/35/24; *El Redactor General*, 23 August 1811, p. 267, HMM. 6/3.
25 Walker to Liverpool, 18 September 1810, PRO. WO.1/261, p. 42; Schepeler, *op. cit.*, II, p. 388.
26 Carvajal to Mahy, 3 February 1810, SHM. AGI.5/8/2, No. 25.
27 Mahy to La Romana, 9 December 1808, SHM. AGI.4/2/10, No. 10; Broderick to Castlereagh, 18 November 1808, PRO. WO.1/231, p. 31; Jackson, *op. cit.*, II, p. 410.
28 Southey, *History of the Peninsular War* (London, 1823–32), II, p. 219 (hereafter Southey, *Peninsular War*).
29 Alos to Copons, 27 October 1809, RAH. 9-31-6:6965; *El Conciso*, 30 April 1813, p. 4, HMM. AH2-5(351); *Indagación de las causas de los malos sucesos de nuestros ejércitos y medios de removerlos* (Cádiz, 1811), p. 10 (hereafter *Indagación*); Schepeler, *op. cit.*, II, p. 468.
30 F. Guervos to his parents, 20 January 1809, RAH. 11-5-7:9003, No. 13; Girón to Copons, 19 March 1809, RAH. 9-31-6:6965; *El Redactor General*, 11 August 1811, 217–18, HMM. 6/3; Jacob, *op. cit.*, 16–17.
31 Girón, *op. cit.*, I, 113–14; *Indagación*, 9–10.
32 F.X. de Cabanes, *Ensayo acerca del sistema militar de Bonaparte* (Isla de León, 1811), p. 57 (hereafter Cabanes, *Sistema Militar*).
33 Alos to Copons, 27 October 1809, RAH. 9-31-6:6965; Pro de Bayona to Sabasona, 26 January 1809, AHN. Estado, 17/10-2, p. 21; González Carvajal, *Intendente del ejército*, 248–9; *Indagación*, p. 9.
34 Roche to Wellington, 15 September 1809, US. WP.1/277; cf. also González Carvajal, *Intendente del ejército*, p. 168.
35 Whittingham to Bentinck, 28 October 1808, PRO. WO.1/230, 140–1.
36 Bentinck to Castlereagh, 2 November 1808, PRO. WO.1/230, p. 134.
37 Wellington to R. Wellesley, 24 August 1809, US. WP.1/275; Whittingham, *op. cit.*, p. 96; Doyle to Cooke, 26 June 1809, PRO. WO.1/241, p. 303; Blake to Cornel, 22 June 1809, *cit. Gazeta Extraordinaria de Gobierno*, 3 July 1809, 665–7, HMM. AH2-5(2925bis).
38 Wellington to H. Wellesley, 22 May 1811, US. WP.1/332, f. 2.
39 Wellington to H. Wellesley, 1 November 1812, US. WP.1/351, f. 9.
40 Doyle to Cooke, 1 March 1809, PRO. WO.1/241, 191–4; D'Urban to Cradock, 9 April 1809, PRO. WO.1/240, 477–9; Rocca, *op. cit.*, p. 128.
41 J. Moscoso, *Avisos militares al Ejército de la Izquierda para la presente guerra* (Tarragona, 1809), 7–8.
42 Doyle to Castlereagh, 4 August 1808, PRO. WO.1/227, p. 99; Whittingham to Dalrymple, 26 August 1808, PRO. WO.1/234, 113–14; Dalrymple to Castlereagh, 11 September 1808, PRO. WO.1/234, p. 105.
43 Wellington to Liverpool, 23 May 1811, US. WP.1/344; Roche to Wellington, 15 September 1809, US. WP.1/277; Schepeler, *op. cit.*, II, p. 390.

44 Wellington to Castlereagh, 25 August 1809, US. WP.1/275.
45 *Memorial Militar y Patriótico del Ejército de la Izquierda*, 1 June 1810, p. 310, HMM. AH3-3(536).
46 Girón, *op. cit.*, I, p. 207; D. Chlapowski, *Mémoires sur les guerres de Napoléon, 1808–13* (Paris, 1908), p. 90.
47 T. González Carvajal, *Meditaciones sobre la constitución militar presentadas a la Comisión de Constitución Militar formada de orden de las Cortes* (Cádiz, 1813), 12–13 (hereafter González Carvajal, *Constitución militar*); Cooke to Skerret, 14 October 1811, PRO. WO.1/252, p. 504; Ballesteros to Skerret, 13 November 1811, PRO. WO.1/252, p. 579.
48 E.g. *Semanario Patriótico*, 13 July 1809, p. 172, HMM. AH1-6(195).
49 *Memorial Militar y Patriótico del Ejército de la Izquierda*, 10 April and 4 May 1810, 17, 70, HMM. AH3-3(536); Cabanes, *Sistema militar*, p. 56.
50 Wellington to Castlereagh, 25 August 1809, US. WP.1/275.
51 Bentinck to Castlereagh, 19 October 1808, PRO. WO.1/230, 89–90.
52 Vaughan to Holland, 28 September 1809, cit. Holland, *op. cit.*, p., 407; Priego López, *op. cit.*, III, 32–3.
53 *Semanario Patriótico*, 24 November 1808, 232–3, HMM. AH1-6 (195).
54 *Semanario Patriótico*, 1 September 1808, 8–11, HMM. AH.1-6 (195); Schepeler, *op. cit.*, II, p. 14.
55 Oman, *op. cit.*, I, p. 360.
56 Real Orden, 18 November 1808, SHM. CDF.DCCCLXIV, p. 69; Jackson, *op. cit.*, II, p. 309.
57 Leith to Castlereagh, 13 September 1808, PRO. WO.1/229, p. 202; Spencer to Castlereagh, 6 and 21 June 1808, PRO. WO.1/226, p. 477; decrees of Junta of Seville, 6 and 30 June 1808, SHM. CDF.DCCCL-XIV, 50, 63; Schepeler, *op. cit.*, II, 140–1, 291.
58 E.g. decree of Junta of Seville, 13 August 1808, SHM. CDF.DCCCL-XIV, p. 65; Junta of Vizcaya to Roche, 12 August 1808, PRO. WO.1/233, p. 472; decree of Junta of Santander, 16 August 1808, PRO. WO.1/229, 55–7.
59 E.g. Moore to Castlereagh, 24 November 1808, PRO. WO.1/236, 74–5; Jackson, *op. cit.*, II, p. 22; R. Porter, *Letters from Portugal and Spain written during the march of the British troops under Sir John Moore* (London, 1809), p. 104.
60 Oman, *op. cit.*, I, 611, 636, 639.
61 Doyle to Castlereagh, 28 and 31 August 1808, PRO. WO.1/227, 213, 225–6; Dalrymple to Castlereagh, 27 September 1808, PRO. WO.1/234, p. 219; Birch to Leith, 8 September 1808, PRO. WO.1/229, p. 227; Holland, *op. cit.*, p. 404.
62 Castaños, *op. cit.*, p. 183.
63 Oman, *op. cit.*, I, 384–7, 636.
64 Doyle to Castlereagh, 11 September 1808, PRO. WO.1/227, 317–19; Cuesta, *op. cit.*, p. 12.
65 Doyle to Castlereagh, 4 August 1808, PRO. WO.1/237, p. 99; Doyle

to Stewart, 12 August 1808, PRO. WO.1/227, p. 135; 'Ejército de la Izquierda' (MS), p. 6, SHM. AGI.3/4/28, No. 1.
66 Cf. Doyle to Castlereagh, 1 October 1808, PRO. WO.1/227, p. 414; 'Ejército de Extremadura, 1808, segunda campaña; resumen histórico de los principales acontecimientos occuridos en este campaña' (MS), 9–14, SHM. AGI.2/2/5 (hereafter 'Ejército de Extremadura' (MS)).
67 Castaños, *op. cit.*, 34, 185.
68 Roche to Castlereagh, 16 October 1808, PRO. W0.1/233, 518–19; Doyle to Cooke, 20 November 1808, PRO. WO.1/227, p. 541; *Diario de Badajoz*, 2 December 1808, p. 696, HMM. AH.14-5(2457); *Gazeta Ministerial de Sevilla*, 8 November 1808, HMM. AH2-5 (373 bis).
69 Real Orden, 29 September 1808, AHN. Estado, 17/6-1, p. 2; Garay to Blake, 17 October 1808, SHM. AGI.3/4/28, No. 4; Schepeler, *op. cit.*, II, p. 7.
70 Girón, *op. cit.*, I, 240–6; Garciny, *op. cit.*, p. 44; Toreno, *op. cit.*, II, p. 4.
71 F. Palafox to Blake, 21 October 1808, SHM. AGI.3/4/28, No. 4.
72 Bentinck to Castlereagh, 2 November 1808, PRO. WO.1/230, p. 132.
73 J. Moscoso, 'Memorias para las campañas de la Izquierda Militar de España' (MS), SHM. AGI.3/4/23, No. 1 (hereafter Moscoso (MS)); Jackson, *op. cit.*, II, p. 291.
74 Girón, *op. cit.*, I, 246–7; Castaños, *op. cit.*, 47–54; Villalva, *op. cit.*, 7–8.
75 Anonymous letter from Aranjuez to Spanish Chargé d'Affaires in Lisbon, 17 November 1808, PRO. WO.1/237, 305–6; Holland, *op. cit.*, 417–18.
76 Jackson, *op. cit.*, II, p. 298.
77 Bentinck to Castlereagh, 14 November 1808, PRO. WO.1/230, 157–8.
78 Doyle to Cooke, 21 November 1808, PRO. WO.1/227, 547–8.
79 Oman, *op. cit.*, I, 432–45.
80 F. Palafox to Castanos, 29 November 1808, AHN. Estado, 17/6-1, p. 38; proclamation of J. Palafox, 13 December 1808, cit. *Diario de Badajoz*, 17 January 1809, 66–7, HMM. AH14-1(2457); Castaños, *op. cit.*, 55, 196; Schepeler, *op. cit.*, II, 52–3; Girón, *op. cit.*, I, p. 254.
81 Castaños, *op. cit.*, 11–12; Jacob, *op. cit.*, p. 356; Whittingham, *op. cit.*, p. 54; O'Neill to J. Palafox, 24 November 1808, AHN. Estado, 17/6-1, 29–32; *Gazeta Extraordinaria de Valencia*, 7 December 1808, 655–9, HMM. AH2-6(408); F. Palafox to Junta Central, 29 November 1808, AHN. Estado, 17/6-1, 39–40; J. Palafox to Junta Central, 3 December 1808, AHN. Estado, 17/6-1, p. 41.
82 *Semanario Patriótico*, 20 July 1809, 183–6, HMM. AH1-6(195); Garciny, *op. cit.*, 98–9, 103; 'Ejército de Extremadura' (MS), SHM. AGI.2/2/5, 9–14.
83 T.S., *A Soldier of the Seventy First*, ed. C. Hibbert (London, 1975), 25–6; cf. also Baird to Castlereagh, PRO. WO.1/236, p. 466; La Romana to Junta Central, 9 December 1808, cit. 'Ejército de la

Izquierda' (MS), 32–3, SHM. AGI.3/4/28, No. 1.
84 Duque del Infantado, *Manifiesto de las operaciones del Ejército del Centro* (Seville, 1809), 16–18; cf. also Doyle to Cooke, 10 January 1809, PRO. WO.1/241, 47–8.
85 Junta of Seville to Junta of Murcia, 7 December 1808, *Gazeta de Valencia*, 23 and 27 December 1808, 706–7, 716–17, HMM. AH2-6(408); Jackson, *op. cit.*, II, p. 326.
86 Reales Ordenes, 1 and 4 December 1808, AHN. Estado, 17/7, 3, 36.
87 *Reglamento de Juntas Provinciales*, 1 January 1809, AHN. Estado, 60/H, p. 142; Oman, *op. cit.*, II, p. 22.
88 Real Orden, 11 January 1809, SHM. CDF.DCCLXXXIX, p. 21.
89 Real Orden, 28 December 1808, *cit. Gazeta del Gobierno*, 3 February 1809, 82–87, HMM. AH17-2(2925bis).
90 Report of Comisión de Guerra to Junta Central, 14 September 1809, AHN. Estado, 60/L, p. 275.
91 Reales Ordenes, 4 and 25 May 1809, *cit. Gazeta del Gobierno*, 9 and 16 June 1809, 578–9, 672; Salas, *op. cit.*, 156–7; Moya y Jiménez, *op. cit.*, p. 913.
92 E.g. Junta of Soria to Castaños, 11 November 1808, RAH. 11-2-2: 8154, VIII-1B; Copons to Cartaojal, 26 February 1809, RAH. 9-31-6: 6965.
93 Schepeler, *op. cit.*, II, 100–1, 309–10; *Junta de Cataluña*, 35–9; Garciny, *op. cit.*, p. 152; Toreno, *op. cit.*, I, 371–2.
94 Cf. proclamation of Alguacil of Valencia, 18 May 1809, AHN. Estado, 17/9-2, p. 47; F. Salvatierra to Garay, 12 June 1809, AHN. Estado, 17/9-3, 1–2; Toreno, *op. cit.*, I, p. 376; Alcalá Galiano, *op. cit.*, I, 227–31.
95 Mackenzie to Castlereagh, 24 February 1809, PRO. WO.1/233, 209–12.
96 Cuesta, *op. cit.*, 24, 26; *Diario de Badajoz*, 1 January 1809, 3–4, HMM. AH14-1(2457); Jackson, *op. cit.*, II, p. 331.
97 Calvo de Rozas to Garay, 14 April 1809, AHN. Estado, 60/L, 265–6; F. Palafox to Floridablanca, 2 January 1809, AHN. Estado, 17/6-1, p. 53; Doyle to Cooke, 25 February 1809, PRO. WO.1/241, p. 187.
98 F. Palafox to Junta Central, 2 May 1809, AHN. Estado, 17/6-2, 31–2; Schepeler, *op. cit.*, II, 385–6; Toreno, *op. cit.*, II, 4–5; Holland, *op. cit.*, 321–2, 361; Southey, *Peninsular War*, II, p. 233; Jackson, *op. cit.*, II, p. 408.
99 Doyle to Cradock, 30 March 1809, PRO. WO.1/237, p. 457; Schepeler, *op. cit.*, II, 384, 487; Toreno, *op. cit.*, II, p. 9; Holland, *op. cit.*, p. 359.
100 Decree of Junta Central, 22 May 1809, *cit. Gazeta del Gobierno*, 5 June 1809, 567–8, HMM. AH17-2(2925bis).
101 Cf. Garay to Sabasona, 30 April 1809, AHN. Estado, 17/9-2, p. 28; Cuesta, *op. cit.*, p. 21; Whittingham, *op. cit.*, 68, 79; Toreno, *op. cit.*, I, p. 378; Southey, *Peninsular War*, II, 220–1; Schepeler, *op. cit.*, II, p. 385;
102 Doyle to Cooke, 3, 13, 23 and 29 January, 10 February, 13 and 23

March 1809, PRO. WO.1/241, 17–18, 39, 57, 106, 129, 241, 251–2; Doyle to Frere, 10 February 1809, PRO. WO.1/241, p. 133; Walker to Liverpool, 8 October, 23 November and 16 December 1810, PRO. WO.1/261, 104, 123, 147; Carroll to Castlereagh, 2 February and 22 March 1809, PRO. WO.1/241, 360, 409–11; *Semanario Patriótico*, 30 May 1811, p. 231, HMM. AH1-6(197); Whittingham, *op. cit.*, p. 156; Schepeler, *op. cit.*, I, 237–8.
103 Doyle to Castlereagh, 4 August 1808, PRO. WO.1/227, p. 100; Doyle to Stewart, 16 August 1808, PRO. WO.1/227, 155–7.
104 Wellington to Liverpool, 27 November 1811, PRO. WO.1/251, 225–7; Schepeler, *op. cit.*, I, 420–1; Stanhope, *op. cit.*, p. 22.
105 Schepeler, *op. cit.*, II, p. 388.
106 *El Redactor General*, 17 September 1811, 325–6, HMM. 6/3; Alcalá Galiano, *op. cit.*, I, 224–5;
107 *Gazeta de Valencia*, 22 November, 16 and 30 December 1808, 3 and 17 January 1809, 691–2, 728–34, 746, 799–80, HMM. AH.2-6 (408); *Diario de Málaga*, 17 October, 23 and 25 November, 4, 6 and 7 December 1808, 527, 678, 685, 720–1, 729, 733–4, SHM. CDF.XL.
108 Graham to Liverpool, 27 May 1811, PRO. WO.1/252, 331–2.
109 Toreno, *op. cit.*, I, p. 418.
110 E.g. Veri to Garay, 26 February 1809, AHN. Estado, 17/10-1, p. 28; Doyle to Cooke, 7 March 1809, PRO. WO.1/241, 208–9; cf. also *Memorial Militar y Patriótico del Ejército de la Izquierda*, 10 April 1810, 18–19, HMM. AH.3-3(536); Castaños, *op. cit.*, 139–40.
111 Birch to Leith, 8 September 1808, PRO. WO.1/229, 225–6; Bouligny (MS), 6–8, SHM. AGI.2/2/8, No. 6; Cuesta, *op. cit.*, 82–3; Infantado, *op. cit.*, 80–1; *Pensamientos militares de un paisano* (Seville, 1809), 21–3 (hereafter *Pensamientos militares*).
112 Calzada, *op. cit.*, p. 116.
113 Cf. Frere to Wellington, 28 July 1809, *cit.* Cuesta, *op. cit.*, 80–2; Junta Central to Venegas, 17 July 1809, *cit. ibid.*, p. 118.
114 Wellington to Castlereagh, 24 August 1809, US. WP.1/275; Porlier to Mahy, 25 March 1811, SHM. AGI. 25/35/24; Carroll to Wellington, 2 January 1810, PRO. WO.1/243, 32–3.
115 E.g. Moore to Castlereagh, 16 December 1808, PRO. WO.1/236, 207–8; *bandos* of General Areizaga, 26 and 30 November 1809, RAH. 9-31-6: 6965.
116 Wellington to Bathurst, 17 October 1812, US. WP.1/351, f. 5. Wellington to H. Wellesley, 29 May 1811, US. WP.1/332, f.3.
117 *Diario de Granada*, 18 May 1809, SHM. CDF.XXXIV.
118 Schepeler, *op. cit.*, III, p. 32.
119 Toreno, *op. cit.*, I, p. 375.
120 Wellesley to Garay, 21 August 1809, PRO. WO.1/242, 30–1.
121 Girón to Copons, 19 March 1809, RAH. 9-31-6:6965; *Semanario Patriótico*, 11 April 1809, 60–2, HMM. AH1-6(197); *El Redactor General*, 7 November 1811, p. 211, HMM. 6/3; *ibid.*, 24 December 1811, 755–6; *ibid.*, 1 February 1812, 901–2; *Indagación*, 11–14;

Schepeler, *op. cit.*, II, p. 455.
122 Broderick to Castlereagh, 5 November 1808, PRO. WO.1/233, p. 61; Taboada to Mahy, 25 April 1809, SHM. AGI.5/8/1; Spencer to Wellesley, 15 July 1808, PRO. WO.1/228, 124–7; Birch to Leith, 1 September 1808, PRO. WO.1/229, p. 222; Copons to Areizaga, 31 October 1809, RAH. 9-31-6:6965; Orgaz to Copons, 25 April 1809, RAH. 9-31-6:6965; Girón to Copons, 19 March 1809, RAH. 9-31-6: 6965.
123 F. Guervos to his parents, 18 November 1808, RAH. 11-5-7:9003, No. 4; Narciso de Pedro to La Peña, 14 November 1808, RAH. 11-2-2:8154, VI–II.
124 *El Redactor General*, 13 September 1813, p. 3353, HMM. 6/3; Jacob, *op. cit.*, p. 42; Cuesta, *op. cit.*, p. 63; Castaños, *op. cit.*, p. 64.
125 E.g. *El Redactor General*, 31 January 1812, 897–8, HMM. 6/3.
126 Wellington to Wellesley, 8 August 1809, US. WP.1/274.
127 E.g. *Gazeta del Gobierno*, 27 January 1809, 68–9, HMM. AH17-2 (2925bis); Infantado, *op. cit.*, 83–4.
128 E.g. Adam to Murray, 24 March 1813, US. WP.1/368, f. 1.
129 E.g. Mahy to Del Parque, 6 October 1809, SHM. AGI.5/8/4, No. 16 bis; Bonnet to Cafarelli, 31 August 1811, PRO. WO.1/261, p. 500; La Romana to Mahy, 25 July 1809, SHM. AGI.5/8/2, No. 5.
130 Real Orden, 25 February 1809, *cit. Diario de Badajoz*, 10 March 1809, 261–2, HMM. AH14-1(2457); Cabanes, *Ejército de Cataluña*, I, p. 48; Schepeler, *op. cit.*, III, p. 171; Sydenham to H. Wellesley, 10 October 1812, US. WP.1/361.
131 F. Guervos to his parents, 18 November 1808, RAH. 11-5-7:9003, No. 4; Villalva, *op. cit.*, p. 45; Schepeler, *op. cit.*, II, p. 430; Castaños to Wellington, 27 June 1813, US. WP.1/368, f. 4.
132 E.g. O'Donnell to Mahy, 18 February 1809, SHM. AGI.5/8/9, No. 20; Doyle to Castlereagh, 20 August 1808, PRO. WO.1/227, p. 196; Santa Cruz de Marcenado to Leith, 6 September 1808, PRO. WO.1/229, p. 122; *Apuntaciones militares para la actual guerra* (Cádiz, 1811), 45–7, SHM. CDF.CXIV (hereafter *Apuntaciones militares*).
133 Wellington to Wellesley, 1 September 1809, US. WP.1/277.
134 Wellington to Wellesley, 24 August 1809, US. WP.1/275.
135 Holland, *op. cit.*, p. 365; Toreno, *op. cit.*, II, 70–2; Schepeler, *op. cit.*, II, 494–6.
136 Moore to Castlereagh, 31 December 1808, PRO. WO.1/236, 253–4.
137 Marqués de Quintanilla to Junta Central, 26 and 28 December 1808, 12 February 1809, AHN. Estado, 17/7, 32, 36–9, 74–5.
138 Marqués de la Romana, 'Manifiesto del Marqués de la Romana sobre la conducta de la junta extinguida del Principado de Asturias' (MS), RAH. 2-MS134, No. 5; Parker Carroll to Castlereagh, 7 May 1809, PRO. WO.1/241, p. 486; Toreno, *op. cit.*, I, p. 406; Schepeler, *op. cit.*, III, 352–3; Alvarez Valdés, *op. cit.*, 147–51.
139 Schepeler, *op. cit.*, II, p. 352; Toreno, *op. cit.*, I, 422–3.
140 Toreno, *op. cit.*, II, 70–4; Jacob, *op. cit.*, 58–9.

141 E.g. Jacob. *op. cit.*, 33–4.
142 *Representación del Exmo. Sr. Marqués de la Romana a la Suprema Junta Central*, 14 October 1809, SHM. CDF.DCCLX, 109–15.
143 Toreno, *op. cit.*, II, 73–5, 79–80; Schepeler, *op. cit.*, II, 449–50, 458–9.
144 Toreno, *op. cit.*, II, 77–8, 89; Schepeler, *op. cit.*, II, 492–8.
145 'Memorandum on the state of Spain' (MS), 27 December 1809, US. Carver MSS, No. 100.
146 Wellington to Liverpool, 31 January 1810, PRO. WO.1/243, p. 169; Frere to Wellington, 24 January 1810, PRO. WO.1/243, 217–8; *El Espectador Sevillano*, 27 January 1810, p. 465, HMM. AH2-4(347); notebook in the hand of R. Wellesley II of events in Spain and Portugal, October 1809–January 1810 (MS), US. Carver MSS, No. 53; Toreno, *op. cit.*, II, 93–103; Jacob, *op. cit.*, p. 367.

Chapter 5

The army and the liberals, 1810–14

The fall of the Junta Central in January 1810 marks a turning point in the history of the Spanish War of Independence. Until that point it may fairly be said that the Spaniards themselves had borne the main weight of the struggle against the French. Despite the crucial importance of the aid received from Great Britain, it was the Spaniards who had performed most of the actual fighting: though the British army had twice driven the French from Portugal, its incursions into Spain had been short lived and interspersed with long periods of inactivity. Following the French conquest of Andalucía the balance of the alliance began steadily to tilt in favour of the British. Thanks to the inexorable advance of the French armies from 1810 onwards and the outbreak of revolution in Latin America, the Spanish government was deprived of an ever greater proportion of its revenue. The result was that the patriot cause fell into a state of paralysis. Denied the logistical support which they required, the regular armies could not even defend the provinces that still remained to the Spaniards, let alone regain the ground which they had lost. In consequence, by January 1812 the only areas of Spain that were still free were Galicia, the hinterland of Alicante and Cartagena, the interior of Catalonia, and the besieged city of Cádiz. The Spaniards were rescued from their predicament by the successful offensive launched by Wellington's army in January 1812, but they were never able to regain the preeminence which they had enjoyed before 1810. Although this situation must in part be attributed to the political and physical disruption engendered by years of warfare, a large part of the responsibility must also be borne by the liberals who came to dominate the patriot régime after 1810. Devoted to the pursuit of national liberty, they were driven by a dogmatic anti-militarism that led them fiercely to oppose the only measures that might have rendered the army an efficient fighting force, and to embark upon a ferocious attack upon the remaining prerogatives of the military estate.

The ascendancy of the liberals after 1810 was initially the product of the weakness of the so-called 'Regency of the Five' that was established in Cádiz after the fall of the Junta Central in January 1810. Hopes that the Regency would be able to exercise absolute power soon proved chimerical as its effective leader, General Castaños, was simply too mild a character to provide dynamic leadership.[1] Cut off from the rest of Spain by the French blockade of Cádiz, its writ did not even run unchallenged in its own capital. A new Junta of Defence had been formed in Cádiz which had taken advantage of the general confusion to proclaim itself to be the sovereign government of Spain. Although it eventually agreed to recognise the Regency, its *de facto* control of the customs revenues allowed it to retain considerable influence.[2] Even had this not been the case, the Regency was as inefficient and unrealistic as any of its predecessors. As one British officer complained to Wellington, 'From the little I have seen of the Regency, they appear to differ from the Junta but in name ... with one exception ... which is that your brother [i.e. Henry Wellesley, who was British ambassador] has only five blockheads to transact business with instead of thirty four'.[3] So weak a body had little chance of withstanding the rising clamour for a Cortes, or of influencing the manner in which it was formed. As Cádiz's powerful commercial community made it by far the most radical city in Spain, the Regency had to abandon all hope of giving separate representation to the Church and the nobility, and instead to agree to a unicameral assembly. Although the franchise was still effectively limited to the propertied classes, there was therefore nothing to stand in the way of the general pressure for reform whose existence had been confirmed by the response to the Junta Central's appeal of June 1809 to all *sabios y personas ilustradas* to submit their views on the priorities for a new Cortes. Interestingly, in addition to calling for a wide range of political, social, legal, economic and educational reforms, the *Informes sobre Cortes* laid much stress on demands for the abolition of the privileges of the military estate and for the replacement of the army by a national militia.[4] Of course, this reformism did not necessarily amount to a desire to transform society, for many reformers drew their inspiration from an idealised view of traditional institutions and wished only to build upon the existing foundations of the *ancien régime*. However, for the group of men who were to become known as the liberals, the time had come for a true revolution.

Although it is conventional to regard the liberals as being the representatives of the revolutionary bourgeoisie, such a definiton is misleading. Whilst their ranks certainly included men such as lawyers, merchants and minor officials, they also contained noblemen, dissident clergymen and army officers. If the ideas of the Enlightenment and the French Revolution had played some part in their political formation, the war itself had been equally important as a factor in their radicalisation. What distinguished the liberals from the rest of the political nation was therefore not so much their social origins as their vision: unlike their fellows they were convinced that neither the political gains of 1808, nor Spain herself, could be saved unless the *ancien régime* was swept away once and for all. In the eyes of the liberals, the disasters of 1808 had been the product of centuries of despotism. Spain had to be given her liberty, or else she would inevitably have to endure similar humiliations in the future; indeed, she would have no future at all, for the French would eventually overcome her resistance and reduce her to slavery. The powers of the monarchy therefore had to be limited by means of a constitution, and the sovereign power restored to the Spanish people assembled in its Cortes. In addition, it would also be necessary to remedy the archaic nature of Spanish society. Henceforward all men were to enjoy full civil rights and equality before the law. The privileges and exemptions of the army, the Church, the Mesta, the guilds, the municipalities, the historic kingdoms and principalities, the nobility and the military orders were all to be abolished. In their place Spain was to be given a unified code of law, a common fiscal structure, and a centralised and uniform system of government. Drawing upon the writings of earlier reformers such as Jovellanos, the liberals were also convinced that the regeneration of Spain required massive social and economic change. Above all, the individual must enjoy complete control of his own property, whilst the vast tracts of land held in entail by the Church and the nobility should be made available for profitable exploitation. The liberals were accordingly to abolish all restrictions upon the acquisition and sale of land, and to expropriate the lands of the municipalities and the religious orders. Mention of the latter brings us to the question of the liberals' policy with regard to the Church. Though far from being anti-catholic, the liberals were not prepared to tolerate the theocratic pretensions entertained by some members of the hierarchy, and desired the reform of those elements of the Spanish Church that they deemed to be harmful to progress, or conducive to despotism. Hence their attack upon the religious orders and the Inquisition, and their support of the freedom of the press.[5]

The number of committed liberals was actually very small, and yet between 1810 and 1813 they were able to dominate Spanish politics, and to force through almost all their proposals. In large part this was due to the circumstances in which the Cortes was elected. Voting could only be conducted with any facility in those areas that remained unoccupied by the French. Deputies for the occupied regions had to be selected from those of their inhabitants who happened to be resident in Cádiz with the result that many of them were far more liberal than might otherwise have been the case. As long as the Cortes was based in Cádiz, the liberals also enjoyed local support from both the press and the crowd. Yet for all the fluctuating nature of their parliamentary majority, which was often seriously reduced over particularly radical measures, they had little need of such assistance. They had a coherent plan, their very lack of numbers allowed them to function as a tightly organized caucus, and their leaders numbered many of the most able figures in the Cortes. As a result they were enabled to exploit the vaguely reformist leanings of the bulk of their fellow deputies, whilst sweeping aside the very few outright reactionaries. Nicknamed the *serviles* (the slavish ones), the conservatives' very sobriquent stands witness to their initial unpopularity.[6]

The liberals' first objectives were to establish the sovereignty of the people, and to neutralise the highly conservative Regency. Since there was general agreement that the Cortes should hold absolute power in the absence of the King, this was a simple task. When the assembly finally met on 24 September 1810 a motion was immediately introduced declaring the sovereign power to reside in the Cortes, and requiring all the authorities of the state, including the Regency, to take an oath of allegiance. The resistance of certain of the regents to this demand provided a pretext for their replacement by a new 'Regency of the Three', whose members, General Blake and Admirals Ciscar and Agar, were all noted for their docility. As far as the army was concerned, the only opposition came from the notoriously traditionalistic Marqués del Palacio, who refused to take the required oath of allegiance and was promptly imprisoned. For the rest, even such noted *frondeurs* as La Romana and Infantado placed themselves unreservedly at the orders of the Cortes.[7] However tempting it might be to suspect that such support was largely the product of political opportunism, it is clear that many generals were genuinely delighted at the advent of the Cortes. As Manuel La Peña proclaimed, 'The hope of saving the fatherland is reborn'.[8] Their optimism rested on the hope that the new régime would at last be able to put the Spanish war effort on a proper footing. Until 1810, in their own eyes at least, they had consistently been denied the means that they needed to fight the war whilst nevertheless being held responsible for defeats whose real origin lay in the chaotic legacy of the national uprising of 1808. The ad hoc nature of Spain's mobilisation had led to the army being swamped by large numbers of new regiments composed entirely of raw recruits officered by men of neither talent nor experience. The resultant disruption had been magnified by the collapse of the supply system, the complete indiscipline of the guerrillas, the insubordination of the provincial juntas, and the refusal of the Junta Central to appoint a commander-in-chief. Considering the superiority of the French forces, defeat had been inevitable.[9] With the greater prestige that had now accrued to the central government, it was possible to hope that the Cortes would now address itself to a thorough reorganization of the army, the provision of an adequate system of recruitment and supply, the militarisation of the guerrillas, and the establishment of a *mando único*.[10]

The priorities of the liberals were entirely different, however, for they insisted that the Spanish people had gone to war with France, not simply to sustain the rights of an absolute monarch, but to regain their liberties.[11] According to this theory, the fervour which had thus inspired the insurgents of 1808 had enabled them to achieve great victories, but thereafter their 'holy fury' had been allowed to subside: political reforms had not been instigated and the revolution had degenerated into a mere war. Once more upon familiar ground, the French had thereupon naturally gained the advantage.[12] It followed that Spain could only be saved by 'a true revolution in which the general effervescence would lend her the strength to resist armies born of a similar upheaval'.[13] The first task of the Cortes was thus to restore the liberty of the nation, for the best way of winning the war was not military reform but the introduction of a constitution. After its promulgation *El Redactor General* could even go so far as to argue that the Constitution of 1812 'has been the most formidable army that the French have had to face, for it has transformed what they regarded as a horde of savages into a nation of free men'.[14]

For the first eighteen months of the Cortes' existence, its attention was therefore wholly absorbed by the formulation of the famous Constitution of 1812. However, far from bringing about the liberation of Spain, the constitutional debate coincided with a further decline in Spain's fortunes. Not only did Cádiz remain besieged, but the French armies occupied an ever greater area of patriot Spain. Following the close of the Austrian campaign in 1809, Napoleon had determined to bring an end to the 'Spanish ulcer'. Heavy reinforcements were therefore poured into the Peninsula so as to enable the French commanders to form a powerful striking force with which to drive the British from their stronghold in Portugal. In the face of such a threat, Wellington could not but adopt a defensive strategy. Retaining his army within the Portuguese frontier, he remained a passive observer whilst the French armies reduced the Spanish fortresses of Astorga and Ciudad Rodrigo. When the French finally invaded Portugal in August 1810, he withdrew before them to the impregnable lines of Torres Vedras outside Lisbon. There he remained throughout the winter until starvation finally forced the French to retreat in March 1811. Wellington was soon back on the Portuguese frontier, but for the rest of the year the French remained sufficiently strong to frustrate any further advances.

For the best part of two years the French were therefore left free to concentrate upon reducing the remaining patriot enclaves. By January 1812 they had occupied Oviedo, Lérida, Tortosa, Badajoz, Tarragona and Valencia. Whilst it is true that disaster was occasionally precipitated by the ineptitude of certain generals, the Spaniards for the most part lacked the strength to make head against these offensives, for their troops remained as ragged, starving, disease-ridden, ill-equipped and unpaid as ever. So desperate was the position in some areas that the soldiers actually had to be dismissed to their homes for want of food and clothing.[15] Most of the armies could field only a small proportion of their available strength (6,000 out of 23,000 in the case of the Army of Galicia in September 1810), and they were often only able to do so at all after their copious wants had been made up by the British.[16] In short, for the most part the

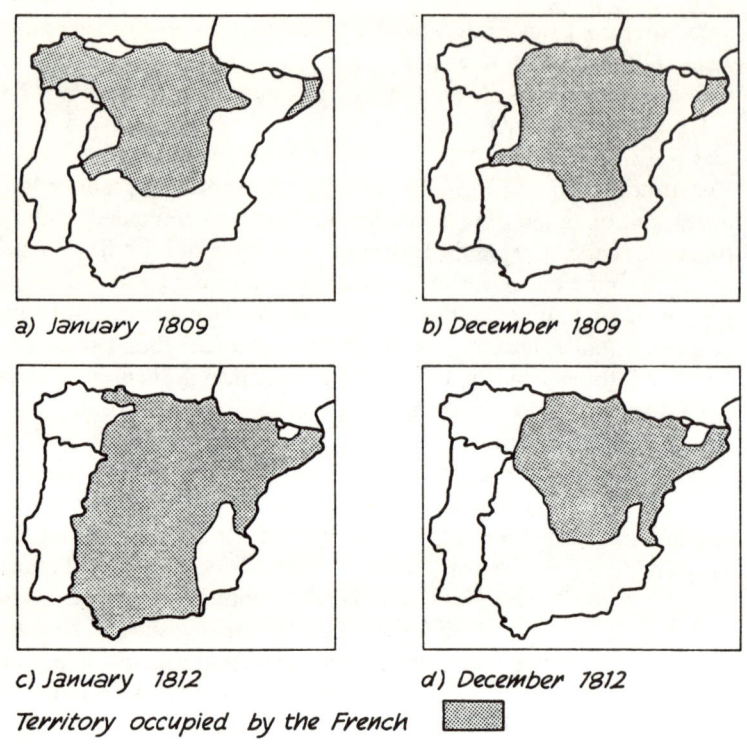

a) January 1809
b) December 1809
c) January 1812
d) December 1812
Territory occupied by the French

5 The Spanish War of Independence, 1808–14

Spanish armies remained 'unfit for anything more than mere guerrilla warfare'.[17] In this capacity it has to be said that the Spanish army often performed with distinction. For example, for most of 1811 and 1812, General Francisco López Ballesteros' division of the Army of the Left operated with considerable success against the French forces in Andalucía. Originally based in the mountains of western Andalucía, in September 1811 his forces were sent round by sea to Algeciras, from where they launched repeated raids against the French positions around Ronda and Málaga. Every time that the invaders concentrated a field force against him, Ballesteros would simply retreat under the guns of Gibraltar whence he could defy them with impunity. In the meantime he would have invariably given considerable assistance to the guerrillas, for the French would have been forced to abandon their pursuit of the irregulars and strip their garrisons so as to provide a respectable field force. Left to their own devices, the *partidas* would then swarm down from their mountain strongholds and attack the inadequately protected French bases, with the result that the invaders would have no option but to give up their operations against Ballesteros.

With their operations complemented in this fashion by those of the regular army, the guerrillas attained their maximum importance during this period. According to one Spanish estimate, by the end of 1812 they numbered 38,520 men organized into twenty-two different *partidas*.[18] They may even have saved Spain from being overcome altogether, keeping resistance alive until Wellington's army was at last able to break free of the stalemate on the Portuguese frontier: thanks to the guerrillas, the conquest of Spain required a much larger army than that which Napoleon had been able to deploy there, but, as Wellington had pointed out in 1810, the invaders 'cannot increase their force in the Peninsula, even admitting that they possess the military means, without increasing their pecuniary and other difficulties and distress'.[19] Yet for all the damage that these forces inflicted upon their opponents, they could not prevent the French advance. As Sir Thomas Graham noted in 1810:

There are points where it is of infinite consequence to the cause that there should be armies for, useful and important as the services of the guerrillas are, that is not enough, let them be ever so much spread over the face of the country. They never can stop the march of a considerable body of the enemy and protect a country as Blake has done lately in Murcia, and O'Donnell has so successfully done in Catalonia.[20]

Although many guerrilla leaders formed their bands into disciplined military units, the irregulars were frequently just as poorly trained, officered and equipped as their colleagues in the rest of the army.[21] Particularly towards the end of the war, they were frequently able to get the better of small forces of the enemy, but a major French offensive left them with no choice but to take evasive action. Nor were the guerrillas any more able to reconquer territory that had fallen to the invaders as the French had only to retreat within one of the fortified bases from which they held down the countryside to be entirely safe: until they had been supplied with artillery by the British after 1812, the guerrillas had no means of conducting formal sieges.[22] Yet another problem was presented by the guerrillas' lack of co-ordination. Many of their chieftains were as intent upon establishing themselves as petty dictators in their own localities as they were upon fighting the French. Not only did they refuse to co-operate with one another militarily, but they ruthlessly suppressed any bands that emerged to challenge their predominance in their home districts.[23] Nor were most of the guerrilla leaders prepared to accept the authority of the military commanders (to whom they were officially subordinated).[24] To have relied upon them as the chief instruments of any concerted plan of operations would therefore have been impossible. Yet even had the guerrillas been free of these deficiencies, they could not have taken the place of a regular army. As the Duke of Wellington pointed out:

> Independent small bodies operating upon the enemy may be extremely useful when these operations are connected and carried on in concert with those of a large body of troops which . . . occupy the whole of the enemy's attention . . . but when the enemy is relieved from the pressure of the larger body, the smaller body must discontinue its operations or be destroyed.[25]

In short, it is impossible to believe that the guerrillas could ever have achieved 'the considerable and lasting advantages . . . that would have provided the government with the means of raising armies'.[26]

So sharp a critique of the guerrillas may well appear incongruous in view of the undoubted successes which they scored in northern Spain in the course of 1812 and 1813. With the assistance of a British naval squadron, the Cantabrian *partidas* of Longa, Jaureghui and Porlier succeeded in temporarily clearing the French from most of the Basque coast, and in capturing the major port of Santander (3 August 1813). In Navarre, meanwhile, the redoubtable Francisco Espoz y Mina built up a force of nearly 10,000 men with which he bottled the French up in Pamplona. So complete was his domination that he established an effective provincial administration, complete with its own hospitals and armament workshops. Finally, in Aragón, the garrisons of Marshal Suchet were faced by the *partidas* of Durán, Gayán and Villacampa, as well as by expeditions dispatched from the direction of Catalonia. Moreover, the major Spanish formations were no longer mere bands of irregulars, but disciplined formations of veteran troops that were often stronger than the punitive columns that the French were able to dispatch against them. They had even been supplied with a certain amount of artillery. Towards the end of 1812 their operations received a tremendous boost from the advance of the Duke of Wellington into the hinterland of Old Castile after the battle of Salamanca. Forced to concentrate all their forces to repel his offensives, the French had no option but to bring forward the troops who had hitherto been fighting the guerrillas. In Aragón, whose garrison was left more-or-less intact, the invaders managed to hold their own, but in Navarre and the Basque country the guerrillas were able to run amok. Communications with France were badly disrupted, whilst in February 1813 Mina forced the surrender of the French garrison of Tafalla, having first defeated a column of over 3,000 troops that had been sent to relieve it (11 February 1813). This exploit was followed in March by the storm of Fuenterrabía on the very borders of France, and the annihilation of two battalions at Lerín (31 March 1813). Attacks on the towns of Huesca and Sos were both beaten off, but the French nevertheless decided to evacuate the latter and almost suffered the destruction of the column sent to its relief when Mina attacked it at Castiliscar (2 March 1813). In response to this activity, the French Army of the North launched a powerful offensive against the *partidas*. To ensure their defeat, its commander was authorised to draw upon the Army of Portugal, five of whose six divisions were eventually to be sucked into the struggle. Although communications with France were placed on a more secure footing, and Mina forced to retreat into Aragón, the guerrillas had not been destroyed. Furthermore, Mina's arrival in Aragón coincided with the withdrawal of a significant proportion of its garrison in response to Suchet's fears of an allied advance on Valencia from the direction of Alicante. The French hold on Navarre and the Basque country had merely been strengthened at the expense of their control of Aragón. Still worse, the reverse inflicted on Mina and the Cantabrians had been achieved by detaching troops from the forces whose task it was to contain Wellington. Though it is hard to see an alternative to this decision, it was one for which the French were to pay dearly.[27]

These campaigns clearly illustrate the limitations of guerrilla warfare. Although Mina and his colleagues were able to score significant successes whenever the French were short of manpower or otherwise distracted, they could not hold their ground in the face of a determined counter-offensive. Unless there was a serious failure of political will on the part of Napoleon – which still could not be foreseen even in the aftermath of the Retreat from Moscow – the French would therefore have to be forced to disgorge their conquests by conventional means. In order to build an army that would be capable of such a task, it was essential that 'effectual measures should be adopted to feed, pay, clothe and discipline the Spanish troops'.[28] How this was to be achieved was by no means clear, for the Cádiz government was effectively bankrupt. Cut off from most of the territory that still remained free from French occupation, its resources were confined to such taxes and patriotic contributions as it could raise in Cádiz itself, the shipments of bullion that were periodically received from Latin America, and the limited financial assistance that could be provided by Great Britain. These resources were simply insufficient to meet the demands on the public treasury, which were calculated early in 1811 as a minimum of 1400,000,000 *reales* per year. Nor was it possible for the régime to raise additional revenue in the form of loans, for it was hardly an attractive target for investment. Finally, the administration was in such disorder that the government could not make effective use of the limited resources that it still possessed.[29] Matters were now to deteriorate still further, for in 1810 revolution broke out in Latin America with effects that can only be described as devastating. In 1809 alone 344,000,000 *reales* had been received from the American colonies, but the figure was reduced by eighty per cent in 1811, and ninety-three per cent in 1812. In 1810 overall revenue had amounted to 407,700,000 *reales*, in 1811 to 201,600,000, and in 1812 to 138,000,000.[30] Although the British repeatedly attempted to persuade the Spaniards that the best means of solving the crisis was to grant the colonies a significant measure of self government, the Regency was in no position to make such concessions, for it was effectively in thrall to the commercial interests that dominated Cádiz. In alliance with the liberals, who maintained that the Constitution of 1812 had freed the Americans from despotism by making them equal citizens of a united Spanish empire, they rejected all forms of compromise and demanded that the *facciosos* should be put down by force. The result was that between November 1811 and October 1813 no fewer than 12,784 troops were sent to America in fourteen separate expeditions.[31] Dispatched in small groups that never amounted to more than two thousand men, these expeditions served only to exacerbate resentment in the colonies and to drain Spanish strength at home. Moreover, even when order was temporarily restored, as in Mexico, such was the disruption to the colonial economy that there was no resumption in the flow of bullion.[32] Had the British government not agreed to supply the Cádiz government with a subsidy of £600,000 in 1812, it is impossible to see how the Spaniards could have continued the struggle at all.[33]

The pecuniary difficulties of the Regency placed the patriot cause in a quandary from which there was no easy escape. The only hope of restoring the Spanish army to a position in which it could not only resist, but also turn back the tide of French conquest was for the government to regain control of the territory that had been lost between 1810 and 1812. However, this territory could not be regained except through the very conventional operations that were beyond the capabilities of the patriot forces. In short, the Spaniards could only hope to maintain their resistance until such time as the Duke of Wellington was once more able to advance across the Portuguese frontier. Yet however much they were powerless to effect their own liberation, it cannot be said that they did not earn their eventual deliverance. The sheer tenacity of Spanish resistance forced the French to garrison every square mile of captured territory. With every step that they advanced, the invaders therefore became more and more over-stretched, and more and more vulnerable to Wellington's army. Until the end of 1811 the French commanders had found it possible to deploy sufficient forces against the Duke to prevent him from advancing far into Spain, but the moment inevitably came when the forces facing him had to be drawn upon to provide reinforcements for the operations that were being carried on elsewhere. Seeing his chance, Wellington immediately pounced upon the inadequately protected border fortresses of Ciudad Rodrigo and Badajoz, and followed up their capture by the victory of Salamanca (22 July 1812). Madrid was liberated on 12 August 1812, the siege of Cádiz was lifted, and the French forced to evacuate Andalucía. Having thus been forced to give up much of their conquests, the French were enabled to concentrate against Wellington in such numbers as to drive him back to the Portuguese frontier. Although Andalucía remained free, its liberation did not put an end to Spain's prostration, it being left to the Duke of Wellington actually to defeat the French. Once again, the simple fact that the French did not have enough troops in Spain to carry out all the tasks with which they were faced was to prove their downfall. Even on the defensive, they could not simultaneously contain the allied regular armies, Spanish as well as Anglo–Portuguese, and put down the *partidas*. By sending the Army of Portugal to restore order in Navarre and the Basque country, Napoleon had presented the Duke of Wellington with a second opportunity to break the stalemate. Catching the French off balance, he struck into Old Castile and forced them into a precipitate retreat. Unlike in 1812, this time there was no mistake: following the decisive battle of Vitoria (21 June 1813), the French were driven across the Pyrenees, leaving Suchet with no choice but to retreat from Valencia, and ultimately Catalonia as well.

The Spanish armies only played an auxiliary role in this success. They fought well enough when they actually came to grips with the enemy, but Wellington deliberately made as little use of them as possible. Even had he wanted to place more reliance upon them, it is clear that the government's bankruptcy would have prevented him from doing so. Far from providing the wherewithal for a revivified war effort, the liberated territories proved to be a ruined land: stripped of their resources by the French, they were also ravaged by bandits and bands of sometime guerrillas, who preferred to prey upon the civilian population and the allied supply trains rather than the retreating enemy.[34] The danger of such a situation had been revealed as early as 1809 when the French evacuation of Galicia had been followed by an upsurge of banditry.[35] With their villages burnt by the enemy, many of the erstwhile insurgents simply had no other means of support. In addition, they had acquired a taste for pillage that far outweighed their desire to fight the French, let alone their willingness to be absorbed into the regular army.[36] A certain proportion of the guerrillas had never been anything more than bandits garbed in a cloak of patriotic fervour, and their activities had often had to be repressed by the regular army.[37] With the departure of the French more of them began to appear in their true colours. At the very same time that Mina was inflicting such havoc upon the French in Navarre, the bands of Borbón, Puchas, Marquínez and Príncipe were turning to highway robbery *en masse* in the Castiles.[38] Individual members of other bands that had been incorporated into the regular army, such as Julián Sánchez's Lanceros de Castilla, registered their own protest by becoming renegades.[39] Finally, even such guerrillas as remained loyal continued to oppress the civilian population with their merciless requisitioning, and to act as an obstacle to the recruitment and supply of the regular army.[40] In November 1813 the Regency attempted to remedy the situation by establishing a rural volunteer militia whose members were charged with the maintenance of order, but this force made little difference; as Wellington complained to the Minister of War the following month:

The wants of the troops and the state in which the army is are to be attributed to the deficiency of public authority in the provinces... The fact is, Sir, that the Intendants of the provinces are unable or unwilling to perform their duty, all authority has been annihilated in Spain, and, at the moment the greatest exertions are required to form and maintain armies to save the state, there is no authority in existence capable of enforcing the most simple order of the government. That is the truth, and, till a remedy is applied, the evil will become worse.[41]

The serious nature of these difficulties reinforced the need to remedy the problems occasioned by the hasty and totally uncontrolled expansion of the armed forces in 1808. Not only were there too many regiments for the number of troops available, but many of the numerous officers who had been left without employment flocked to Cádiz where their salaries consumed much of the government's limited revenue.[42] Yet instead of taking action to ensure that its resources were put to the best possible use, the Regency was forced to give way to the vested interests of the officer corps in maintaining the current disorder. For example, rather than reducing the number of units, in May 1812 it decreed that each infantry regiment should consist only of a single battalion, a measure that not only institutionalised three times as many regiments as was necessary, but left no means by which recruits could be channelled to the front.[43] A similar effort was made to accommodate the generals, of whom there were 690 in 1814 compared with 422 in 1808: when a permanent system of higher formations was finally introduced late in 1812, the size of a brigade was limited to four battalions, and that of a division to eight, although in both cases this was two thirds or even one half the size of the European norm.[44] The fundamental problem of the army's structure therefore remained unresolved, with the result that when the Cortes did turn its attention to military affairs its efforts were totally ineffective. Despite the liberals' fixation with the Constitution, the period from 1810 to 1812 had not been entirely bereft of developments with regard to the army, as witness the establishment of a general staff in 1810 and the introduction of the principle of universal military service in 1811. In addition, a training depot was established outside Cádiz under the command of the British liaison officer, Charles Doyle, several new military academies were created, and the appointment of new officers was brought firmly under the control of the central government.[45] However, with no change discernible in Spain's military position, pressure for the Cortes to pay more attention to the needs of the army became ever greater, and in June 1812, it was finally agreed that a special *comisión de constitución militar* should be established to elaborate a programme of action.[46] The following month new regulations were introduced that placed rigorous controls on the activities of the guerrillas.[47] Finally, in September 1812 a group of liberal and anglophile deputies succeeded in persuading their fellows to offer the Duke of Wellington the supreme command of the Spanish armies in the Peninsula.[48]

Why the liberals should have been the ones to take the lead in this matter is somewhat obscure, for they were certainly not interested in military reform in the conventional sense. On the contrary, they were convinced that history had shown regular armies to be 'incompatible with the liberty of nations'.[49] Completely segregated from the rest of society, soldiers could have no interest in the liberty of their fellow citizens, and were as likely to repress them as they were to defend them against external aggression.[50] Little else could be expected, for their ordnances were 'truly despotic and suitable for slaves', being designed to make them 'the instrument of tyranny'.[51] Bound by rigid discipline and accustomed to violence and killing, soldiers automatically became 'the natural enemies of liberty', for 'they are unable to recognize any other right than that of force, any other law than the demands of their officers'.[52] As proof of this argument, the liberals argued that in ancient Rome, imperial Spain, and revolutionary France the substitution of a regular army for a citizens' militia had led to the emergence of despotism.[53] The unregenerate conduct exhibited by the army confirmed the liberals' anti-militarism. Civilian officials were frequently ill-treated by army officers; arbitrary forced requisitioning was imposed with devastating regularity; and the dues of *bagajes y alojamiento* were exploited to provide for the swollen suites that accompanied many generals.[54] A particularly glaring example of such arrogance occurred when the Marqués del Palacio arrived at Badajoz in 1812 to take up his appointment as Captain General of Extremadura: in spite of the town having recently been thoroughly sacked by the British, the Marquess immediately imposed a levy of 30,000 *reales* for the upkeep of his personal household.[55] An alarming tendency towards caesarism was also apparent. Encouraged by the adulation that they frequently received in the press, a number of commanders such as Francisco Ballesteros seized the opportunity offered by the political vacuum left by the retreat of the French armies in 1812–13 to establish petty dictatorships in the cities occupied by their forces.⁵⁶ When the Cortes appointed the Duke of Wellington to the supreme command of the Spanish army, Ballesteros even launched an abortive *pronunciamiento* against the government.⁵⁷

Convinced that a standing army was a threat to liberty, the liberals sought to prove that such a body was also a military liability. The essence of their claim was that the very existence of an army guaranteed the establishment of despotism, which in its turn led to national impotence. 'A slave people', it was maintained, 'is incapable of any act of true valour because its sacrifices cannot bring it any reward.'⁵⁸ It followed that a nation's military strength depended 'on the grade of perfection of the institutions of society'.⁵⁹ Hence the decline of all the empires of the past, and the prosperity enjoyed by Great Britain: whereas the former had all fallen into despotism, the British had experienced a steady growth in their political freedom.⁶⁰ Even had this not been the case, the liberals held that a regular army was no match for a free people. Regular soldiers could not be expected to fight bravely because they could not hope to improve their lot. Subjected to a fierce and brutal discipline, they could hardly be expected to show any fervour in defending freedoms which they did not enjoy themselves.⁶¹ The liberal ideal was therefore a citizens' militia. Not only would such a force pose no threat to liberty, but it would be fighting for its own homes and its own freedom, surely the most powerful of all possible motivations. As for the soldiers themselves, they would be far better prepared for war by a healthy life in the fields, than by the boredom, discomfort and disease of the barracks. A further barrage of historical precedent was laid down to justify this conclusion, the glories of ancient Greece and Rome, the Reconquista, the successful defence of Swiss independence, and the American War of Independence all being attributed to citizen armies. Further testimony to the superiority of the Nation-in-Arms was found in the prodigies attributed to the Spanish guerrillas and the Voluntarios Distinguidos de Cádiz, the civic militia that had garisoned the walls of the capital during the siege of 1810–12.⁶² To reinforce their argument, the liberals drew a comparison between the events of the French and Spanish revolutions. According to their version of events, at the start of the Revolutionary Wars France had possessed a powerful regular army, but had nevertheless been consistently beaten until she had instigated the *levée en masse*. In Spain, the opposite had occurred, the armed people having everywhere defeated the French until they had been formed into regular armies. In the same way, defeat had allegedly been changed into victory in the Russian campaign of 1812 when 'the cabinet war waged by the Russians was converted into a national war by the people taking an interest in their own defence'.[63]

The liberals' deprecation of the army was closely connected with their deep distrust of the executive power, for they were convinced that human nature made kings, regents, and commanders-in-chief alike the enemies of liberty. It was natural for all human beings to strive for the achievement of total happiness, but for rulers of all kinds 'happiness' was synonymous with unfettered power. As constitutions limited their power, it was inevitable that they should seek their overthrow.[64] As for the generals, the liberals could not rid themselves of the belief that 'the first fortunate and victorious general with sufficient forces to put himself at the head of the nation would irremediably destroy our present government and constitution . . . [and] . . . enslave us once more in the chains we have just broken'.[65] The danger posed by the Regency became more acute in January 1812 following the fall of the subservient 'Regency of the Three' in the wake of the capture of its titular president, Joaquín Blake, at the siege of Valencia. Headed from the beginning by the legitimist Duque del Infantado, the new Regency became still more pronounced in its conservatism when the only one of its members who was even moderately sympathetic to the liberals, the Conde del Abisbal, resigned in a fit of pique in July 1812.[66] The new Regency's *servilismo* became still more apparent in the autumn of 1812, when it was discovered that it had secretly been funding the violently anti-liberal *Procurador General de la Nación y del Rey*.[67] Rumours that a plot was afoot to suppress the Cortes came to a head early in March 1813 when the liberal military governor of Cádiz was suddenly replaced by a *servil*. At the same time, the Regency also refused to implement a decree of the Cortes that the recently passed bill for the abolition of the Inquisition should be read in all Spain's churches. For a brief moment a coup seemed imminent, but the Regency apparently had very little support, for when the Cortes voted that it should be dismissed it surrendered without a struggle.[68]

A new three-man Regency was now elected whose members were weak enough to pose no threat to the liberals, but by that time the latter had discovered a new enemy in the person of the Duke of Wellington. The prospect of a commander-in-chief had always been distasteful to the notables who had ruled Spain since 1808. Confronted by military demands for a *mando único*, until 1812 they had evaded the issue by maintaining that the command of the armed forces resided in the sovereign government. It was in order to give some verisimilitude to this argument that a general staff – the Estado Mayor General – had been established in 1810 in order to provide the Regency with tecnical assistance and to transmit its orders to the Spanish armies.[69] Although circumstances had forced the liberals to appoint Wellington as *generalísimo*, they seem to have done so under the impression that he would merely lead the armies to victory. As far as the Duke was concerned, however, he had no intention of being encumbered with the Spanish army unless he had the power to turn it into an efficient fighting force. He therefore demanded a wide range of powers affecting the internal organisation of the army, and the subordination of the provincial authorities to the Captains General.[70] In the event his demands were only conceded in part – for example, the *jefes políticos* were only subordinated to the military authorities in matters pertaining to the conduct of the war[71] – but the liberals remained convinced that the Constitution was in great danger, especially in view of the manner in which the British had already remodelled the Portuguese forces in the style of a despised 'cabinet army'.[72]

Whilst they were certainly eager to defeat the French, the liberals' priorities with regard to the armed forces were far more political than they were military. Their objectives were essentially two-fold: to ensure that the struggle against France should on no account be allowed to deteriorate into a mere 'cabinet war', and to neutralise the army as a factor in Spanish politics – after all, it was as futile to expect 'the mercenary slaves who until now have been the instruments of despotism by some prodigy to become the zealous guardians of liberty' as it was to hope that the executive power would voluntarily respect the constitutional system.[73] In short, the liberals' chief interest lay in making certain that the War of Independence should be a national war waged by a citizens' army. In the eyes of some of the more exalted liberals, the obvious conclusion was that the regular army should be dissolved altogether, or at the very least be merged with the guerrillas. The fight would thus once more devolve upon the armed people, who would be set free to resurrect the triumphs of 1808.[74] On a slightly less radical note, an officer named Albo proposed a scheme whereby the regular army would be transformed into a citizens' militia that in peacetime wold be employed in public works such as the reclamation of Spain's immense *despoblados*. In order to eradicate all traces of the old army, the new force would be modelled upon the troops of the Roman republic: divisions would be replaced by legions, and the soldiers themselves known as *agricolas*.[75] Although more practical views prevailed, the liberals nevertheless could not forget that in its present state the army was 'in absolute contradiction with . . . the liberty of the fatherland'; hence the need to create a new army that 'has an incomparably greater interest in liberty than in slavery, an army that cannot be . . . seduced by the false glory of a warrior king or a lucky general'.[76] To do this it was necessary to ensure that the army was 'constituted in such a manner that its members have the same direct share in civil interests as that possessed by all the other citizens'.[77] The first priority was therefore to end the rigid distinction that had hitherto existed between soldier and civilian. Instead of being composed of criminals and foreigners who had no stake in the freedoms which they were being expected to defend, the army would henceforth be recruited from free Spanish citizens serving 'in the greatest number and for the least time possible'.[78] Not only was the system cheap, particularly if the conscripts only served with the colours for a few months in every year, but it also provided the perfect means whereby they could be indoctrinated with liberal civic virtue.[79]

The Cortes had already declared all Spaniards to be 'soldiers of the Fatherland' in January 1811.[80] However, in the eyes of the liberals the soldiers could never be turned into citizens whilst the army retained any features that constituted a threat to liberty. Hence the restrictions that were imposed upon the *fuero militar*, the numerous plans that were entertained for the reform or abolition of the Royal Guards, the abolition of the privileges of the nobility in the officer corps, and the creation of a more equitable system of rewards.[81] Great importance was also placed upon the reform of the Ordenanzas. The old emphasis upon blind obedience was to be swept away lest the army be used to overthrow the Constitution; instead, the troops were to be taught that there were limits to the authority of their officers, and that they had a positive duty to disobey orders that jeopardised the public good. In short, it had to be established that 'the soldier is human before he is military and a citizen before he is a soldier, that the army's law is inferior to the natural and civil laws, that the army must have no other object than to defend the liberty of the citizens'.[82]

Considerable attention was also given to the question of the army's relations to the executive power. Fears that the Regency might use the army to overthrow the Constitution gave rise to frequent demands for the army to be placed under the direct control of the Cortes.[83] In order to allow the monarchy to retain a measure of dignity, a compromise was eventually reached in the Constitution of 1812, which gave the command of the army to the King, together with the control of all patronage – appointments, promotions, decorations and rewards. However, the Cortes was given the right to vote upon the size of the army, and to determine its ordinances. At the same time, all the Viceroys, Captains General and military governors were henceforth to be excluded from the civil government: their places were taken by civilian nominees of the Cortes known as *jefes políticos* to whom the generals were officially subordinated.[84] In case these provisions should still not be sufficient to prevent the army from being used against the Constitution, it was also decided that a new armed force should be created that was wholly under the control of the civil authorities. Known as the National Guard, this force was effectively to be a self-sufficient army in its own right, but its members were to be part-time militiamen who could be relied upon to retain their links with their communities and to remain free of the corruption of military life.[85] The formation of the National Guard had been prefigured in the Constitution of 1812, and the liberal military writer, Sancho, eventually produced a detailed scheme for such a force, taking as his model the Voluntarios Distinguidos de Cádiz.[86] However, it was not until 15 April 1814, that the Cortes finally decreed its formation, by which point it was far too late, for the newly returned Fernando VII was already on the point of overthrowing the Constitution.[87]

The advent of military reform as the subject of regular discussion in the Cortes soon revealed its divisive nature as an issue. The liberals bitterly opposed every attempt to discipline the guerrillas, and condoned their many excesses.[88] The gulf between liberal and orthodox military opinion became still more apparent with the formation of the Comisión de Constitucion Militar in June 1812. As far as the officers who made up the bulk of its membership were concerned, its task was to restore order, system and discipline to the army.[89] In contrast, the liberals believed that its aim should be to make the

Ordenanzas 'perfectly analogous with the political system'.[90] This contradiction was brought to light when the liberals ensured the defeat of a motion introduced by General Llamas, one of a number of soldiers with seats in the Cortes, calling for the commission's purview to be limited solely to military affairs.[91] Writers such as Flórez Estrada also claimed that the officers of the old army from whom the commission was largely recruited could hardly be expected to carry out their duties in the right spirit.[92] Even avowedly liberal officers took offence at this attitude, whilst they pointed out that, unless adequate measures were taken to ensure the pay and supply of the army, no beneficial effects could be expected from the most laudable reform of its Ordenanzas.[93] Despite their protests, in October 1813 the Cortes decided to establish a second commission drawn from its own members to examine the all-important question of the Ordenanzas, leaving the original body to deal solely with the anodyne questions of organisation and tactics.[94]

However logical this decision may have been from the liberal point of view, many officers would be certain to construe it as a deliberate abdication of the Cortes' responsibilities with regard to the army, whose situation remained as parlous as ever throughout 1812 and 1813. The immense amount of clothing and equipment that was received from Great Britain did something to remedy the various material deficiencies, but nothing could ameliorate the chronic shortage of money: by 1813 the failure of their pay had driven some officers to beg in the streets, whilst others are reputed to have died of starvation.[95] Even the considerable abilities of the Duke of Wellington proved insufficient to the task of setting the army to rights. Although he introduced a series of administrative and organisational reforms that should have done much to assuage its difficulties, their effect was undermined on the one hand by the chaotic domestic situation of patriot Spain, and on the other by a wave of growing anglophobia. Encouraged by the anti-British sentiments that were voiced with ever greater frequency by the liberal press, the Regency and its ministers did everything in their power to obstruct the Duke's activities. Angry and frustrated, Wellington was driven to resign his command in August 1813. He was eventually reinstated by the Cortes, but nothing could be done to remedy the effects of the long months of inter-allied conflict. The problems of the Spanish army remained unresolved, as was graphically shown when Wellington was forced to leave most of his allies behind when he invaded France at the end of 1813 for fear that otherwise their pillaging would turn the French peasantry against him.[96]

In the face of this situation, the liberal programme was an irrelevance, unless, as one officer was overheard to remark, the soldiers were expected to clothe themselves in the pages of the military constitution.[97] Nor was the liberal programme any more satisfactory in terms of its analysis of the Spanish war effort. The liberals maintained that Spain's successes in 1808 — which they greatly exaggerated — had been gained by the unaided efforts of the Spanish people, whereas in reality it had been shown beyond all doubt that an armed citizenry was no match for a regular army. As for the only field battle won by the Spaniards, Bailén had been gained by the despised 'slave soldiers' of the *ancien régime*. Nor were the parallels that were drawn with the French Revolutionary Wars any more appropriate. France's early defeats were caused not by reliance upon the old regular army but by its disintegration. As for the *levée en masse*, it could never have been forged into a powerful weapon of war had it not been for the organisational and tactical legacy of the *ancien régime*, the genius of the revolutionary leaders, and the numerous veterans of the old army to whom the revolution had for the first time offered the chance of professional satisfaction. Developments since 1808 had undermined the liberal arguments still further. Much emphasis had been placed upon the Voluntarios Distinguidos de Cádiz as the model for a new army, for this regiment not only conformed to liberal theories of military organisation, but had also supposedly performed prodigies of valour during the siege of Cádiz. However, the Volunteers had taken advantage of the riots of 1809 to secure a guarantee that they would never have to serve outside the walls of the city; indeed, there is a strong possibility that its members had fomented the disorder with precisely this end in mind.[98] Since Cádiz is situated upon a promontory that juts out into the sea from an island off the coast of southern Spain, such service as they performed was anything but arduous: even during the siege of 1810–12, all that they had to endure was an occasional bombardment. The other feature of the war effort on which the liberals looked with particular favour was the guerrillas. Yet the *partidas* could not take the place of the regular army, whilst popular resistance was not nearly so all pervasive as the liberals inferred. In the first place, the urban population (in which number were included a considerable number of the peasantry and the agricultural proletariat) was generally noted to be indifferent or even openly sympathetic towards the French.[99] Furthermore, as the war progressed the guerrillas became more and more separate from the civilian population. Rather than slipping back to their homes after every operation, they coalesced into individual bands, adopted military forms, and established semi-permanent bases. Thereafter they lived off the people as much as they lived among them. Although they might provide the guerrillas with various degrees of support, most of the inhabitants remained aloof from their operations and 'very lukewarm' to the allied cause because the *partidas* could offer them no protection against French reprisals.[100] They hated the French, but as the British diplomat, Thomas Sydenham, complained:

> It is a passive feeling, which murmurs under the oppression and tyranny which it suffers without exerting itself to remove or diminish what it complains of. The people pay their contributions . . . whenever they are demanded . . . by the enemy. Of course they complain of these exactions and are happy to see the English, who relieve them from the continuance of these exactions . . . But if they complain in secret, or to us when the French have left them, it does the enemy no harm, nor us any good.[101]

The Spanish people might have taken a leading role in precipitating the struggle against the French, but their participation in it had been considerably less than the liberals imagined. The whole rationale underlying the programme of reform that had culminated in the Constitution of 1812 was therefore open to question. At all events, as the *serviles* gleefully pointed out, it had not saved Spain from her prostration.[102] So great was the liberal refusal to take account of reality that it is hard to escape from the conclusion that their military policy was motivated by factors other than than an objective consideration of the strategic situation. In their drive to create a Nation-in-Arms and to ensure that the army could never again be used as a tool of despotism, they had simultaneously redressed many of the grievances which the civilian notables, from whose ranks they sprang, had felt against the military estate before the outbreak of war. A satisfactory career in the officer corps was now open to all men of a reasonable degree of property and education, the military courts had been stripped of much of their competence over disputes between officers and civilians, and the army had been deprived of all share in the local administration. If only on a subconscious level, the liberals had allowed their sectional interests to colour their thinking with regard to the war. Had they been able to bring about a significant change in the army's fortunes, then it is possible that they might have been able to secure their political objectives without too much difficulty. However, with the army utterly humiliated by its experiences during the campaigns of 1812 and 1813, a violent reaction was inevitable.

It is possible to argue that the army could never have been brought to accept the changes that had been effected in its relationship with the rest of society, particularly as the war does not seem to have caused the bourgeoisification of the officer corps with which it has often been credited.[103] Evidence has already been given to suggest that many of the officers who were employed in the new regiments that were raised in 1808 already possessed commissions. The same is true of the *generalato*: of the 458 new Spanish generals appointed in the course of the War of Independence, at least 174 had already been officers before 1808, whereas only eight had definitely been civilians and another one a member of the rank and file. Furthermore, although the percentage of titled noblemen had declined from twenty-three per cent to only fourteen, there were still complaints that the aristocracy continued to enjoy greater favour than their fellows.[104] Several important changes had nevertheless taken place. The decree of 17 August 1811 that abolished the privileges of the nobility had still not opened the officer corps to every Spaniard, as the military academies charged their cadets eight *reales* a day for their tuition.[105] However, at least it was now possible for prosperous commoners to embark upon a military career. Only time would tell whether merit really would triumph over inherited privilege, but there were still numerous officers who knew that they owed everything to the revolution and therefore could not afford a return to the *ancien régime*. At the same time a desire to emulate the triumphs of the French armies led many others to espouse the cause of social and political reform within the army itself. Self interest and conviction therefore coincided to produce a nucleus of liberal support within the officer corps, particularly in the Estado Mayor General.[106]

Yet the writings of liberal soldiers such as Sancho and Albo often betray a residual belief that the army officer was not simply one more citizen, but rather a being set apart to whom society owed a special debt of gratitude. In their frequent emphasis on the need to abolish the privileges of the Royal Guards and the nobility there is also a hint that their liberalism stemmed as much from professional frustration as it did from conviction. At all events, if most officers could agree on the need to place the internal dynamics of the military profession upon a more equitable basis, few of them were likely to be willing to abandon the privileges which it brought them, and particularly not if they had only just been able to gain access to them. These privileges were still of great importance even among the guerrillas, who are often represented as an important source of liberal support within the army.[107] In reality, there was no reason why this should have been the case. Many of the guerrilla leaders, such as Villacampa, Durán, Gayán, Porlier and Longa, were actually regular officers whom the vicissitudes of war had separated from the colours. In one or two cases, of whom Villacampa is again an example, they had actually become guerrillas on the instructions of their superiors.[108] As for those who did not possess commissions, the privileges of the officer corps, the scorn with which they were often treated by regular soldiers, and the hope of obtaining supplies and munitions from the government, all constituted excellent reasons for them to petition the authorities to regularise the ranks held by themselves or their subordinates.[109] In short, the guerrillas had just as much interest in defending military privilege as the rest of the officer corps. The later involvement of some of them in liberal *pronunciamientos* does not constitute proof of their liberalism in the War of Independence. Not only were some of them, notably Durán and Merino, avowed *serviles*, but even those who did declare for the liberals after 1814 were often motivated by their injured pride as much as by their political convictions. This was certainly the case with the leader of the first attempted coup against Fernando, Francisco Espoz y Mina. Although he later made a great show of his liberalism, he had initially welcomed the return of absolutism, only turning his back upon it when he was snubbed at court and deprived of his command.[110]

The vested interest of the entire officer corps in defending its corporate privileges made it essential for the liberals to treat the army with caution. Yet as time progressed military opinion became more and more alienated. To a certain extent this was inevitable, for the army could not possibly have remained immune from the powerful conservative reaction generated by the liberal attack upon the Church and the monarchy: in the course of 1812 and 1813 *servil* elements in the officer corps on several occasions petitioned Wellington for support against the liberals.[111] In addition, there was no shortage of disaffected interest groups within the officer corps who could be expected to oppose the liberals. Many pre-war officers were bitterly jealous of the newcomers who had gained commissions since 1808.[112] The Royal Guards were incensed at the hostility that had been shown towards them.[113] Finally, the generals resented the manner in which they had been excluded from the control of strategy, as witness the frequent proposals for the establishment of a *junta de generales* that would assume this role.[114] These essentially sectional grievances might have been counter-balanced by the equally large numbers of officers who stood to gain from the breakdown of privilege within the military estate had it not been for the liberals' assault upon the privileged status of the army in relation to the rest of society. According to the numerous pamphlets that were published in response to this attack, by excluding the army from the civil administration, subordinating the generals to the *jefes políticos*, and curtailing the *fuero militar*, the Constitution of 1812 had deprived Spain's soldiers of all tangible reward for their services.[115] Spain would thus be left without any defence against her foreign enemies: because human beings would not risk their lives in the defence of their country without the promise of substantial material rewards and the respect of their fellow citizens, nobody would embark upon a military career. She would also be deprived of all her grandeur, for history had shown that a country's stature was solely dependant upon its military power, whose conservation in turn depended upon the army being showered with honours and rewards.[116] Far from being treated with the deference, let alone the gratitude, to which it believed it was entitled, the army felt humiliated and despised. Deserving generals were subordinated to civilian *jefes políticos* of inferior social status and no reputation; deprived of their role in government, Captains General found themselves without any proper function; and officers with years of distinguished service had their characters 'besmirched by some effeminate fop', or were harrassed by arrogant civilian officials, who constantly invoked 'the sacred name of the Constitution . . . as a safeguard for their egotism'.[117] In short, in the eyes of many officers, it really seemed that 'anybody now has the right to insult us solely by calling themselves a citizen . . . we are considered mercenaries, hired servants or paid assassins'.[118] Much of this outrage was pure cant, however. Although for the most part camouflaged by a veneer of patriotic disinterest, the real motive for the unrest was the liberals' refusal to admit the officer corps' pretensions to be regarded as 'the first citizens of the state'.[119]

The blatant egotism that was implicit in such protests enabled some liberals to argue that military opposition to their rule stemmed solely from 'a few old men' who could not reconcile themselves to the loss of their privileges. However, as at least one worried liberal officer pointed out, many of his fellows genuinely believed that the Cortes had done nothing for the army, and therefore broke out in 'imprecations which a lover of the Fatherland cannot hear without horror'.[120] Considering that the liberal idea of military reform offered no hope of an improvement in the army's situation, this was hardly surprising, particularly as more conventional solutions were rejected as 'seditious, insulting, alarmist and incendiary'.[121] At the same time, the attitude of many liberals towards the army was wounding and vindictive. Their plans were often needlessly provocative, whilst it was also particularly maladroit to accuse the army of being a danger to liberty when it had been fighting since 1808 to sustain the very freedom that it was supposed to threaten. Most outrageous of all was the tendency of many civilians – not just liberals in this case – to hold the army responsible for Spain's misfortunes. Not only were defeats invariably blamed upon the generals, but they were followed by demands that 'no commanders should be employed except those formed and almost born in the revolution'.[122] Frequent calls were also heard for all generals who lost a battle or surrendered a fortress to be shot.[123] Incapable though some commanders may have been, such attacks were clearly pushed to unacceptable lengths. The same was true of the criticism attracted by the opulence of certain officers. Whilst a minority certainly contrived to live a life of comparative luxury, blanket reductions in the perquisites allowed to the officer corps was not an appropriate solution to the problem.[124]

The effect of these attacks was still further to inflame military opinion against the liberals in particular, and the constitutional system in general. It was bad enough to be lectured by 'armchair generals' who had sat out the war ensconced in the safety of Cádiz.[125] However, at times the army's critics seemed openly hypocritical. The problem was exemplified by the question of forced requisitioning. As far as most officers were concerned, the Cortes had manifestly failed to provide for the pay and supply of the army. Although they had no option but to feed their men with whatever they could seize from the countryside, as soon as they did so they found that they were accused of military despotism.[126] At the same

The army and the liberals, 1810–14

time, the Cortes would not do anything to remedy the defects of which it complained: officers were told that they could not expect the government to be able to remedy their wants when the entire country was experiencing such extreme privation, and even that to strengthen the army would be positively dangerous because it might cause the British to reduce the size of their forces in the Peninsula.[127]

Mention of the British was unwise, for the fact that they had become 'rather first agents than auxiliaries' in the struggle was a constant source of frustration to the Spanish officer corps.[128] Although a few of the more reactionary generals had attracted the Duke of Wellington's favour, the relationship between the allied forces had never been particularly cordial, being marred by frequent storms of mutual recrimination such as that occasioned by the battle of Barrosa (5 March 1811).[129] The Spaniards were bitterly jealous of the glories won by the British army, and believed that their own efforts merited greater approbation than they had received. It must also be admitted that the British did nothing to assuage their irritation, the repeated proposals that the Spanish army should be provided with British officers being especially tactless in this respect. As Wellington himself remarked, 'I am quite convinced that the majority of officers in the Spanish army would prefer submitting to the French to allowing us to have anything to say to their troops'.[130] It is therefore somewhat surprising that Ballesteros should have received so little support when he 'pronounced' against the Duke's appointment as *generalísimo*. Instead, his actions were publicly repudiated by several officers, including so noted a *servil* as Francisco Elió, the leader of the absolutist coup of 1814.[131] Perhaps he was simply too vainglorious a figure to attract anything but the jealousy of his fellow commanders. At the time, however, the conditions that Wellington was to place upon his acceptance of the command were still unknown, whilst the hopes aroused by the formation of the Comisión de Constitución Militar had not yet been dispelled. Yet the gestures of support that Ballesteros received from various officers after his arrest suggest that had the coup come in October 1813 rather than October 1812, it might well have succeeded.[132] The armies that fought in the Pyrenees in the autumn of 1813 suffered privations that surpassed anything that the much-tried Spanish soldiery had yet had to endure.[133] In protest at this situation, at least one regiment mutinied, refusing to march against the enemy until its wants had been attended to, whilst the commander of the Fourth

Army, General Freyre, attempted to resign.[134] Insult was added to injury when Wellington publicly disgraced Morillo's division of the Fourth Army on account of its pillaging, which was, of course, the only means by which it could survive.[135]

The miserable state of their armies, and their consequent inability to play a major role in the invasion of France was a source of considerable embarassment to the Spanish generals.[136] Naturally enough they attributed their loss of face to the Spanish government, of whom the Conde del Abisbal wrote, 'it appears that our Regency has entirely forgotten the war'.[137] Although liberal views continued to survive in the officer corps – as witness the numerous messages of congratulations received by the Cortes concerning the abolition of the Inquisition and the overthrow of the Infantado Regency[138] – many officers now began to turn to resistance. Whilst some of them urged their superiors to overthrow the Cortes, others physically attacked liberal journalists.[139] The Duke of Wellington refused to become involved in the unrest, but as he wrote to Lord Bathurst in September 1813, 'It is quite impossible that such a system can last... If I was out of the way, there are plenty of generals who would overturn it. Ballesteros positively intended it, and I am much mistaken if O'Donnell [i.e. the Conde del Abisbal] and even Castaños ... are not equally ready'.[140] As if to prove the point, in January 1814 Abisbal had suggested to Wellington that he station a division within striking distance of Madrid, whether the Cortes had moved at the end of 1813.[141]

Had matters carried on in the same vein, it is probable that the worsening state of civil-military relations would have made a coup inevitable. In the event, however, a crisis was precipitated by the decision of Napoleon to release the imprisoned Fernando VII in a desperate attempt to put an end to the Peninsular War. Devout and autocratic, Fernando was unlikely to accept the Constitution of 1812, but such was his personal timidity that he would not have opposed it unless he could be certain of widespread support.[142] That he was likely to be assured of such support soon became apparent. Two of Fernando's fellow exiles, the Duque de San Carlos and José Palafox, were dispatched to Spain to ratify the Emperor's terms for Fernando's release, which were effectively that Spain should agree to expel the Anglo–Portuguese army from the Peninsula. In the course of their mission they discovered not only that the liberals were highly unpopular with all classes of society, but that elements of the army were ready to revolt against their rule. Interestingly enough, one of the generals whom they contacted was the Conde del Abisbal, who at that very period was suggesting that preparations be made for a military coup. The Count's disaffection stemmed from motives that were personal as much as they were political, for he had always been regarded as a liberal. Eager to secure a more prominent role in the war for himself in particular and the Spaniards in general, in the summer of 1813 he had proposed that all the Spanish armies in the Pyrenees should be united into a single force under his own command, only to be told by the Duke of Wellington that he 'had not lately heard of any Spanish troops acting together as a one corps that had not been destroyed and that the last that had so acted [i.e. that commanded by Abisbal's brother, José O'Donnell, at Castalla in July 1812] had been destroyed by half their numbers'.[143] Furious at this rebuff, Abisbal had ever since been searching for revenge, to which end he had kept most of his troops in their cantonments in the interior of Spain so that they might be ready for whatever might ensue.[144]

If anything was needed to confirm Fernando in his determination to overthrow the Constitution, it was the rapturous welcome that he received from army and population alike as soon as he crossed the frontier of Catalonia on 24 March 1814. He was egged on by the same group of aristocratic conspirators who had intrigued for the establishment of a puppet monarchy in 1808: among those who returned with him from exile or who flocked to join his suite once he had crossed the frontier were the Duque de Osuna, the Duque de San Carlos, the Duque del Infantado, José Palafox, and the Conde de Montijo. After a series of discussions, Montijo was dispatched to Madrid in order to raise the mob against the Cortes by means of his usual weapons of rumour and innuendo: stories were soon abroad that Fernando would have gone to the scaffold within six months of swearing to the Constitution. However, the final rising did not take the form of a popular tumult but of a *pronunciamiento*. As soon as the royal party arrived in the city of Valencia on 16 April, the Captain General, Francisco Elió, paraded his troops before Fernando and publicly swore to uphold the absolute power of the monarchy. He then knelt before the King and surrendered his baton of command, only for it to be immediately restored by the royal hand.[145]

Elió's gesture unleashed the whirlwind. The King's return had already provoked a number of demonstrations on the part of absolutists in the army, as in Cádiz where on 6 April a number of Guards officers had attacked the offices of the liberal newspaper, *El Duende de los Cafés*.[146] Their behaviour was probably the exception rather than the rule, but even so few officers could be found who would defend the liberals. The few exceptions knew that they were unlikely to be followed by their subordinates, and in any case received no encouragement from their superiors, most of whom seem to have been concerned only to protect their own persons. Abisbal is even reputed to have sent a courier to Madrid with two messages, the first congratulating Fernando on the downfall of the Cortes, and the second congratulating the Cortes on the downfall of Fernando.[147] When troops from Elió's Second Army and Whittingham's División de Mallorca set out for Madrid on 5 May, there was therefore no resistance. On the contrary, joyful crowds greeted them en route, and rioted against the constitutional authorities. The defencelessness of the liberals was underlined when the commander of the division from the Second Army refused to obey orders to return to his cantonments on the grounds that he was responsible only to General Elió. A similar response was received from Whittingham, who agreed to stay his hand only for so long as it took him to consult with Fernando VII.[148] On the night of 10–11 May absolutist troops entered Madrid, and arrested the liberal leaders. The Spanish revolution was over. As for the army, it simply fell into line behind the new régime. The commander of the garrison of Cádiz, the liberal Cayetano Valdés, suppressed a royalist rising that broke out at San Lúcar de Barrameda on 10 May. However, the commander of the First Army, Francisco Copóns y Navía, who had been supposed to be equally loyal, published the decree for the dissolution of the Cortes without demur. Hamnett argues that but for the intervention of the Duke of Wellington, the commanders of the Spanish armies which had eventually been sent into France would have declared for the liberals, but the possibility seems an unlikely one in the Third Army a *servil* plot was uncovered against the Príncipe de Anglona, whilst in the Fourth resistance was opposed by General Freyre.[149]

The absence of a *contragolpe*, and thus the restoration of absolutism, was implicit in the failure of the liberals to effect any change in Spain's military situation. As the radicalism of their policies alienated them from an ever greater proportion of the Spanish nation, so the support of the army became all important, for it soon became clear that were they left without its protection the liberals would be doomed as soon as *el rey deseado* should lift a finger against them. With the liberals determined to eradicate the privileges of the military estate and to abolish the role which the army had played in the governance of Bourbon Spain, their only hope of retaining its acquiescence was to flatter its self esteem by other means, such as enabling it to play a leading role in the liberation of patriot Spain. The war had engendered a considerable degree of social change within the officer corps by opening it to a wider spectrum of society and breaking down the erstwhile domination of the military aristocracy, a development that the liberals themselves had fostered by their abolition of the privileges of the nobility. However, the change had not brought with it the liberalisation of the officer corps. Indeed, if anything it had made it more conservative: whereas in 1808 the subaltern officers had often had good reason to break ranks with their superiors and join forces with the insurgents, by 1814 the erosion of social barriers within the officer corps had given all its members a common interest in defending their professional status. This is not to say that the nucleus of liberal officers could not have been expanded, for the return of Fernando VII carried with it the possibility that the military aristocracy would once more acquire the royal favour. However, to gain such support it is clear that the liberals would have had to achieve success in the war against France.

Far from providing the army with a salve for its injured pride, the liberals succeeded in alienating it altogether. Instead of applying themselves to practicalities, they substituted rhetoric for reality, whilst presiding over a further period of national humiliation. Between 1810 and 1812, the French occupied most of the territory still left to the patriots, and then between 1812 and 1814 Spain was for the most part forced to be a passive spectator of her liberation at the hands of a widely detested foreign army. Spanish resistance may have continued with undiminished ferocity, but the glory had all been usurped by the British redcoats. Already angered by the liberal attack upon its prerogatives, the officer corps therefore allowed itself to be persuaded by the minority of *serviles* within its ranks that the wrongs it had suffered would be redressed by a grateful Fernando VII. As for the army, its politicisation, already implicit in the events of 1808, was now confirmed, for which reason it is fitting that the Spanish revolution ended as it had begun – with a military coup.

Chapter 5 Notes

1. Toreno, *op. cit.*, II, 110–11; Schepeler, *op. cit.*, II, 671–2.
2. Graham to Liverpool, 9 and 24 May, 24 July, 4 September 1810, PRO. WO.1/247, 236, 244, 460–2, 568; Duque de Alburquerque, *Manifiesto del Duque de Alburquerque acerca de su conducta con la Junta de Cádiz* (London, 1810), 7–8, 11–12; Jacob, *op. cit.*, 383, 389–90.
3. Roche to Wellington, 6 March 1810, PRO. WO.1/243, 490–4; cf. also H. Wellesley to Marquess of Wellesley, 12 March 1810, *cit. The Diary and Correspondence of Henry Wellesley, First Lord Cowley*, ed. F. Wellesley (London, 1930), p. 54.
4. P. Casado Burbano, *Las fuerzas armadas en el inicio del constitucionalismo español* (Madrid, 1982), 45–61.
5. For the liberals see R. Carr, *Spain, 1808–1975* (Oxford, 1982), 92–101; G. Lovett, *Napoleon and the Birth of Modern Spain*, II, 415–90; W. Callahan, *Church, Politics and Society in Spain, 1750–1874* (London, 1984), 93–102.
6. Cf. Lovett, *op. cit.*, II, 432–4, 460–78.
7. Toreno, *op. cit.*, II, 213, 221–4, 249–50; Schepeler, *op. cit.*, III, 24–5; proclamation of La Romana, 27 October 1810, *cit. El Patriota Compostelano*, 25 December 1810, 710–12, HMM. A581.
8. Proclamation of La Peña, 26 September 1810, *cit. Gazeta de la Regencia de España e Indias*, 2 October 1810, p. 741, HMM. AH16-2(2776); cf. also Alburquerque, *op. cit.*, 11–12.
9. Cf. Girón, *op. cit.*, I, 252–3; *Periódico Militar del Estado Mayor General*, 19 February 1812, p. 118, SHM. CDF.CXVI; *Memorial Militar y Patriótico del Ejército de la Izquierda*, 10 April 1810, 15–19, HMM. AH3-3(536); *ibid.*, 4 May 1810, 69–71; *ibid.*, 5 June 1810, 151–3; Castaños, *op. cit.*, 180–1, 185–6; Cabanes, *Sistema militar*, 54–7.
10. Cf. *Memorial Militar y Patriótico del Ejército de la Izquierda*, 5 June 1810, 152–3, HMM. AH3-3(536); *ibid.*, 17 July 1810, 258–60; *ibid.*, 22 October 1810, 396–404; *Periódico Militar del Estado Mayor General*, 12 March 1812, 172–4, SHM. CDF.CXVI.
11. E.g. *El Observador*, 27 July 1810, p. 63, SHM. CDF.CX; *Diario Redactor de Sevilla*, 9–11 December 1812, SHM. CDF.CXXXII.
12. *El Tribuno del Pueblo Español*, 9 March 1813, p. 179, HMM. AH1-4(121); *El Español*, 30 April 1810, p. 14, HMM. AH4-2(710).
13. *El Español*, 30 April 1810, 24–5, HMM. AH.4-2(710).
14. *El Redactor General*, 1 March 1813, p. 2513, HMM. 6/3; *ibid.*, 22 September 1813, p. 3395.
15. Walker to Liverpool, 23 November 1810, PRO. WO.1/261, p. 123; *Semanario Patriótico*, 1 August 1811, HMM. AH1-6(198).
16. Walker to Liverpool, 18 September 1810, PRO. WO.1/261, p. 42; Wellington to Liverpool, 27 October 1810, PRO. WO.1/246, 122–3; Cooke to Skerret, 14 October 1811, PRO. WO.1/252, p. 505.
17. Skerret to Cooke, 8 November 1811, PRO. WO.1/252, 544–5.

18 *Diario Redactor de Sevilla*, 5 November 1812, SHM. CDF.CXXXII.
19 Wellington to Liverpool, 18 August 1810, PRO. WO.1/245, 357–8.
20 Graham to Bunbury, 27 September 1810, PRO. WO.1/247, p. 629.
21 Walker to Liverpool, 1 and 18 September 1810, PRO. WO.1/261, 42, 116; Johnston to Walker, 6 September 1811, PRO. WO.1/261, 415–16.
22 Cf. Douglas to Wellington, 19 September 1811, PRO. WO.1/261, 541–2; Christian to Cotton, 26 August 1811, PRO. WO.1/261, 386–7; Walker to Liverpool, 18 September 1810, PRO. WO.1/261, p. 48; *Diario de Algeciras*, 24 April 1811, 357–61, HMM. A227.
23 E.g. *El Tribuno del Pueblo Español*, 29 October 1813, 529–40, HMM. AH1-4(121); *ibid.*, III, 309–10, 347; Christian to Cotton, 26 August 1811, PRO. WO.1/261, p. 386; *Diario de Gobierno de Sevilla*, 19 March 1813, SHM. CDF.CXL; Wimpffen to Wellington, 26 October 1813, US. WP.1/389; L. Picado Franco, *Historia del origen, acontecimientos y acciones de guerra de la sexta división del Segundo Ejército (o sea de Soria) durante nuestra sagrada lucha al mando del Excmo. Sr. D. José Joaquín Durán y Barazábal, Mariscal de Campo de los Reales Ejércitos* (Madrid, 1817), II, 129–35, 138–9, 192–3, 196–8, 209–14; Toreno, *op. cit.*, II, p. 169; Schepeler, *op. cit.*, II, 585–6; *ibid.*, III, p. 464.
24 *The Military Exploits of Don Juan Martín Díez, the Empecinado* (London, 1823), 85–6 (hereafter *The Empecinado*); Picado Franco, *op. cit.*, I, 17, 188–9; Castaños to Wellington, 11 March 1813, US. WP.1/367, f. 10.
25 Wellington to Villiers, 20 November 1809, PRO. WO.1/242, 420–2.
26 *El Redactor General*, 14 September 1812, 1808–10, HMM. 6/3.
27 D. Alexander, *Rod of Iron: French Counter Insurgency Policy in Aragón during the Peninsular War* (Wilmington, 1985), 203–23; Oman, *op. cit.*, VI, 252–74.
28 Wellington to Liverpool, 2 January 1811, PRO. WO.1/248, p. 175.
29 Graham to Liverpool, 24 July and 6 October 1810, PRO. WO.1/247, 460–61, 641; Graham to Bunbury, 30 June 1810, PRO. WO.1/247, 408–9; J. Canga Argüelles, *Apuntes para la historia de la hacienda pública de España en el año de 1811* (Cádiz, 1813), 5–11, 25–6, SHM. CDF.CCLXI.
30 T. Anna, *Spain and the Loss of America* (Lincoln, 1983), 57, 83.
31 *El Conciso*, 28 February 1813, HMM. AH2-5(349); *Memoria presentada a las Cortes por el Secretario del Despacho de la Guerra en dos de octubre de 1813* (Cádiz, 1813), 26–7, SHM. CDF.CCC-XLVIII.
32 H. Wellesley to Castlereagh, 6 November 1812, Public Record Office, Foreign Office Papers (hereafter PRO. FO.) 72/132, 211–13; Maclean to Bathurst, 5 January 1813, US. WP.1/382, f. 2.
33 Cf. H. Wellesley to Wellington, 28 April 1812, US. WP.12/2/3, 78–9; H. Wellesley to Castlereagh, 12 May 1812, US. WP.1/345; H. Wellesley to Castlereagh, 20 January 1813, US. WP.1/364, f. 4.
34 E.g. Maitland to J. O'Donnell, 16 August 1812, US. WP.1/359;

Wellington to Hill, 1 December 1812, US. WP.1/355, f. 1; Beresford to Wellington, 4 February 1813, US. WP.1/366, f. 3; *El Conciso*, 1 April 1813, HMM. AH2-5(351).
35 Southey, *Peninsular War*, II, 336.
36 E.g. *Memorial Militar y Patriótico del Ejército de la Izquierda*, 12 June 1810, 169–73, HMM. AH.3-3(536).
37 Schepeler, *op. cit.*, III, 517–8; Morillo to Concejo Permanente de Guerra, 4 June 1811, SHM. AGI.3/6/34, No. 6; F. Ballesteros, *Respetuosos descargos que el Tnte. Gral. D. Francisco Ballesteros ofrece a la generosa nación española* (Cádiz, 1813), 21–2, SHM. CDF.CLIV.
38 *The Empecinado*, 135–6; Guillen to Wellington, 27 February 1813, US. WP.1/382, f. 2; Espoz y Mina to Castaños, 12 March 1813, US. WP. 1/368, f. 2; *Diario Crítico y Erúdito de Granada*, 10 April 1813, 37–8, HMM. AH5-5(1046).
39 Mejía to Wellington, 7 December 1812, US. WP.1/354, f. 3; Escobeda to Wellington, 8 March 1813, US. WP.1/367, f. 3.
40 Castaños to Wellington, 30 August 1812, US. WP.1/349, f. 7; 'Manifiesto de los leales Castellanos' (MS), 9 November 1812 , US. WP.1/364, f. 7; Escobeda to Wellington, 12 March 1813, US. WP.1/367, f. 3; Junta Superior de Burgos to Wellington, 9 June 1813, US. WP.1/371, f. 2; *Diario de Gobierno de Sevilla*, 22 March 1813, 769–70, SHM.CDF.CXL.
41 Real Orden, 26 November 1813, cit. *El Imparcial: Diario Político y Mercantil de la Ciudad de Alicante*, 27–9 December 1813, SHM. CDF. CCLV; Wellington to O'Donoju, 7 December 1813, US. WP.1/381, f. 5.
42 Schepeler, *op. cit.*, III, p. 103; Graham to Liverpool, 6 October 1810, PRO. WO.1/247, p. 610.
43 Real Orden, 8 May 1812, cit. *El Redactor General*, 18 May 1812, 1331–2, HMM. 6/3; Castaños to Wellington, 12 March 1813, US. WP.1/382, f. 3.
44 Real Orden, 8 December 1812, cit. *El Patriota Ausonense*, 4 February 1813, 127–8, HMM. AH1-2(65).
45 *El Patriota en las Cortes*, 25 February 1811, p. 89, HMM. A215; *Diario de las Cortes*, III, 38, 51–9, 320–4; *El Redactor General*, 11 November 1811, 583–4, HMM.6/3; Real Orden, 1 March 1811, BS. 041970; Whittingham, *op. cit.*, 162, 187–8.
46 *Diario de las Cortes*, II, 141–2, 274–8; *ibid.*, XI, 48–50, 302; *ibid.*, XIII, 475–82; *ibid.*, XIV, 38–48.
47 *Reglamento para las partidas de guerrillas*, 11 July 1812, SHM. ML.1812/4.
48 Toreno, *op. cit.*, III, 148–51.
49 V. Sancho, *Ensayo de una constitución militar deducida de la constitución política de la monarquía española* (Cádiz, 1813), p. 2 (hereafter Sancho, *Constitución militar*).
50 *El Tribuno del Pueblo Español*, 30 March 1813, p. 290, HMM. AH1-4(121).
51 Sancho, *Constitución militar*, 25–33.

52 Semanario Patriótico, 27 October 1808, p. 153, HMM. AH1-6(195).
53 V. Sancho, Proyecto de una constitución de las milicias nacionales (Madrid, 1814), 11–12 (hereafter Sancho, Milicias nacionales); El Tribuno del Pueblo Español, 9 March 1813, p. 161, HMM. AH.1-4(121); La Abeja Española, 19 January 1813, p. 153, HMM. AH6-5(1251).
54 El Redactor General, 17 July 1812, p. 1567, HMM. 6/3; ibid., 15 August 1812, p. 1687; ibid., 2 March 1813, p. 2517; El Patriota, 14 November 1812, 66–7, 69, HMM. AH1-5(158); ibid., 28 July 1813, HMM. AH1-5(158bis); El Conciso, 6 February 1813, HMM. AH2-5(349).
55 El Redactor General, 19 October 1812, p. 1960, HMM. 6/3.
56 El Articulista Español, 13 January 1813, 51–3, HMM. AH13-6(2449); El Redactor General, 12 November 1812, p. 2062, HMM. 6/3; ibid., 30 October 1812, 2007–8; ibid., 23 December 1812, p. 2232; El Conciso, 5 January 1813, p. 8, HMM. AH2-5(348); Toreno, op. cit., II, p. 135.
57 Cf. Ballesteros to Carvajal, 24 October 1812, SHM. CDF.DCCCXCI, p. 162; Manifiesto que S.A. ha tenido a bien expedir y publicar por la Secretaría del Despacho de la Guerra sobre cesación en el mando del Cuarto Ejército y Capitanía General de las Andalucías de dicho Señor Ballesteros (Cádiz, 1812), SHM. CDF.DCL, 99–114; La Abeja Española, 10 November 1812, 85–6, HMM. AH6-5(1250); Toreno, op. cit., III, 148–52.
58 El Tribuno del Pueblo Español, 30 March 1813, p. 286, HMM. AH1-4(121).
59 El Redactor General, 11 April 1812, p. 1183, HMM. 6/3.
60 El Tribuno del Pueblo Español, 9 March 1813, 177–8, HMM. AH1-4(121); ibid., 30 March 1813, p. 282.
61 Ibid., 30 March 1813, p. 282, HMM. AH.1-4(121); ibid., 8 October 1813, 433, 437–8, HMM. AH1-4(123).
62 La Abeja Española, 1 December 1812, 9–10, HMM. AH6-5(1250); ibid., 19 January 1813, 158–9, HMM. AH6/5(1251); El Tribuno del Pueblo Español, 18 December 1812, 197–8, HMM. AH1-4(120); ibid., 5 March 1813, p. 158, HMM. AH1-4(121); ibid., 9 March 1813, p. 178; El Fanal, 7 December 1812, 1–4, SHM. CDF.CXLVI.
63 El Tribuno del Pueblo Español, 9 March 1813, 178–83, HMM. AH1-4(121).
64 Sancho, Constitución militar, 147–8; El Tribuno del Pueblo Español, 23 April 1813, p. 399, HMM. AH1-4(121).
65 J. Alvarez Guerra, Indicaciones político-militares del estado de la nación española (Madrid, 1814), p. 32.
66 Toreno, op. cit., III, 72, 141; Alcalá Galiano, op. cit., I, 297– 317.
67 El Conciso, 11 April 1813, 3–4, HMM. AH2-5(351).
68 H. Wellesley to Castlereagh, 7 and 9 March 1813, US. WP.1/388.
69 Diario de las Cortes, VI, 523–6.
70 Wellington to Carvajal, 4, 25 and 27 December 1812, US. WP.1/355, f. 3.

71 Real Orden, 6 January 1813, US. WP.1/364, f. 3.
72 Cf. *El Redactor General*, 11 November 1811, 583–4, HMM. 6/3; *Semanario Patriótico*, 19 December 1811, 83–4, HMM. AH1-6(199); *El Tribuno del Pueblo Español*, 15 January 1813, 332–4, HMM. AH.1-4(120); *ibid.*, 19 January 1813, 345–60, HMM. AH1-4(120).
73 Cf. Sancho, *Constitución militar*, 4–5, 33; *El Tribuno del Pueblo Español*, 22 December 1812, 206–7, HMM. AH.1-4(120); *ibid.*, 9 March 1813, p. 182, HMM. AH.1-4(121).
74 *El Patriota*, 14 November 1812, p. 73, HMM. AH1-5(158); *Carta de un paisano a un militar amigo suyo sobre nuestra situación y sobre los medios de mejorarla* (Ayamonte, 1811).
75 J. Albo, *Memorias en que se discurre el modo de constituir la infantería sobre bases solídas y análogas a la constitución política de la monarquía* (Cádiz, 1813), 12–18.
76 Sancho, *Constitución militar*, 24, 38–9.
77 Albo, *op. cit.*, p. 6.
78 Sancho, *Constitución militar*, 58–65, 70–1.
79 *Ibid.*, 40–7; González Carvajal, *Constitución militar*, 39–40, 50–1, 69–70.
80 *Semanario Patriótico*, 17 January 1811, p. 202, HMM. AH1-6(196); *El Patriota en las Cortes*, 25 February 1811, p. 89, HMM. A215; *Diario de las Cortes*, III, 38, 51–9, 320–4.
81 Cf. *El Redactor General*, 21 May 1812, p. 1345, HMM. 6/3; *Medios de salvar el reino* (Cádiz, 1810), 51–3; *Diario de las Cortes*, VII, 383–94, 393–9, 402–11, 413–7, 418–29; *Diario Crítico y Erúdito de Granada*, 9 April 1813, p. 35, HMM. AH5-5(1046).
82 *La Abeja Española*, 25 April 1812, 197–9, HMM. AH6-5(1250); *ibid.*, 26 April 1812, 205–9; A. Alvarez Guerra, *Ensayo de una constitución militar interino o de campaña* (Seville, 1813), p. 7; *El Redactor General*, 11 July 1811, p. 93, HMM. 6/3; *El Tribuno del Pueblo Español*, 18 December 1812, 191–5, HMM. AH1-4(120); *ibid.*, 30 March 1813, p. 287, HMM. AH.1-4(121).
83 *El Espectador Sevillano*, 2 January 1810, 366–7, HMM. AH2-4(347); Sancho, *Constitución militar*, 147–8; *El Tribuno del Pueblo Español*, 30 March 1813, 291–5, HMM. AH1-4(121); *ibid.*, 9 April 1813, 329–38; *La Abeja Española*, 26 November 1812, 209–13, HMM. AH6-5(1250); *ibid.*, 27 November 1812, 217–20; *ibid.*, 29 November 1812, 233–4;
84 *Constitución política de la nación española* (Cádiz, 1812), articles 30, 171, 354–5.
85 *El Tribuno del Pueblo Español*, 23 April 1813, 393–5, HMM. AH1-4(121); *El Espectador Sevillano*, 21 January 1810, 441–2, HMM. AH4-2(347); Sancho, *Constitución militar*, 143–6; *El Español*, 30 November 1810, 128–42, HMM. AH4-2(711).
86 Cf. Sancho, *Milicias nacionales*, 10–91.
87 *Reglamento provisional para la milicia nacional local*, 15 April 1814, SHM. CDF.CCCXLVIII, 129–36.

88 *El Redactor General*, 11 August 1811, p. 220, HMM. 6/3; *Semanario Patriótico*, 31 October 1811, 337–49, HMM. AH1-6(198); *El Conciso*, 1 April 1812, 3–5, HMM. AH2-5(351).
89 *Exposición de la Comisión de Constitución Militar* (Madrid, 1814), 20, 24–5.
90 Albo, *op. cit.*, p. 6; A. Alvarez Guerra, *op. cit.*, 10–11.
91 *El Redactor General*, 21 June 1812, p. 1466, HMM. 6/3.
92 Sancho, *Constitución militar*, 153–4; *El Redactor General*, 14 December 1812, p. 2196, HMM. 6/3; *El Tribuno del Pueblo Español*, 2 March 1813, 133–43, HMM. AH1-4(121).
93 *El Redactor General*, 4 February 1813, p. 2405, HMM. 6/3; Moscoso, Landaburu *et al* to Flórez Estrada, 3 March 1813, *cit. El Tribuno del Pueblo Español*, 9 March 1813, 188–90, HMM. AH1-4(121).
94 *El Tribuno del Pueblo Español*, 2 October 1813, 447–8, HMM. AH1-4(123).
95 *El Redactor General*, 26 October 1813, p. 3358, HMM. 6/3; *Diario Mercantil de Cádiz*, 10 November 1813, 171–2, HMM. AH4-1(686); *ibid.*, 9 December 1813, 299–90; Whittingham, *op. cit.*, p. 173.
96 Wellington to Bathurst, 21 November 1813, US. WP.1/381, f. 4.
97 *Diario Mercantil de Cádiz*, 18 November 1813, p. 243, HMM. AH14-1(686).
98 Toreno, *op. cit.*, I, p. 376; Alcalá Galiano, *op. cit.*, I, 227–31.
99 E.g. E. Cocks, *Intelligence Officer in the Peninsula: Letters and Diaries of Major the Hon. Edward Charles Cocks, 1786–1812*, ed. J. Page (Tunbridge Wells, 1986), 134–5; 'A Peninsular Brigadier: Letters of Major General Sir F.P. Robinson, KCB, Dealing with the Campaign of 1813', ed. C.T. Atkinson, *Journal of the Society for Army Historical Research*, XXXIV, No. 140, p. 157.
100 E.g. Popham to Wellington, 29 September 1812, US. WP.1/350, f. 5.
101 Sydenham to H. Wellesley, 12 September 1812, US. WP.1/361.
102 E.g. *La Tía Nórica a los Críticos de Malecón*, No. 20, 78–9, SHM. CDF.CDLXVI.
103 E.g. Busquets, *op. cit.*, p. 52; Ramón Alonso, *op. cit.*, p. 148.
104 *Estado Militar*, 1807, 8–20; *ibid.*, 1815, 9–27; Calzada, *op. cit.*, 101–2.
105 Real Orden, 1 March 1811, BS. 041970.
106 *El Tribuno del Pueblo Español*, 31 August 1813, p. 272, HMM. AH1-4(123).
107 E.g. Busquets, *op. cit.*, p. 53; Lovett, *op. cit.*, II, p. 720.
108 Schepeler, *op. cit.*, II, p. 238.
109 Cf. Graham to Wellington, 5 July 1813, US. WP.1/372, f. 4; Longa to Wellington, 21 September 1813, US. WP.1/382, f. 8; Longa to Wellington, 20 October 1813, US. WP.1/378, f. 3.
110 Girón, *op. cit.*, II, 19–21.
111 Palacio to Wellington, 25 August 1812, US. WP.1/364, f. 5; Belisario to Wellington, 26 August 1813, US. WP.1/374, f. 4.
112 Representation of the subaltern officers of the Regimiento de Murcia

to Cartaojal, 20 February 1809, RAH. 9-31-6:6965; Walker to Liverpool, 18 September 1811, PRO. WO.1/261, p. 43; *Diario Crítico y Erúdito de Granada*, 12 April 1813, p. 46, HMM. AH5-5(1046); Marqués de Lazan, *Exposición de la conducta militar del Teniente General Marqués de Lazan y de las causas de su permanencia en Cádiz* (Cádiz, 1811), 10–11.

113 E.g. *Diario Mercantil de Cádiz*, 24 November 1813, 225–7, HMM. AH1- 4(686).

114 Cf. *Semanario Patriótico*, 18 April 1811, p. 90, HMM. AH1-6(197); *El Redactor General*, 4 January 1812, p. 794, HMM. 6/3.

115 *La milicia desatendida por las leyes en tiempo de guerra* (Madrid, 1814), 5–15.

116 Cf. *Indagación*, 7, 23–6, 28–31; Finestra, *op. cit.*, 3–5, 11–13; *El ejército destruido por las leyes*, 7–10, 14–15, 23–5, 34–5; J. Liano, *Breve discurso que hace Don Josef Liano, Capitán de Husares de Granada, agregado a Cazadores de Sevilla, a los generales sobre la decadencia de los ejércitos* (Isla de León, 1813), p. 1; *Diario Mercantil de Cádiz*, 2 November 1813, 134–5, HMM. AH1-4(686); *Apéndice al Procurador General de la Nación y del Rey*, No. 40, HMM. RVP.T46.

117 Cf. *El Procurador General de la Nación y del Rey*, 17 June 1813, p. 3046, HMM. AH3-2(529); *El Redactor General*, 10 April 1813, p. 2680, HMM. 6/3; *ibid.*, 14 March 1813, p. 2567; *Diario Crítico y Erúdito de Granada*, 1 July 1813, 2–3, HMM. AH5-5(1046); *Apéndice al Procurador General de la Nación y del Rey No. 40*, HMM. RVP.T46.

118 Liano, *op. cit.*, 2–3.

119 *Ibid.*, p. 5.

120 J. Alvarez Guerra, *op. cit.*, 50–1.

121 Liano, *op. cit.*, p. 2.

122 *El Patriota*, No. 1, p. 5, HMM. AH1-5(158).

123 Cf. *El Redactor General*, 18 August 1812, 1699–1700, HMM. 6/3; *ibid.*, 19 August 1812, 1702–3; *El Patriota en las Cortes*, 4 February 1811, 65–6, HMM. A215; *Semanario Patriótico*, 21 March 1811, 432–9, HMM. AH1-6(196); *ibid.*, 27 March 1811, p. 14.

124 Cf. *El Redactor General*, 23 February 1811, p. 2512, HMM. 6/3.

125 *Ibid.*, 24 December 1811, 755–6; *Suplemento al Patriota*, 8 September 1813, p. 236, HMM. AH1-5(158bis).

126 *La milicia desatendida por las leyes en tiempo de guerra*, 44–5; *Periódico Militar del Estado Mayor General*, 20 February 1812, 119–20, SHM. CDF.CXVI; Whittingham, *op. cit.*, p. 235.

127 Cf. J. Segovia, *Sátira contra Don Tomas Finestra por haber escrito la 'Exposición a sus compañeros de armas sobre la decadencia de los ejércitos nacionales'* (Cádiz, 1813).

128 Finestra, *op. cit.*, 5–6.

129 Cf. J. Lardizábal, *Contestación a la falsa e injuriosa idea que el papel numero doce intitulado El Español da de la memorable acción del cinco de marzo en los campos de Chiclana* (Cádiz, 1811); M. La Peña,

The army and the liberals

Representación hecha a las Cortes por el Capitán General de Andalucía y General en Jefe interino del Cuarto Ejército (Cádiz, 1813).
130 Wellington to H. Wellesley, 29 August 1811, US. WP.12/1/4.
131 *El Redactor General*, 5 March 1813, p. 2532, HMM. 6/3; *Un militar español, tan amante como el primero del bien de su patria y celoso del honor de su profesión, al considerar la conducta del Teniente General D. Francisco Ballesteros en ésta última época no ha podido prescindir de manifestar al público los hechos de que esta cerciorado y las siguientes reflexiones a que da imagen el reciente que ha motivado su separación del mando del Cuarto Ejército* (Cádiz, 1812), SHM. CDF.CXXXIV, 45–6.
132 *El Redactor General*, 17 December 1812, p. 2208, HMM.6/3; *Diario de la Tarde*, 10 October 1813, p. 40.
133 España to Wellington, 4 August 1813, US. WP.1/374, f. 5; Freyre to Wellington, 2 September 1813, US. WP.1/376, f. 1; Girón to Wellington, 10 and 30 November 1813, US. WP.1/382, f. 10; Abisbal to Wellington, 7 December 1813, US. WP.1/389; Morillo to Wellington, 19 December 1813, US. WP.1/389.
134 Walker to Hill, 7 November 1813, US. WP.1/379, f. 1; Wellington to Wimpffen, 12 November 1813, US. WP.1/379, f. 5; O'Donoju to Freyre, 18 November 1813, US. WP.1/379, f. 5.
135 Morillo to Freyre, 30 December 1813, US. WP.1/391.
136 E.g. Abisbal to Wellington, 23 December 1813, US. WP.1/389.
137 Abisbal to Wellington, 10 December 1813, US. WP.1/389.
138 E.g. *Diario Crítico y Erúdito de Granada*, 10 June 1813, 38–9, HMM. AH2-5(351); *El Amante de la Libertad Civil*, 1 December 1813, 80–4, HMM. AH2-5(371).
139 E.g. Liano, *op. cit.*, 3–4; Finestra, *op. cit.*, 7–8.
140 Wellington to Bathurst, 5 September 1813, US. WP.1/377, f. 1.
141 Abisbal to Wellington, 31 January 1814, US. WP.1/394.
142 H. Wellesley, *op. cit.*, p. 76.
143 Wellington to H. Wellesley, 16 August 1813, US. WP.1/375, f. 5.
144 Toreno, *op. cit.*, III, 343–4.
145 *Ibid.*, III, 357–61; Palafox, *op. cit.*, 35–9, 91–7; Whittingham, *op. cit.*, 257, 269.
146 Hamnett, *op. cit.*, p. 185.
147 Toreno, *op. cit.*, III, p. 159.
148 Whittingham to Moreno, 4 May 1814, AHN. Estado, 3566; Lavalle to Moreno, 5 May 1814, AHN. Estado, 3566.
149 Hamnett, *op. cit.*, 187, 197–98; Toreno, *op. cit.*, III, p. 365.

Epilogue

1814 and after

The restoration of Fernando VII to absolute power in May 1814 did not equate to *carte blanche* for a restoration of the *status quo ante*. Instead, as Henry Wellesley remarked, 'Much will depend upon the King's future proceedings being conducted with good sense and moderation.'[1] For all the power of the *servil* rhetoric, and the isolation of the liberals, nothing could alter the fact that Spain had experienced a genuine revolution. The torrent of social and political change unleashed by the Motín de Aranjuez could not be reversed by royal decree. Although domestic opposition to the liberals had grown apace in proportion to the attention which they had paid to the religious question, *servilismo* was not necessarily exclusive of a desire for reform. The small group of diehards who were opposed to all forms of progress had increasingly been joined by moderates whose reformism did not extend to a willingness to countenance the wholesale transformation of society. Whilst opposing the liberals, they continued to desire the regeneration of Spain, and thus, by implication, an end to the abuses that had characterised the *ancien régime*. What distinguished them from the liberals was the belief that these goals could be achieved in conjunction with an absolute monarchy.

The clearest statement of these aims may be found in the so-called *Manifiesto de las Persas*, an absolutist manifesto that had been signed by sixty-nine *servil* deputies to the Cortes in May 1814. Although this document denounced the liberals, it also called for an end to the incompetence, extravagance and 'ministerial despotism' that was held to have characterised the reign of Carlos IV, and for the convocation of Spain's traditional Cortes.[2] At first, Fernando seemed to be ready to meet these petitions, for he promised that he would neither be a despot himself, nor permit the return of 'ministerial despotism', and that he would rule in accordance with Spain's ancient constitution in conjunction with the Spanish people. He also gave specific assurances that he would summon the Cortes as quickly as possible, respect individual liberty, restore probity to the government, place the nation's finances upon a respectable footing, and allow a certain degree of press freedom.[3] Such a programme might well have brought Fernando a temporary respite, but no attempt was made to put it into effect. The Cortes was not called, the liberal leaders remained under arrest, and Fernando surrounded himself with an aristocratic *camarilla*. As early as 17 June 1814, Henry Wellesley noted that, 'The delay in issuing the proclamation for assembling the Cortes, together with the prolonged confinement of the persons who have been arrested without any apparent cause have occasioned great discontent.'[4] Implicit in this discontent was the revitalisation of Spanish liberalism, for many of those who had initially rallied to the *serviles* would now come to see that reform was incompatible with absolute monarchy.

Fernando's answer to the growing discontent was to rely on the one hand upon popular traditionalism, and on the other upon the influence of the Church, which he encouraged in a campaign of reaction.[5] No safety was to be found in such measures, however, for they took no account of the army, which had already become the true arbiter of Spain's destiny. For example, even assuming that the populace was as fervently absolutist as is commonly supposed, a royalist militia would have been as militarily ineffective as a liberal civic guard. As Christiansen has pointed out, for Fernando the voice of the army was very much the voice of God.[6] In 1814 the officer corps had fallen solidly into line behind the absolutist *pronunciamiento* because the bulk of its members could unite in a shared resentment of the liberals. Yet the army's restoration of Fernando did not necessarily mean that it was wholeheartedly absolutist in its sympathies: most officers had merely refused to defend the liberals rather than actively working for their overthrow. If a minority of aristocrats had a powerful vested interest in returning to the days before 1808, a large number of their fellows had actually gained enormous benefits from the war and had only been alienated by the liberals' dogmatic anti-militarism. Neither the pre-war subalterns, nor the bulk of those officers who had entered the officer corps in the course of the war could have the slightest interest in the *status quo ante*. Matters were further complicated by the return of the 4,000 officers who had been prisoners of war at the close of hostilities. Not only did they come home expecting to enjoy some reward for their sacrifices, but many of them had been introduced to freemasonry and liberal ideals during their imprisonment.[7]

In order to maintain the support of the apolitical majority, it was essential that Fernando should meet the army's wants in terms of pay, food, uniforms and equipment, and restore it to its erstwhile pre-eminence. Furthermore, he would have to reward the officers for their wartime services and provide them with employment, whilst eschewing the favouritism that had characterised his predecessors. Such aspirations had been implicit even in Elió's crucial declaration of support for Fernando in Valencia, which Busquets has interpreted as an attempt to put pressure on a king whose views were still very much an unknown quantity.[8] These hopes were soon disappointed, however. If the Captains General were restored to their former glory, the army remained in the greatest disorder. Satisfying the demands of every member of the officer corps would have been impossible as it now contained some 16,000 members, of whom only 8,200 could be accommodated even by the 184,000-strong army which Spain possessed in 1814.[9] However, the burdens incumbent upon the reduction in its size necessitated by Spain's desperate financial situation were not shared equally. The regiments that were disbanded were those formed in the course of the war, just as the officers who were placed on half-pay were the commoners and petty *hijosdalgo*. As for those officers who were fortunate enough to retain some appointment, their material conditions remained as bad as ever. In December 1814 Francisco de Paula Guervos complained of having gone unpaid for three months; when he did finally receive some wages, it was in the form of *una porción de papel para irlo de cobrar Dios sabe donde*. Left 'without money or health', he saw himself reduced to the choice of 'death or robbery'.[10] Guervos' regiment – Soria – was reduced to such straits that in 1815 its commander refused to march against Napoleon unless his men were paid.[11] As for Guervos himself, weak from old wounds as well as imprisonment at the hands of the French, he fell ill and died on 30 November 1815.[12] Meanwhile, as El Empecinado protested, Fernando continued to shower his favours upon young noblemen who had not even served in the war and 'persons who retired to Cádiz, Ceuta and other places of safety and looked down from the midst of their pleasures on the massacre of their brethren'.[13]

In this atmosphere it was not long before the original nucleus of liberal officers was joined by many others whose discontent stemmed from disappointed hopes of promotion or a sincere conviction that Fernando was betraying the army's professional interests. The spread of liberalism was further aided by the widespread penetration of freemasonry amongst the officer corps, for this provided conspirators with a safe medium of communication.[14] The first evidence of the growing military opposition came in September 1814 when Francisco Espoz y Mina led an abortive coup at Pamplona. Although he was a noted *servil*, the famous guerrilla had been refused the viceroyalty of Navarre, and deprived of the command of his division of sometime guerrillas, which was disbanded. Furthermore, when Mina travelled to the court, he was snubbed in public by Fernando. Furious at this treatment, he returned to Pamplona and attempted to raise the garrison in revolt. However, the rank and file refused to heed his appeals, and Mina was left with no option but to flee across the Pyrenees.[15]

Mina's coup was only the first in a series of military conspiracies and rebellions that beset Spain between 1814 and 1820. Aside from several more-or-less shadowy intrigues which were uncovered before they could come to fruition, the chief revolts were those of Porlier in 1815 at La Coruña, and Lacy and Miláns del Bosche in Catalonia in 1817. As in the case of Mina, however, the rebels came to grief on the refusal of the rank and file to join a revolt against *el rey deseado* and the chief protagonists were shot. Yet in 1819 a new threat emerged to Fernando in the form of the unrest that began to take hold of the army that had been assembled in Andalucía for dispatch against the American rebels. For want of ships to take them across the Atlantic, in some cases the troops had been waiting in their camps since 1815, where they had been forced to endure the usual privations commensurate with service in the Spanish army. Many of them had been pressed into the ranks by force or were convicted criminals, and none of them had any enthusiasm for the war in America. Meanwhile, a group of liberal officers led by Rafael Riego, Evaristo de San Miguel and Antonio Quiroga had begun to lay plans for revolt. They were initially able to persuade their commander, the Conde del Abisbal, to join them. For the first time they also won over the soldiery by promising them that they would not be sent to America, and that they would be paid in full, given land and allowed to go home. The coup was initially scheduled to take place in the summer of 1819, but had to be postponed at the last minute when Abisbal suddenly defected from the plot, apparently because he had suddenly lost faith in its success. Yet for reasons which are unknown, the conspirators were allowed to remain undisturbed, and continued to prepare for revolt.

On 1 January 1820 Riego duly 'pronounced' in favour of the Constitution of 1812 at Las Cabezas de San Juan, assuring his troops that the mere promulgation of this document would be enough to bring the war in America to an end. However, when the rebels attacked Cádiz they were driven off by a young absolutist officer named Luis Fernández de Córdoba: unlike the troops of the expeditionary army, the garrison was not faced with the prospect of being shipped across the Atlantic and thus had no reason to abandon Fernando. A period of stalemate ensued in which the rebel forces marched from one Andalucían city to the next in a desperate attempt to acquire popular support, whilst the Madrid government attempted to put a field force together with which to quell the insurrection. Although this did not prove easy, for a time it appeared that the rebels were doomed. However, kept alive almost solely by the courage of Rafael Riego, the flickering flame of the Andalucian revolt gave fresh heart to Fernando's opponents in the rest of Spain. On 21 February a second military rebellion broke out in La Coruña, which was swiftly followed by other risings in Zaragoza, Barcelona, Tarragona, Gerona and Pamplona. The final blow was delivered by Abisbal, who was now in command of the forces that had been sent against Riego. Sensing which way events were moving, he changed sides yet again and led his army over to the rebels. Deserted on all sides, Fernando was left with no option but to surrender.[16]

By 1820 a large part of the officer corps may therefore be said to have been won over to the cause of liberalism, or at least to have become so disillusioned with *el rey deseado* that they were no longer prepared to defend him. Yet that does not mean that most officers had become liberals. Whilst it is true that some of the conspirators had been motivated primarily by ideological considerations, others were clearly influenced chiefly by their personal ambitions, or even by sheer opportunism. Still others, such as the Conde del Montijo (who – inevitably – was implicated in many of the intrigues of the period 1815–19) were mere adventurers. Bored and frustrated by the realities of peacetime life, many young officers became addicted to the *gesto heróico* for which the *pronunciamiento* offered so many opportunities. Success – as in 1820 – brought instant advancement, and failure the prospect of a glorious death. Personal characteristics and considerations aside, however, what united these officers and enabled them to win the support of their fellows was a growing sense that the aspirations of the army could be as safe in the hands of the liberals as of the absolutists.

For a great many officers, the alliance with the forces of revolution had been no more than a marriage of convenience designed to attain their professional ends. They were no more liberal in 1820 than they had been in 1814, as was suggested by their desertion of the constitutional regime in the face of the French invasion of 1823. Their experiences of the years immediately following the *trienio liberal*, during which Fernando temporarily disbanded the army and instead relied upon a royalist popular militia, were more than sufficient to alienate them from the cause of absolutism. Most officers therefore fought for the liberals during the Carlist War of 1833–39, but as the nineteenth century wore on so the general trend of military opinion was to become more and more reactionary. In part this was a reflection of the increasing tendency of the bourgeoisie – to whom most officers could trace their origins – to become conservative rather than revolutionary as it gained an ever greater stake in the political system. Yet it was also a reflection of the perceptions acquired in the course of the War of Independence, whose humiliations the officer corps attributed to the breakdown of discipline and national unity.[17] The chaos caused by the guerrillas, the collapse of the central government, the parochialism of the provincial juntas, the failure to appoint a *mando único*, and the anti-militarism of the liberals were therefore regarded as evils that must never be repeated. The result was a strong belief in the need to uphold the unity of Spain, to maintain a strong government, to protect the authority and integrity of the army, and to ensure the continuance of law and order. As the army regarded these interests as being synonymous with those of the nation as a whole, it followed that it possessed the duty to overthrow any government whose actions militated against them.

The chief legacy of the War of Independence was thus to afflict Spain with an army that not only possessed a tradition of political interventionism, but equated its own interests with the national good. By burdening her with a swollen officer corps that far outstripped her actual needs, it also made the military's aspirations in terms of employment, promotion, and conditions of service so much the harder to satisfy. With the proclivities of many officers towards *caudillismo* encouraged by the contempt for civilian authority that had been stimulated by the events of 1808–14, a lasting obstacle had been erected to Spain's emergence as a modern democracy. Yet at the same time change had become inevitable, for the politicisation of the Spanish army sounded the death knell of the *ancien régime*. So long as the military had remained an unthinking tool of royal power, for all the changing structure of Spanish society and the emergence of revolutionary ideologies, absolutism might have hoped to emulate the survival of the eastern European empires. In Spain as in so many other countries, war was indeed the midwife of revolution.

Epilogue Notes

1. H. Wellesley, *op. cit.*, p. 73.
2. M. Pintos Vieites, *La política de Fernando VII entre 1814 y 1820* (Pamplona, 1958), 95–102.
3. Real Orden, 4 May 1814, *cit.* Toreno, *op. cit.*, III, 400–5.
4. Wellesley, *op. cit.*, p. 74; cf. also Whittingham, *op. cit.*, p. 265.
5. Callahan, *op. cit.*, 112–14.
6. E. Christiansen, *The Origins of Military Power in Spain, 1800–1854* (Oxford, 1967), p. 18.
7. E.g. Alcalá Galiano, *op. cit.*, I, p. 410.
8. Busquets, *op. cit.*, p. 14.
9. C. Seco Serrano, *Militarismo y civilismo en la España contemporánea* (Madrid, 1985), p. 38; *Estados de la organización y fuerza de los ejércitos españoles beligerantes en la península durante la guerra de España contra Napoleón Bonaparte* (Barcelona, 1822), p. 218.
10. F. Guervos to his parents, 24 December 1814 and 17 January 1815, RAH. 11-5-7:9003, Nos. 58, 60.
11. F. Guervos to his parents, 9 May 1815, RAH. 11-5-7:9003, No. 62.
12. Death certificate of F. Guervos, RAH. 11-5-7:9003.
13. Remonstrance of El Empecinado to Fernando VII, cit. Wellesley, *op. cit.*, 79–80; Girón, *op. cit.*, II, 18, 22–4.
14. Alcalá Galiano, *op. cit.*, I, p. 424.
15. Girón, *op. cit.*, II, 12–14; Whittingham, *op. cit.*, p. 367.
16. Alonso, *op. cit.*, 152–4; Seco Serrano, *op. cit.*, 43–5.
17. Cf. J. Gómez de Arteche, 'Juan Martín, El Empecinado: la Guerra de la Independencia bajo su aspecto popular', *La España del Siglo XIX*, I, 81–132.

Appendix 1

Order of battle of the Spanish Army, 1788

(a) **Royal Guard**

Guardias de Corps (three companies),
Guardias de Alabarderos (one company),
Guardias Españolas (six battalions),
Guardias Walonas (six battalions),
Carabinieros Reales (four squadrons).

(b) **Infantry**

Twenty-seven Spanish line infantry regiments, each of two battalions:
 Rey, Galicia,[1] Príncipe, Saboya, Corona, Africa, Zamora, Soria, Córdoba, León, Guadalajara, Sevilla, Granada, Lisboa,[2] España, Toledo, Mallorca, Burgos, Murcia, Cantabria, Asturias, Navarra, Aragón, América, Princesa, Extremadura, Vitoria.[3]
Eight foreign line infantry regiments, each of two battalions:
 Irlanda, Hibernia, Ultonia, Milán,[4] Nápoles, Flándes,[5] Brabante,[6] Bruselas.[7]
Two garrison infantry regiments, each of two battalions:
 Fijo de Ceuta, Fijo de Orán.[8]
Four Swiss infantry regiments, each of two battalions:
 Schwaller, Rutiman, Reding, Preux.
Three light infantry regiments:
 1er Voluntarios de Cataluña (two battalions), 2° Voluntarios de Cataluña (two battalions), Voluntarios de Aragón (one battalion).

(c) **Cavalry:**

Twelve line cavalry regiments, each of four squadrons:
 Rey, Reina, Príncipe, Infante, Borbón, Farnesio, Alcántara, España, Algarve, Calatrava, Santiago, Montesa.
Eight dragoon regiments, each of four squadrons:
 Rey, Reina, Almansa, Pavía, Villaviciosa, Sagunto, Numancia, Lusitania.
Two regiments of light cavalry, each of four squadrons:
 Costa de Granada,[9] Voluntarios de España.

(d) Royal Regiment of Artillery:
Staff, six battalions, each of eight companies, one company of cadets.

(e) Royal Corps of Engineers:
Staff of 150 officers.

(f) Provincial Militia:
Forty-three regiments, each of one battalion:
Jaén, Badajoz, Sevilla, Burgos, Lugo, León, Granada, Oviedo, Córdoba, Murcia, Trujillo, Tuy, Ecija, Ciudad Rodrigo, Logroño, Salamanca, Toro, Jérez, Sigüenza, Laredo, Santiago, Pontevedra, Soria, Orense, Betanzos, Málaga, Guadix, Ronda, Bujalance, Cuenca, Alcázar de San Juan, Toledo, Chinchilla, Ciudad Real, Valladolid, Mondoñedo, Lorca, Avila, Plasencia, Segovia, Monterrey, Compostela, Mallorca.

Grand total at full establishment strength

	Officers	Men
Royal Guard	559	9,867
Infantry	2,669	66,702
Cavalry	990	14,376
Artillery	320	4,900
Engineers	150	—
Provincial militia	1,443	41,190
	6,131	136,785

Notes
1. Renamed Reina, 1789(?).
2. Renamed Zaragoza, 1791.
3. Renamed Valencia, 1791.
4. Disbanded, 1792.
5. Disbanded, 1792.
6. Disbanded, 1792.
7. Disbanded, 1792.
8. Disbanded, 1788(?).
9. Renamed Cazadores de Valencia, 1802.

Appendix 2

Order of battle of the Spanish Army, 1808

(a) **Royal Guard**

Guardias de Corps (three companies),
Guardias de Alabarderos (one company),
Guardias Españolas (three battalions),
Guardias Walonas (three battalions),
Carabinieros Reales (six squadrons).

(b) **Infantry**

Thirty-nine line infantry regiments, each of three battalions:
Rey, Reina, Príncipe, Saboya, Corona, Africa, Zamora, Soria, Córdoba, Guadalajara, Sevilla, Granada, Valencia, Zaragoza, España, Toledo, Mallorca, Burgos, Murcia, León, Cantabria, Asturias, Fijo de Ceuta, Navarra, Aragón, América, Princesa, Extremadura, Málaga, Jaén, Ordenes Militares, Voluntarios de Castilla, Voluntarios de la Corona, Voluntarios del Estado, Irlanda, Hibernia, Ultonia, Nápoles, Borbón.
Six Swiss infantry regiments, each of two battalions:
Wimpffen, Reding *mayor*, Reding *menor*, Bertschart, Traxler, Preux.
Twelve light infantry regiments, each of one battalion:
1er Voluntarios de Cataluña, 2° Voluntarios de Cataluña, 1er Voluntarios de Aragón, 2° Voluntarios de Aragón, 1er de Barcelona, 2° de Barcelona, Tarragona, Gerona, Cazadores de Barbastro, Voluntarios de Valencia, Campo Mayor, Navarra.

(c) **Cavalry**

Twelve line cavalry regiments, each of five squadrons:
Rey, Reina, Príncipe, Infante, Borbón, Farnesio, Alcántara, España, Algarve, Calatrava, Santiago, Montesa.
Eight dragoon regiments, each of five squadrons:
Rey, Reina, Almansa, Pavía, Villaviciosa, Sagunto, Numancia, Lusitania.
Two regiments of chasseurs, each of five squadrons:
Cazadores de Olivencia, Cazadores Voluntarios de España.
Two regiments of hussars:

Husares de María Luisa, Husares Españoles.

(d) Artillery
Staff, four regiments, each of ten companies, nineteen garrison companies, five pioneer companies, one company of cadets.

(e) Engineers
Staff, Regimiento de Zapadores-Minadores.

(f) Provincial militia
Four divisions of grenadiers, each of two battalions:
Castilla la Vieja, Castilla la Nueva, Andalucía, Galicia.
Forty-three regiments, each of one battalion:
Jaén, Badajoz, Sevilla, Burgos, Lugo, León, Granada, Oviedo, Córdoba, Murcia, Trujillo, Tuy, Ecija, Ciudad Rodrigo, Logroño, Salamanca, Toro, Jérez, Sigüenza, Laredo, Santiago, Pontevedra, Soria, Orense, Betanzos, Málaga, Guadix, Ronda, Bujalance, Cuenca, Alcázar de San Juan, Toledo, Chinchilla, Ciudad Real, Valladolid, Mondoñedo, Lorca, Avila, Plasencia, Segovia, Monterrey, Compostela, Mallorca.

Grand total

	Establishment strength		Actual strength
	Officers	Men	(Men only)
Royal Guard	444	7,850	7,184
Infantry	3,240	116,922	71,034
Cavalry	960	16,164	14,440
Artillery	675	6,647	6,344
Engineers	197	1,275	1,049
Provincial militia	1,271	33,997	30,527
	6,787	182,855	130,578

Appendix 3

Regiments of new creation, 1808

A. Infantry

(a) *Catalonia*
1er Tercio de Miqueletes de Tarragona (1), 2° Tercio de Miqueletes de Tarragona (1), 1er Tercio de Miqueletes de Lérida (1), 2° Tercio de Miqueletes de Lérida (1), 3er Tercio de Miqueletes de Lérida (1), 4° Tercio de Miqueletes de Lérida (1), 1er Tercio de Miqueletes de Gerona (1), 2° Tercio de Miqueletes de Gerona (1), 3er Tercio de Miqueletes de Gerona (1), Tercio de Miqueletes de Manresa (1), 1er Tercio de Miqueletes de Cervera (1), 2° Tercio de Miqueletes de Cervera (1), Tercio de Miqueletes de Tortosa (1), 1er Tercio de Miqueletes de Vich (1), 2° Tercio de Miqueletes de Vich (1), Tercio de Miqueletes de Mataro (1), Tercio de Miqueletes de Seo de Urgel (1), Tercio de Miqueletes de Berga (1), 1er Tercio de Miqueletes de Talarn (1), 2° Tercio de Miqueletes de Talarn (1), Tercio de Miqueletes de Cerdaña (1), Tercio de Miqueletes de Val de Aran (1), Tercio de Miqueletes de Barcelona (1), Tercio de Miqueletes de Ampurdán (1), Tercio de Miqueletes de Igualada (1), Tercio de Miqueletes de Figueras (1), Tercio de Miqueletes de Granollers (1).

(b) *Andalucía*
Osuna (3), 1er Voluntarios de Sevilla (1), 2° Voluntarios de Sevilla (1), 3er Voluntarios de Sevilla (1), 4° Voluntarios de Sevilla (1), 5° Voluntarios de Sevilla (1), 1er Voluntarios de Granada (1), 2° Voluntarios de Granada (1), 3er Voluntarios de Granada (1), 4° Voluntarios de Granada (1), 5° Voluntarios de Granada (1), 6° Voluntarios de Granada (1), Voluntarios de Marchena (1), Vélez Málaga (2), Real Maestranza de Ronda (1), Alpujarras (2), 1er de Guadix (1), Baza (2), Loja (2), Campo de Ujijar (2), Santa Fé (2), Illiberia (2), Almería (2), Bailén (3), Cazadores de Granada (2), Tiradores de Cádiz (1), Cazadores de Carmona (1), Cazadores de Antequera (2), Cazadores de las Navas de Tolosa (1), Cazadores de Bailén (1), Tiradores Voluntarios de España (1), Cazadores de Vélez Málaga (1), Voluntarios de Cádiz (3), Granaderos del General del Ejército del Centro (1)*.

(c) *Aragón*
1er Voluntarios de Aragón (1), 2° Voluntarios de Aragón (1), 3er Voluntarios de Aragón (1), 4° Voluntarios de Aragón (1), 5° Voluntarios de Aragón (1),

Voluntarios de Borja (1), Voluntarios de Jaca (1), Voluntarios de Daroca (1), 1er Voluntarios de Calatayud (1), 2° Voluntarios de Calatayud (1), 1er Voluntarios Rebajados de Teruel (1), 2° Voluntarios Rebajados de Teruel (1), Voluntarios de Caspe (1), Voluntarios de Albarraicín (1), Voluntarios de Alcañiz (1), Voluntarios de Tauste (1), 1er Voluntarios de Huesca (1), 2° Voluntarios de Huesca (1), 3er Voluntarios de Huesca (1), Nuestra Señora del Pilar (2), Reserva de Aragón (1), 1er Fusileros de Aragón (1), 2° Fusileros de Aragón (1), 1er Voluntarios de Barbastro (1), 2° Voluntarios de Barbastro (1), 3er Voluntarios de Barbastro (1), Voluntarios de la Canal de Verdun (1), Gastadores de Aragón (1), Puerta Quemada (1), Puerta de Santa Engracia (1), Suizos de Aragón (1)*, 2° de la Princesa (2)*, Reunión de Aragón (3), Granaderos de Palafox (2), 2° del Infante Don Carlos (2), Voluntarios de Zaragoza (3), 1er Ligero de Zaragoza (1), 2° Ligero de Zaragoza (1), 3er Ligero de Zaragoza (1), Carmen (1), Portillo (1), Torrero (1), Puerta del Sol (1), Tiradores de Calatayud (1), Cazadores de Palafox (1), Tiradores de Doyle (1), Tiradores de Rivagorza (1).

(d) *Levante/Baleares*
Voluntarios de Cartagena (3), Voluntarios de Chelva (1), 1er Voluntarios de Murcia (1), 2° Voluntarios de Murcia (1), 3er Voluntarios de Murcia (1), 4° Voluntarios de Murcia (1), 5° Voluntarios de Murcia (1), La Fé (2), Voluntarios de Turia (3), 2° de Valencia (2)*, 2° de Saboya (2)*, Voluntarios de Borbón (1), Voluntarios de Palma (1), Almansa (3), 1er Cazadores de Orihuela (1), 2° Cazadores de Orihuela (2), 1er Cazadores de Valencia (1), 2° Cazadores de Valencia (2), 1er Tiradores de Murcia (2), 2° Tiradores de Murcia (2), 3er Tiradores de Murcia (1), Voluntarios de Alicante (3), 2° Cazadores de Fernando VII (1), Cazadores de Segorbe (2).

(e) *Asturias*
1er de Fernando VII (1), 1er del Infante Don Carlos (1), Cangas de Tineo (1), Navia (1), Langreo (1), Llanes (1), Castropol (1), Siero (1), Salas (1), Villaviciosa (1), Grado (1), Candas y Luanco (1), Infiesto (1), Covadonga (1), Pravia (1), Cangas de Onís (1), Rivadesella (1), Gijón (1), Avíles (1), Lena (1), Colunga (1).

(f) *Extremadura*
Badajoz (3), Legión de Voluntarios Extranjeros (1)*, Voluntarios de Plasencia (1), 4° Batallón de Guardias Españolas (1)*, 4° Batallón de Guardias Walonas (1)*, Cazadores de Llerena (1), Tiradores de Mérida (1), Voluntarios de Valencia de Alburquerque (1), Cazadores Extranjeros (1)*, Cazadores de Alcántara (1), Cazadores de Zafra (1), Cazadores de la Serena (1), Tiradores de Badajoz (1).

(g) *Castilla la Vieja*
1er Voluntarios Escolares de León (1), 1er Voluntarios de León (2), 2° Voluntarios de León (2), 3er Voluntarios de León (2), 4° Voluntarios de León (2), 5° Voluntarios de León (2), Escolares de Benavente (1), Voluntarios Castellanos de Fernando VII (2), 1er Voluntarios de Ciudad Rodrigo (1), 2°

Appendix 3

Voluntarios de Ciudad Rodrigo (1), 3ᵉʳ Voluntarios de Ciudad Rodrigo (1), Voluntarios Literarios de Valladolid (1), Voluntarios de Alava (2), Tiradores de Ledesma (1), 1ᵉʳ Tiradores de Castilla (1), 3ᵉʳ Cazadores de Fernando VII (1), 1ᵉʳ Cántabro (2), 2° Cántabro (2), Cazadores de León (3), 1ᵉʳ Tercio de Castilla (1), 2° Tercio de Castilla (1), 3ᵉʳ Tercio de Castilla (1).

(h) *Castilla la Nueva*
Peñas de San Pedro (3), 2° de Fernando VII (2), Voluntarios de Honor de la Real Universidad de Toledo (1), 1ᵉʳ Voluntarios de Madrid (3), 2° Voluntarios de Madrid (2), Imperial de Toledo (3), Voluntarios Leales de Fernando VII (3), Voluntarios de la Patria (3), Voluntarios Numantinos (1), Voluntarios de Villanueva de los Infantes (1).

(i) *Galicia*
Batallón del General del Ejército de la Izquierda (1)*, Buenos Aires (1)*, 1ᵉʳ Cazadores de Fernando VII (2), Voluntarios Literarios de Santiago (1), Voluntarios de la Victoria (2), Cazadores del General del Ejército de la Izquierda (2)*.

Total

	Regiments	Battalions
Catalonia	27	27
Andalucía	34	49
Aragón	47	55
Levante/Balcares	24	41
Asturias	21	21
Extremadura	13	15
Castilla la Vieja	22	33
Castilla la Nueva	10	22
Galicia	6	9
Grand total	214	272

B. Cavalry

(a) *Line Cavalry*
Guardias de Honor de Sevilla (1), Perseguidores de Andalucía (4)*, Voluntarios de Sevilla (4), Voluntarios de Ciudad Rodrigo (2), Carabinieros Reales de Extremadura (1)*, Granaderos a Caballo de Fernando VII (3), 2° de Alcántara (2)*, Voluntarios de Madrid (4).

(b) *Dragoons*
2° de Lusitania (4)*, Cáceres (4)*, Castilla (2), Granada (4).

(c) *Light Cavalry*
Cazadores Voluntarios de Alcántara (3), Cazadores de la Maestranza de Valencia (4), Cazadores Voluntarios de Trujillo (4), Cazadores de Fuen Santa (3), Cazadores de Sevilla (4)*, Lanceros de Utrera (1), Lanceros de Jérez (1), Lanceros de Carmona (1), 1ᵉʳ Regimiento de Húsares de

Extremadura (5)*, 2° Regimiento de Husares de Extremadura (5), Husares Francos de Valencia (3), Husares de Granada (3).

Total

	Regiments	Squadrons
Line Cavalry	8	19
Dragoons	4	14
Light cavalry	12	37
Grand total	24	70

Notes

The figures in brackets refer to the number of battalions or squadrons in a regiment. Units marked with an asterisk were composed of deserters from the French forces, prisoners of war returned from England, or fragments of the regular army. In a few cases, the 'new' regiments had merely been renamed: for example, the Husares de María Luisa became the 1er Regimiento de Husares de Extremadura, and the Tercios de Tejas (a force that had been raised for service in Texas, but had not yet been sent to America) the Cazadores de Sevilla.

This table has been compiled from the lists given in Clonard, *Historia Orgánica*, VI, 303–12.

Appendix 4

Order of battle of the Spanish Army, 1814

(a) **Estado Mayor General**

Chief of the General Staff, thirty-four *ayudantes generales*, forty *ayudantes primeros*, seventy *ayudantes segundos*.

(b) **Royal Guards**

Guardias Españolas (four battalions),
Guardias Walonas (four battalions),
Carabinieros Reales (four squadrons).

(c) **Line Infantry**

120 regiments, each of one battalion, viz:
  (i) Thirty pre-war line infantry regiments – Rey, Príncipe, Corona, Africa, Zamora, Soria, Córdoba, Sevilla, Granada, Valencia, Zaragoza, España, Toledo, Mallorca, Burgos, León, Cantabria, Ceuta, Navarra, América, Princesa, Málaga, Ordenes Militares, Voluntarios de la Corona, Borbón, Irlanda, Hibernia, Ultonia, Aragón, Galicia (ex-Reina).
  (ii) Twenty-six regiments of pre-war provincial militia (the militia was given the status of line infantry in 1810) – Jaén, 2° de Badajoz, 2° de Sevilla, 2° de Burgos, Lugo, Oviedo, Trujillo, Ciudad Real, Sigüenza, Toro, 2° de Soria, Laredo, Orense, Santiago, Pontevedra, Tuy, Betanzos, 2° de Guadix, Ronda, Cuenca, Alcázar de San Juan, Chinchilla, Plasencia, Monterrey, Compostela, Mondoñedo.
  (iii) Sixty-four regiments formed since 1808 (date of formation given in brackets where known) – Granaderos de Castilla, Palma (1808), Almería (1808), 1er de Guadix (1808), Alpujarras (1808), Urgel (1813), Badajoz (1808), Benavente (1808), 2° Voluntarios de Madrid (1808), Bailén (1808), Fernando VII (1808), Lena (1808), Pravia (1808), Castropol (1808), Veteranos de la Patria (1813), Cangas de Tineo (1808), Leales Manresanos (1811), Barcelona (1811), 2° de la Princesa (1808), 1er Voluntarios de Navarra (1809), 2° Voluntarios de Navarra (1809), 3er Voluntarios de Navarra (1809), 5° Voluntarios de Navarra (1811),

Almansa (1808), Canarias, Unión (1809), San Fernando (1812), 1er de Cádiz (1811), Cansados de Galicia (1811), 1er de Guadalajara (1810), 2° de Guadalajara (1812), Reunión (1808), Batallón del General del Cuarto Ejército (1813), Imperial Alejandro (1813), Arlanza, Mataró (1812), 5° Granaderos, 1er de Asturias (1812), 2° de Asturias (1812), 3er de Asturias (1812), Legión Extranjera, Constitución (1812), Granaderos del Tercer Ejército, 1er de Alava (1812), 2° de Alava (1812), 3er de Alava (1812), Batallón del General de la Reserva de Andalucía (1813), Batallón del General del Primer Ejército, 2° de Príncipe (1813), 1er Voluntarios de Aragón (1813), 2° Voluntarios de Aragón (1813), 3er Voluntarios de Aragón (1813), 4° Voluntarios de Aragón (1813), Rivagorza, Provisional de Mahón, Lobera (1809), Murcia (1813), Talavera (1813), 2° Voluntarios de Sevilla (1808), Infiesto (1808), Voluntarios Distinguidos de Cádiz (1808 – five battalions).

(d) **Light Infantry**

Sixty-two regiments, each of one battalion, viz:
  (i) Nine regiments of pre-war light infantry – 1er Voluntarios de Aragón, 2° Voluntarios de Aragón, 1er Voluntarios de Cataluña, 2° Voluntarios de Cataluña, Gerona, Campo Mayor, Voluntarios de Navarra, Voluntarios de Valencia.
 (ii) Fifty-three regiments formed since 1808 (date of formation given where known) – 1er de Guipúzcoa (1810), 2° de Guipúzcoa (1810), 3er de Guipúzcoa (1812), 1er Tiradores de Cantabria (1810), 2° Tiradores de Cantabria (1811), 3er Tiradores de Cantabria (1812), 1er de Vizcaya (1810), 2° de Vizcaya (1812), 3er de Vizcaya (1812), Cazadores de Valencia (1808), Tiradores de Cádiz (1808), Voluntarios de la Victoria (1808), Tiradores de Mérida (1808), Voluntarios de Santiago (1808), Cazadores de Carmona (1808), Tiradores de Busa (1811), Cazadores de León (1808), 1er Tiradores de Castilla (1808), 2° Tiradores de Castilla (1809), 3er Tiradores de Castilla (1811), Voluntarios de Rivera (1809), Cazadores del Rey (1809), Voluntarios de Guadalajara (1810), Tiradores de Bureva (1809), Cazadores de Soria (1810), Voluntarios de Molina (1810), Voluntarios de Rioja (1810), Voluntarios Numantinos (1808), Legión Extremeña (1811), Tiradores de Sigüenza (1811), Voluntarios de Alicante (1808), Voluntarios de Jaén (1811), 1er de Iberia (1811), 2° de Iberia (1811), 3er de Iberia (1811), 4° de Iberia (1812), Tiradores de Cataluña (1812), Cazadores de Cataluña (1811), Voluntarios de Cardona (1811), Cazadores de Mallorca (1811), Voluntarios de Madrid (1811), Guardias Nacionales (1811), Cazadores del Campo de Cariñena (1809), Cazadores de Antequera (1808), Cazadores de la Costa de Levante (1811), Tiradores de Cuenca (1811), Cazadores de Castilla (1811), Voluntarios de Asturias (1811), Cazadores Voluntarios del Ampurdán (1810), Cazadores Extranjeros (1812), Tiradores de Doyle (1808), 1er Cántabro (1808), Albuera (1812).

Appendix 4

(e) Cavalry

Twenty-eight regiments, each of four squadrons:
  (i) Twelve regiments of line cavalry – Rey, Reina, Príncipe, Infante, Borbón, Farnesio, Alcántara, España, Algarve, Calatrava, Santiago, Montesa.
  (ii) Ten regiments of dragoons – Rey, Reina, Almansa, Pavia, Villaviciosa, Sagunto, Numancia, Lusitania, Granada, Madrid.
  (iii) Four regiments of chasseurs – Olivencia, Voluntarios de España, Sevilla, Valencia.
  (iv) Four regiments of hussars – Husares Españoles, Extremadura, Granada, Fernando VII.

(f) Artillery

General Staff, one cadet company, five regiments of foot artillery, six squadrons of horse artillery, twenty-one companies of garrison artillery, five workshop companies, six train battalions.

(g) Engineers

General Staff, one regiment of Zapadores-Minadores.

Total strength of Army, 1 March 1814 (according to report of Minister of War to Cortes, 4 March 1814):

	Disposable strength		*Total strength*	
	Officers	Men	Officers	Men
First Army	778	15,345	1,008	17,061
Second Army	946	26,262	1,205	34,174
Third Army	665	13,861	982	18,648
Fourth Army	2,084	50,807	2,953	70,851
Army of Reserve of Andalucía	400	8,826	567	12,598
Army of Reserve of Galicia	299	3,654	378	5,472
Division of Mallorca	505	8,664	846	13,986
Army of the Province of Cádiz	120	3,402	307	5,856
Garrisons, depots, etc.	—	—	—	5,512
Total	5,797	130,821	8,246	184,158

Select bibliography

A. Archival Sources

Archivo Histórico Nacional, Madrid (AHN)
Sección de Estado, *legajos* 16, 17, 60, 71, 2821, 2959, 2995, 3566.

Biblioteca del Senado, Madrid (BS):
Collección e Arteche, *carpetas* 292–2, 294–2, 301–4, 341–2.

Public Records Office, London (PRO):
War Office Papers, Series 1, Volumes 226–27, 229–52, 260–1.
Foreign Office Papers, Series 72, Volumes 133–4, 144, 153.

Real Academia de Historia, Madrid (RAH):
Legajos 2-MS134; 2-MS135; 9-31-6:6964; 9-31-6:6965; 9-31-6:6966; 9-31-7:7021; 9-31-7:7025; 11-2-2:8154; 11-5-7:9003; 14-9-6:6925.

Servicio Histórico Militar, Madrid:
(a) *Colección Documental del Fraile (SHM. CDF.)*
Volumes XXVII, XXXII–XLI, CX, CXIV–CXVII, CXXXII–CLXIV, CXCI, CCLX, CCLIII–CCLXVIII, CCCXXXVI–CCCLI, CDLII–CDLXVII, DXL, DCXLVII–DCCLXIII, DCCLXXXIX, DCCXCI, DCCCLXIV, CMVIII, CMXXII.
(b) *Archivo de la Guerra de la Independencia (SHM. AGI.)*
Carpetas 1/2/2, 1/2/8, 3/2/4, 3/4/23, 3/4/24, 3/4/28, 3/4/32, 3/6/34, 4/2/10, 5/8/1, 5/8/2, 5/8/4, 5/8/9, 25/35/24, 32/49/21, 32/49/23, 34/52/53, 35/53/59, 36/54/1.

University of Southampton
(a) *Wellington Papers (US. WP.)*
Volumes 1/205, 1/207–14, 1/216, 1/274–77, 1/315, 1/331–2, 1/341–56, 1/358–83, 1/387–99, 12/1/1–3, 12/1/5, 12/2/3.
(b) *Carver Manuscripts (US. Carver MSS.)*
Nos. 8, 53, 100.

Select bibliography

B. Published Contemporary Sources

(a) *Official publications, documentary collections, etc.*

Colección de todas las pragmáticas, cédulas, provisiones, autos acordados, bandos y otras providencias publicados en el actual reinado del Señor Don Carlos IV, ed. S. Sánchez (Madrid, 1794–1801).
Cartas confidenciales de la reina María Luisa y de Manuel Godoy, ed. C. Peyreyra (Madrid, n.d.).
Constitución política de la nación española (Cádiz, 1812).
Diario de las sesiones y actas de las Cortes (Cádiz, 1810–13).
The Dispatches and Correspondence of the Marquess Wellesley during his Mission to Spain as Ambassador Extraordinary to the Supreme Junta in 1809, ed. M. Martin (London, 1838).
The Dispatches of Field Marshal the Duke of Wellington during his Various Campaigns in India, Denmark, Portugal, Spain, the Low Countries and France from 1779 to 1815, ed. J. Gurwood (London, 1837–39).
Estados de la organización y fuerza de los ejércitos españoles beligerantes en la península durante la guerra de España contra Napoleón Bonaparte arreglados por la Sección de Historia Militar en 1821 (Barcelona, 1822).
Extracto puntual de todas las pragmáticas, cédulas, provisiones, circulares, autos acordados y otros providencias publicados en el reinado del Señor Don Carlos III, ed. S. Sánchez (Madrid, 1794).
Guerra de la Independencia: proclamas, bandos y combatientes, ed. S. Delgado (Madrid, 1979).
Kalendario manual y guía de forasteros en Madrid (Madrid 1788–1807, 1815).
Ordenanzas de S.M. para el régimen, disciplina, subordinación y servicio de sus ejércitos (Madrid, 1768).
Supplementary Despatches, Correspondence and Memoranda of Field Marshal Arthur, Duke of Wellington, ed. Second Duke of Wellington (London, 1858–72).

(b) *Newspapers, gazettes, etc.*

La Abeja Española (Cádiz, 1812–13).
El Amante de la Libertad Civil (Cádiz, 1813).
El Articulista Espánol (Cádiz, 1813).
Atalaya de la Mancha en Madrid (Madrid, 1813–14).
El Centinela de la Constitución Española (Cádiz, 1813).
El Ciudadano Imparcial (Cádiz, n.d.).
El Conciso (Cádiz, Madrid, 1812–14).
El Correo de Sevilla (Seville, 1808).
Diario de Algeciras (Algeciras, 1813).
Diario de Badajoz (Badajoz, 1808–09).
Diario Crítico y Erudito de Granada (Granada, 1812–13).
Diario de Gobierno de Sevilla (Seville, 1812–13).
Diario de Granada (Granada, 1808–09).

Diario de Málaga (Málaga, 1808).
Diario Mercantil de Cádiz (Cádiz, 1813).
Diario Patriótico de Cádiz (Cádiz, 1813).
Diario Político de Mallorca (Palma, 1808).
Diario Redactor de Sevilla (Seville, 1812–13).
Diario de la Tarde (Cádiz, 1813).
Diario de Valencia (Valencia, 1809).
El Español (Cádiz, London, 1810–14).
El Espectador Sevillano (Seville, 1808–10).
Gazeta de la Coruña (Coruña, 1808).
Gazeta del Gobierno (Seville, 1809–10).
Gazeta de la Junta-Congreso del Reino de Valencia (Valencia, 1810).
Gazeta Ministerial de Sevilla (Seville, 1808–09).
Gazeta de la Regencia de España e Indias (Cádiz, Madrid, 1810–14).
Gazeta de Valencia (Valencia, 1808–09).
Gazeta de Zaragoza (Zaragoza, 1808–09).
El Imparcial: Diario Político y Mercantil de la Ciudad de Alicante (Alicante, 1813).
Los Ingleses en España (Sevilla, 1813).
Memorial Militar y Patriótico del Ejercito de la Izquierda (Badajoz, 1810).
El Observador (Cádiz, 1810).
El Patriota (Cádiz, 1812–13).
El Patriota (Valencia, 1809).
El Patriota Compostelano (Santiago, 1810).
El Patriota en las Cortes (Cádiz, 1810–12).
Periódico Militar del Estado Mayor General (Cádiz, 1812–13).
El Procurador General de la Nación y del Rey (Cádiz, 1812–13).
El Redactor General (Cádiz, 1811–14).
Semanario Patriótico (Madrid, Seville, Cádiz, 1808–12).
El Tribuno del Pueblo Español (Cádiz, Madrid, 1813–14).

(c) *Apologia, memoirs, manifestos, diaries, histories, etc.*

Aguirre, M. de, *Cartas y discursos del militar ingenuo al 'Correo de los Ciegos de Madrid'*, ed. A. Elorza (San Sebastián, 1973).
Albo, J., *Memorias en que se discurre el modo de constituir la infantería sobre bases sólidas y análogas a la constitución política de la monarquía* (Cádiz, 1813).
Alburquerque, Duque de, *Manifiesto del Duque de Alburquerque acerca de su conducta con la Junta de Cádiz y arribo [sic] del ejército de su mando a aquella plaza* (London, 1810).
Alcaide Ibieca, A., *Historia de los dos sitios que pusieron a Zaragoza en los años de 1808 y 1809 las tropas de Napoleón* (Madrid, 1830).
Alcalá Galiano, A., *Memorias* (Madrid, 1886).
Alvarez, P. P., *Espíritu militar o principios teóricos y prácticos del arte de la guerra, acomodados al servicio de los estados mayores generales de los ejércitos nacionales* (Madrid, 1814).
Alvarez Guerra, A., *Ensayo de un reglamento militar interino o de campaña*

Select bibliography

(Seville, 1812).
Alvarez Guerra, J., *Indicaciones político-militares del estado de la nación española dirigidas a la oficialidad de los ejércitos nacionales y dedicadas al soberano congreso de Cortes* (Madrid,1814).
Alvarez Valdés, A., *Memorias del levantamiento de Asturias en 1808* (Oviedo, 1889).
Apuntaciones militares para la actual guerra (Cádiz, 1811).
Baccigalupí, L., *Indicaciones acerca de las columnas volantes* (Badajoz, 1811).
Bacon, Conde de, *Manual de un joven oficial o ensayo sobre la teoría militar* (Madrid, 1813).
Ballesteros. F., *Respetuosos descargos que el Tnte. Gral. D. Francisco Ballesteros ofrece a la generosa nación española* (Cádiz, 1813).
Beckford, W., *The Journal of William Beckford in Portugal and Spain 1787–1788*, ed. B. Alexander (London, 1954).
Blanco White, J. M., *Letters from Spain* (London, 1808).
Bourgoing, J. F. de, *A Modern State of Spain* (London, 1808).
Brandt, H. von, *The Two Minas and the Spanish Guerrillas* (London, 1825).
Bulow, H. von, *Espíritu del sistema moderno de la guerra*, ed. J. X. de Lardizabal (Madrid, 1806).
Cabanes, F. X., *Historia de las operaciones del Ejército de Cataluña en la primera campaña de la guerra de la usurpación, o sea de la independencia de España* (Tarragona, 1809).
Cabanes, F. X., *Ensayo acerca del sistema militar de Bonaparte* (Isla de León, 1811).
Cadalso, J., *Obras de Don José Cadalso* (Madrid, 1818).
Cadalso, J., *Obras inéditas de Don José Cadalso*, ed. R. Fouché-Delbosc (Madrid, 1894).
Cadalso, J., *Los eruditos a la violeta* (Madrid, 1928).
Calvo de Rozas, L., *Explicación de las equivocaciones que ha padecido el Sr. Marqués de Lazán* (Cádiz, 1811).
Calzada, B. M. de., *Pensamientos militares que da a luz por si fuesen útiles el Teniente Coronel Don Bernardo María de Calzada, Capitán del Regimiento de Dragones de Granada* (Madrid, 1814).
Canga Argüelles, J., *Apuntes para la historia de la hacienda pública de España en el año de 1811* (Cádiz, 1813).
Carta de un paisano a un militar amigo suyo sobre nuestra situación y sobre los medios de mejorarla, (Ayamonte, 1811).
Cartilla militar para el soldado español (Isla de León, 1811).
Castaños, F. X. de, *Reales Ordenes de la Junta Central Suprema de Gobierno del Reino y representaciones de la de Sevilla y del General Castaños acerca de su separación del mando del Ejército de Operaciones del Centro*, (Seville, 1809).
Cevallos, P., *Exposición de los hechos y maquinaciones que han preparado la usurpación de la corona de España y los medios que el emperador de los franceses ha puesto en obra para realizarla* (Mexico, 1808).
Chlapowski, D., *Mémoires sur les guerres de Napoleon, 1806–1813* (Paris, 1908).
Cocks, E. C., *Intelligence Officer in the Peninsula: Letters and Diaries of*

Major the Honourable Edward Charles Cocks, 1786–1812, ed. J. Page (Tunbridge Wells, 1986).
Conjuración de Bonaparte y Don Manuel Godoy contra la monarquía española (Mexico, 1808).
Copons, F. de, *Carta del Mariscal de Campo D. Francisco de Copons y Navia al editor del Semanario Patriótico* (Cádiz, 1811).
Coxe, W., *Historical Memoirs of the Kings of Spain of the House of Bourbon* (London, 1815).
Crusy de Marcillac, L., *Histoire de la guerre entre la France et l'Espagne pendant les années de la révolution francaise* (Paris, 1808).
Dalrymple, H., *Memoir written by General Sir Hew Dalrymple, Bart., of his Proceedings as connected with the Affairs of Spain and the Commencement of the Peninsular War* (London, 1830).
Dalrymple, W., *Travels through Spain and Portugal in 1774* (London, 1777).
Diario exacto o relación circunstanciada de lo acaecido en el real sitio de Aranjuez de resultas de haber creido el pueblo que SS.MM. querían dejar la capital (Córdoba, n.d.).
El ejército español destruido por las leyes o manifestación de los efectos que debe producir el decreto que separa de los gobiernos militares la intervención en lo político y de las Capitanías Generales la presidencia de las Audiencias dejando al ejército aislado a sus empleos interiores (Alicante, 1813).
Elió, X., *Manifiesto que D. Xavier Elió, general del Segundo y Tercer Ejército, hace a todos los españoles exponiéndoles la conducta que observara durante su mando* (Cádiz, 1812).
Escoiquiz, J. de, *Memorias de D. Juan de Escoiquiz* (Madrid, 1915).
Espoz y Mina, F. de, *Memorias del General Don Francisco Espoz y Mina* (Madrid, 1851–52).
Exposición de la Comisión de Constitución Militar acompañando los trabajos que se le pidieron (Madrid, 1814).
Exposición que hacen a las Cortes generales y extraordinarias de la nación española los individuos que compusierion la Junta Central Suprema del mismo de su conducta en el tiempo de su administración (Cádiz, 1811).
Finestra, T., *Exposición que hace un oficial a sus compañeros de armas sobre la decadencia de los ejércitos españoles* (Cádiz, 1813).
Fischer, C. A., *Travels in Spain in 1797 and 1798* (London, 1802).
Fischer, C. A., *A Picture of Madrid* (London, 1808).
Foy, A., *Histoire de la guerre de la péninsule sous Napoléon* (Paris, 1827).
Gámez, P. J. de, *Exposición que hace a las Cortes generales y extraordinarias el Real Cuerpo de Guardias de Corps en contestación de la del Exmo. Sr. Secretario de Estado y del Despacho Universal de la Guerra* (Cádiz, 1811).
García de la Cuesta, G., *Manifiesto que presenta a la Europa el Capitán General Don Gregoria García de la Cuesta sobre sus operaciones militares y políticas desde el mes de junio de 1808 hasta el 12 de agosto de 1809* (Palma, 1811).
García del Barrio, M., *Sucesos militares de Galicia en 1809 y operaciones en*

la presente guerra de Coronel D. Manuel García del Barrio (Cádiz, 1811).
García de León y Pizarro, J., *Memorias* (Madrid, 1953).
García y Loygorri, M., *Colección de ejercicios facultativos aprobadas por S. M. para la uniforme instrucción de la tropa del Real Cuerpo de Artillería* (Madrid, 1814).
García Marín, F., *Memorias para la historia militar de la guerra de la revolución española* (Madrid, 1817).
Garciny, I., *Cuadro de la España desde el reinado de Carlos IV* (Valencia, 1811).
Girón, P. A., *Recuerdos de la vida de Don Pedro Agustín Girón*, ed. F. Suárez and A. Berazluce (Pamplona, 1978).
Godoy, M. de, *Memorias de Don Manuel de Godoy* (Madrid, 1836–46).
González Carvajal, T., *Del oficio y cargos del Intendente del Ejército en campaña* (Valencia, 1810).
González Carvajal, T., *Meditaciones sobre la constitución militar* (Cádiz, 1813).
Hawker, P., *Journal of a Regimental Officer during the Recent Campaign in Portugal and Spain under Lord Viscount Wellington* (London, 1810).
Hernández de Morejón, S., *Idea histórica de los principales sucesos ocurridos en Zaragoza durante el último sitio* (Valencia, 1809).
Holland, Lady, *The Spanish Journal of Elizabeth Lady Holland* (London, 1910).
Impugnación que hacen los individuos que compusieron la Suprema Junta Central al manifiesto del Capitán General Gregorio de la Cuesta (Cádiz, 1812).
Indagación de las causas de los malos sucesos de nuestros ejércitos y medios de removerlas (Cádiz, 1811).
Infantado, Duque del, *Manifiesto de las operaciones del Ejército del Centro* (Seville, 1809).
Jackson, G., *The Diaries and Letters of Sir George Jackson*, ed. Lady Jackson (London, 1872).
Jacob, W., *Travels in the South of Spain* (London, 1811).
Laborde, A. de, *A View of Spain* (London, 1809).
La Peña, M., *Representación hecha a las Cortes por el Capitán General de Andalucía y General en Jefe interino del Cuarto Ejército* (Cádiz, 1811).
Lardizabal, J., *Contestación a la falsa e injuriosa idea que el papel 'El Español' da de la memorable acción del cinco de marzo en los campos de Chiclana* (Cádiz, 1811).
Lazán, Marqués de, *Exposición de la conducta militar y patriótica del Tnte. Gral. Marqués de Lazán y de las causas de su permanencia en Cádiz* (Cádiz, 1811).
Leach, J., *Rough Sketches of the Life of an Old Soldier* (London, 1831).
Liano, J., *Breve discurso de Don Josef Liano, Capitán de Husares de Granada, agregado a Cazadores de Sevilla, a los generales sobre la decadencia de los ejércitos* (Isla de León, 1813).
Llorente, J., *Memorias para la historia de la revolución española* (Paris, 1814).
Lozoya, Marquésa de, *La campaña de Navarra 1793–95 en las cartas de la*

Marquesa de Lozoya, ed. Marqués de Lozoya (Valencia, 1925).
Manifiesto de la Junta Superior del Principado de Cataluña (Tarragona, 1809).
Manifiesto de los procedimientos del Consejo Real en los gravísimos sucesos ocurridos desde octubre del año próximo pasado (Valencia, 1808).
Manifiesto que S.A. ha tenido a bien expedir y publicar por la Secretaría del Despacho de la Guerra sobre cesación en el mando del Cuarto Ejército y Capitanía General de las Andalucías de dicho Señor Ballesteros (Cádiz, 1812).
Martínez Colomer, V. *El filósofo en su quinta o relación de los principales hechos acontecidos desde la caida de Godoy hasta el ataque de Valencia* (Valencia, 1808).
Martínez Colomer, V., *Sucesos de Valencia desde el dia 23 de mayo hasta el 28 de junio del año 1808* (Valencia, 1810).
Medios de salvar el reino (Cádiz, 1810).
Memorias de tiempos de Fernando VII, ed. M. Artola Gallego (Madrid, 1957).
Mesonero Romanos, M. de, *Memorias de un setentón* (Madrid, 1880).
La milicia desatendida por las leyes en tiempo de guerra (Madrid, 1814).
Un militar español, tan amante como el primero del bien de su patria y celoso del honor de su profesión, al considerar la conducta del Tnte. Gral. D., Francisco Ballesteros en este última época, no ha podido prescindir de manifestar al público los hechos de que está cerciorado y los siguientes reflexiones a que da margen el reciente que ha motivado su separación del mando del cuarto ejército (Cádiz, 1812).
The Military Exploits of Don Juan Martín Díez, the Empecinado (London, 1823).
Moore, J., *The Diary of Sir John Moore*, ed. J. Maurice (London, 1904).
Moscoso, J. de, *Avisos militares al Ejército de la Izquierda para la presente guerra* (Tarragona, 1809).
Moscoso, J. de, *Reflexiones sobre la guerra de España e instrucciones para la guerra de partidas o de paisanos* (Cádiz, 1809).
Muñoz Maldonado, J., *Historia política y militar de la guerra de la independencia de España contra Napoleón Bonaparte desde 1808 a 1814* (Madrid, 1833).
Muriel, A., *Historia de Carlos IV*, ed. C. Seco Serrano (Madrid, 1959).
Palafox y Melcí, J., *Don José Palafox: autobiografía*, ed. J. Garcia Mercadel (Madrid, 1966).
Peñalosa y Zuñiga, C., *El honor militar, causas de su origen, progresos y decadencia* (Madrid, 1795).
Peñalosa y Zuñiga, C., *Memoria sobre la artillería volante o de a caballo* (Segovia, 1796).
Pensamientos militares de un paisano (Seville, 1809).
Picado Franco, L. M., *Historia del origen, acontecimientos y acciones de guerra de la sexta división del Segundo Ejército (o sea de Soria) durante nuestra sagrada lucha al mando del Exmo. Sr. D. José Joaquín Durán y Barazábal, Mariscal de Campo de los Reales Ejércitos* (Madrid, 1817).
Pina Ferrer, V., *Páginas de 1808: memorias de un patriota* (Zaragoza,

1889).
Porter, R. K., *Letters from Portugal and Spain written the march of the British troops under Sir John Moore* (London, 1809).
Pradt, M. de, *Mémoires historiques sur la révolution d'Espagne* (Paris, 1816).
Ramírez y Vandama, P., *Táctica general de la infanteriá* (Palma, 1809).
Robinson, F. P., 'A Peninsular Brigadier: letters of Major General Sir F. P. Robinson, K.C.B., dealing with the campaign of 1813', ed. C. T. Atkinson, *Journal of the Society for Army Historical Research*, XXXIV, No. 140, 153–70.
Rocca, A. J. M. de, *Memoirs of the War of the French in Spain* (London, 1815).
Rodríguez de la Buria, P., *El Tnte. Gral. Pedro Rodríguez de la Buria a las Cortes generales y extraordinarios de España e Indias* (Cádiz, 1811).
Sánchez Cisneros, J., *Ideas sueltas sobre la ciencia militar* (Madrid, 1814).
Sancho, V., *Ensayo de una constitución militar deducida de la constitución política de la monarquía española* (Cádiz, 1813).
Sancho, V., *Proyecto de una constitución de las milicias nacionales* (Madrid, 1814).
Schepeler, A. von., *Histoire de la révolution d'Espagne et de Portugal ainsi que de la guerre qui en résulta* (Liège, 1829–31).
Schubert, H., 'Lettres d'un diplomate danois en Espagne (1798–1800)', ed. E. Gigas, *Revue Hispanique*, IX, 395–439.
Segovia, J., *Satira contra Don Tomás Finestra por haber escrito la exposición a sus compañeros de armas sobre la decadencia de los ejércitos españoles* (Cádiz, 1813).
Serrano Valdenebro, J., *Discursos varios del arte de la guerra: tratan el buen uso de la táctica con relación y crítica de la batalla de Almansa* (Madrid, 1796).
A Soldier of the Seventy First, ed. C. Hibbert (London, 1975).
Southey, R. W., *Letters written during a Journey in Spain and a Short Residence in Portugal* (London, 1808).
Southey, R. W., *History of the Peninsular War* (London, 1823–32).
Stanhope, Earl of, *Notes of Conversations with the Duke of Wellington, 1831–1851* (London, 1889).
Suchet, L. G., *Memoirs of the War in Spain from 1808 to 1814* (London, 1829).
Swinburne, H., *Travels through Spain in the Years 1775 and 1776* (Dublin, 1779).
Toreno, Conde de, *Historia del levantamiento, guerra y revolución de España* (Paris, 1838).
Townsend, J., *A Journey through Portugal and Spain in the Years 1786 and 1787* (London, 1792).
Vaughan, C., *Narrative of the Siege of Saragossa,* (London, 1809).
Villalva, L. de, *Zaragoza en su segundo sitio* (Palma, 1811).
Villanueva, J., *Mi viaje a las Cortes* (Madrid, 1860).
Wellesley, H., *The Diary and Correspondence of Henry Wellesley, first Lord Cowley, 1790–1846*, ed. F. Wellesley (London, 1930).

Whittingham, S., *A Memoir of the Services of Lieutenant General Sir Samuel Ford Whittingham*, ed. F. Whittingham (London, 1868).

C. Secondary Sources

Alexander, D. W., *Rod of Iron: French Counter-Insurgency Policy in Aragón during the Peninsular War* (Wilmington, 1985).
Alonso Baquer, M., *El ejército en la sociedad española* (Madrid, 1971).
Anes Alvarez, G., 'La economía española (1782–1829)', *El Banco de España: una historia económica*, ed. Banco de España (Madrid, 1970).
Anes Alvarez, G., *Economía e ilustración en la España del siglo XVIII* (Barcelona, 1972).
Anes Alvarez, G., *El antiguo régimen: los Borbones* (Madrid, 1975).
Anna, T., *Spain and the Loss of America* (Lincoln, 1983).
Artola Gallego, M., *Los origenes de la España contemporanea* (Madrid, 1959).
Aymes, J. R., *La Guerra de la Independencia en España (1808–1814)* (Madrid, 1980).
Benavides Moro, N., and Yaque Laurel, J., *El Capitán General D. Joaquín Blake y Joyes, Regente del Reino y fundador del Cuerpo de Estado Mayor* (Madrid, 1960).
Bueno, J. M., *El ejército y la armada en 1808* (Madrid, 1982).
Busquets, J., *Pronunciamientos y golpes de estado en España* (Barcelona, 1982).
Callahan, W., *Church, Politics and Society in Spain, 1750–1854* (London, 1985).
Carr, R., *Spain, 1808–1975* (Oxford, 1982).
Carrasco y Saiz, A., *Iconobiografía del generalato español* (Madrid, 1901).
Casado Burbano, P., *Las fuerzas armadas en el inicio del constitucionalismo español* (Madrid, 1982).
Castro Bonel, H., 'Manejos de Fernando VII contra sus padres y contra Godoy', *Boletín de la Universidad de Madrid*, 1930, II, 397–408, 493–503; *ibid.*, 1931, III, 93–102.
Chamorro Martínez, M., *1808–1936: dos situaciones históricas concordantes* (Madrid, 1974).
Chastenet, J., *Godoy, Master of Spain 1792–1808* (London, 1953).
Childs, J., *Armies and warfare in Europe, 1648–1789* (Manchester, 1982).
Christiansen, E., *The origins of military power in Spain, 1800–1854* (London, 1967).
Clonard, Conde de, *Historia orgánica de las armas de infantería y caballería españolas* (Madrid, 1851–62).
Corona Baratech, C., *Revolución y reacción en el reinado de Carlos IV* (Madrid, 1957).
Corvisier, A., *Armies and societies in Europe, 1494–1789* (London, 1979).
D'Auvergne, E., *Godoy, the Queen's Favourite* (London, 1912).
Desdevises du Dézert, G. N., *L'Espagne de l'ancien régime* (Paris 1897–1904).
Desdevises du Dézert, G. N., 'La société espagnole au XVIII siècle', *Revue*

Hispanique, LXIV, 225–656.
Domínguez Ortiz, A., *Sociedad y estado en el siglo XVIII español* (Barcelona, 1976).
Fernández Bastarreche, F., *El ejército español en el siglo XIX* (Madrid, 1978).
Fernández Bastarreche, F., 'El ejército español en el siglo XIX: aspectos sociales y económicos', *Revista de Historia Militar*, No. 50 (1981), 69–88.
García Mercadel, J., *Palafox, Duque de Zaragoza, 1775–1847* (Madrid, 1948).
Gates, D., *The Spanish Ulcer: a History of the Peninsular War* (London, 1986).
Gómez de Arteche, J., *Guerra de la Independencia: historia militar de España de 1808 a 1814* (Madrid, 1868–1903).
Gómez de Arteche, J., 'Juan Martín, el Empecinado: la Guerra de la Independencia bajo su aspecto popular', *La España del Siglo XIX*, I, 81–132.
Guillaume, H., *Histoire des Gardes Wallonnes au service d'Espagne* (Brussels, 1858).
Guzmán, F., *La España de Goya* (Madrid, 1981).
Hamilton, E. J., 'War and inflation in Spain, 1780–1800', *Quarterly Journal of Economics*, LXIX, No. 1, 36–77.
Hamilton, E. J., *War and prices in Spain, 1651–1800* (Cambridge, Massachusetts, 1947).
Hamnett, B., *La política española en una época revolucionaria, 1790–1820* (Mexico City, 1985).
Harrison, R. J., *An Economic History of Modern Spain* (Manchester, 1978).
Herr, R., *The Eighteenth-Century Revolution in Spain* (Princeton, 1958).
Horward, D. D., *Napoleon and Iberia: the Twin Sieges of Ciudad Rodrigo and Almeida, 1810* (Tallahassee, 1984).
Izquierdo Hernández, M., *Antecedentes y comienzos del reinado de Fernando VII* (Madrid, 1963).
Izquierdo Hernández, M., 'Godoy', *Revista de Estudios Extremeños*, XIII (1967), 189–208.
Keegan, J., *The Face of Battle* (London, 1979).
Lovett, G., *Napoleon and the Birth of Modern Spain* (New York, 1965).
Madol, H. R., *Godoy, the First Dictator of Modern Times* (London, 1934).
Martí Gilabert, F., *El Motín de Aranjuez* (Pamplona, 1972).
Montón, J. C., *La revolución armada del Dos de Mayo en Madrid* (Madrid, 1983).
Moya y Jiménez, F., and Rey Joly, C., *El ejército y la marina en las Cortes de Cádiz* (Cádiz, 1913).
Murat, Comte, *Murat, lieutenant de l'Empereur en Espagne* (Paris, 1897).
Oman, C., *A History of the Peninsular War* (Oxford, 1902–30).
Pardo González, C., *Don Manuel Godoy, Príncipe de la Paz* (Madrid, 1911).
Payne, S., *Politics and the Military in Modern Spain* (London, 1967).
Pérez de Guzmán y Gallo, J., 'El primer conato de rebelión precursor de la

revolución de España', *España Moderna*, CCL (1909), 105–24; *ibid.*, CCLI, 48–68.
Pérez de Guzmán y Gallo, J., *El Dos de Mayo en Madrid* (Madrid, 1908).
Pintos Vieites, M., *La política de Fernando VII entre 1814 y 1820* (Pamplona, 1958).
Priego López, J., *Guerra de la Independencia, 1808–14* (Madrid, 1972–81).
Prieto y Llovera, P., *El grande de España, Capitán General Castaños, primer Duque de Bailén y primer Marqués de Portugalete* (Madrid, 1958).
Ramón Alonso, J., *Historia política del ejército español* (Madrid, 1974).
Read, J., *War in the Peninsula* (London, 1977).
Rodríguez, L., 'The riots of 1766 in Madrid', *European Studies Review*, III, No. 3 (1973), 223–42.
Rudorff, R., *War to the Death: the Sieges of Saragossa, 1808–1809* (London, 1974).
Salas, R. de, *Memorial histórico de la artillería española* (Madrid, 1831).
Seco Serrano, C., *Godoy, el hombre y el político* (Madrid, 1978).
Seco Serrano, C., *Militarismo y civilismo en la España contemporánea* (Madrid, 1985).
Severn, J. K., *A Wellesley Affair: Richard, Marquess Wellesley, and the conduct of Anglo-Spanish diplomacy, 1809–1812* (Tallahassee, 1981).
Vicens Vives, J., *An Economic History of Spain* (Princeton, 1969).
Vicens Vives, J. (ed.), *Historia de España y América social y económica* (Madrid, 1979).
Vigón, J., *Historia de la artillería española* (Madrid, 1947).

Index

Abisbal, Conde del, 161, 170, 182–4, 197–8
Africa, 52
Agar, Pedro, 157
agregados, 21, 59–60
Aguirre, Manuel de, 23, 26–7
Alagón, 98
Albo, J., 171, 177
Albuera, 121
Alburquerque, Duque de, 17, 136, 145
Alcalá de Henares, 49, 52, 85
Alcolea, 91, 98
Algeciras, 45, 160
Algiers, 8, 15
Alicante, 154, 163
America, 140, 164, 197–8, *see also* Latin America, South America, Spanish Empire
Amiens, Treaty of, 56
Andalucía, 24–5, 95, 144, 154, 160, 165, 197
Andujar, 98–100
Anglona, Príncipe de, 184
Antonio, Infante Don, 83
Aragón, 6, 24, 47, 79, 82, 88, 90, 92–3, 95, 103, 135, 139, 162–3
Aranjuez, 36, 52, 58–9, 65–7, 84, 104–6, 130
aristocracy, 3, 17, 26, 142, 177, 185, *see also* grandees, *grandeza, hidalguía, hijosdalgo*, magnates, nobility, *titulados*
Armies,
  Anglo–Portuguese, 115, 154, 159, 161, 165, 181
  British, 133, 139, 142, 154
  French,
    of Portugal, 163, 165
    of Spain, 126
    of the North, 163
  Spanish,
    First, 184
    Fourth, 16, 119, 181–2, 184
    of Andalucía, 97, 126–7
    of Aragón, 131–2
    of Castile, 106, 120, 135
    of Catalonia, 132
    of Extremadura, 127, 131, 135, 139, 144–5
    of Galicia, 126, 159
    of La Mancha, 138–9, 143–4
    of the Centre, 127, 131–2, 135
    of the Left, 126, 131–2, 143–4, 160
    of the Levante, 139
    of Valencia and Murcia, 127
    Second, 184
    Third, 184
army, Portuguese, 81, 139
army, Spanish,
  after 1814, 195–9
  and coup of 1814, 182–4
  and liberals, 174–85
  and Motín de Aranjuez, 65–8
  and uprising, 79–81, 84–90, 107

attempts at reform, 5, 10, 37, 40–5, 47–53, 167–8, 171
conditions, 11, 46, 61, 140, 174, 181–2, 196
desertion, 13, 41–2, 48, 140–1
discipline, 11, 97, 138, 140–1
opposition to Godoy, 58–62
opposition to reform, 44, 61, 167
organisation, 3–7, 37–8, 48, 51–4, 59, 95, 118, 134, 139, 167
pay and supply, 7–8, 39, 61, 96–7, 117, 139–40, 159
quality, 5, 14, 28–9, 118, 120–3, 138, 140, 159, 166
recruitment, 9–14, 37–8, 41–5, 48, 94–5, 125–6, 142, 167, 172
tactics, 4–5, 40, 45, 49–51, 121, 123
transport, 7–8, 37, 42, 53–4, 140
artillery, 3, 6–7, 17, 37, 41, 43, 45, 53–4, 96–7, 123
artillery park of Monteleón, 77
Astorga, 159
Asturias, 12, 79, 93, 103, 134, 142
Audiencias, 24–5, 92
Auerstadt, 102
Austria, 144
Avila, 58

Badajoz, 84, 102, 135, 159, 165, 168
bagajes, alojamiento y utensilios, 7, 25, 28, 168
Bailén, 53, 94, 96–101, 103, 105, 120–1, 125, 127, 129, 132, 137, 165, 175
Balearic Islands, 102
Ballesteros, Francisco, *see* López Ballesteros, Francisco
Bando de los Alcaldes de Móstoles, 84
Barcelona, 7, 12, 24, 64, 94, 101, 198
Barrosa, 181
Basle, Treaty of, 39
Basque country, 163, 165, *see also* Basque provinces, *señoríos* (Basque)
Basque provinces, 12, 39, 85, *see also* Basque country, *señoríos* (Basque)
Bathurst, Lord, 182
Bayonne, 75–7, 83, 86, 104
Belchite, 121, 139
Bentinck, Lord William, 117, 120, 124, 130
Bilbao, 127, 129
Blake, Joaquín, 89, 93–4, 105, 126–7, 129–31, 137, 139, 157, 161, 170
Blanco White, José, 65
Bonaparte, Joseph, 76, 104
Boulou, 38
Bourbons, 2, 9, 15, 24, 26, 63, 76
Buenos Aires, 57
Burgos, 131

Caballero, José Antonio, 46, 56, 62
Cáceres, 45
caciques, 20–1, *see also* notables
Cadalso, José, 19, 23
cadets, 15–18, 21–23
Cádiz, 24, 57, 81, 84, 87–8, 102, 119–20, 135, 144, 154–5, 157, 159, 164–5, 167, 170, 175, 180, 184, 196, 198
Calvo de Rozas, Lorenzo, 92, 129
Campo del Gibraltar, 84
Canarias, *see* Canary Islands
Canaries, *see* Canary Islands
Canary Islands, 85, 93
Cantabria, 130
Cape St. Vincent, 57
Captain Generalcies, 2, 4, 7, 24
Captains General, 4, 24–5, 55, 84, 89–90, 107, 171, 173, 179, 196
Cardedeu, 132
Carlist War (1833–39), 199
Carlos III, 5, 8, 12, 14, 17, 22, 28, 36, 39–40
Carlos IV, 29, 36, 61, 81, 194
and Ambuscade of Bayonne, 76
and crisis of 1808, 64–5, 67

Index

and Guardias de Corps, 18
and military reform, 40–1
and Treaty of Fontainebleau, 58
appoints Godoy Generalísimo, 47
closes military academies, 22
falls ill, 62
fear of reform, 46, 49, 67
orders re-organisation of Council of War, 3
personal habits, 18
Cartagena, 79, 81, 89, 154
Casa Cagigal, Marqués de, 24, 40, 45, 85
Castalla, 183
Castaños, Francisco Xavier,
and Bailén, 98–101
and plots against Junta Central, 105–6
and Tudela campaign, 126–7, 129–31
attempts to secure Cádiz, 87
chairs Junta General de Guerra, 107
enters Madrid, 96
experiments with new tactics, 50
heads first Regency, 144, 155
heads uprising at San Roque, 84–5
hostility to liberals, 182
imprisoned, 131
rebuffs British pretensions, 88
recalled to Seville, 131
submits to Junta of Seville, 90, 94
supply difficulties, 97
Castelfranco, Príncipe de, 67
Castile, 24, 48, see also Castiles, Old Castile
Castiles, 12, 122, see also Castile, Old Castile
Castiliscar, 163
Castlereagh, Lord, 120
Catalonia, 6, 37, 39, 47, 64, 90, 95, 103, 161–2, 166, 183, 197
caudillismo, 200
cavalry, 3, 5–6, 38, 41, 43, 51–2, 96–7, 122–3
Ceuta, 88, 196
Chancillerías, 24–5

Church, 11, 37, 40, 46, 75, 79, 155–7, 178, see also, Inquisition, religious orders
Ciscar, Gabriel, 157
Ciudad Rodrigo, 89, 159, 165
civil–military relations, 11, 14, 20, 23–9, 82, 84–5, 93–5, 104, 107, 141, 158–9, 168, 176–81, 184–5
Cochrane Johnstone, Andrew, 116
Comisión de Constitución Militar, 168, 173–4, 181
Concejo Supremo del Almirantazgo, 84
Conquista, Conde de, 91
Constitution of 1812, 81, 159, 164, 167, 171–3, 176, 179, 182–3, 198
Continental System, 58
Copóns y Navía, Francisco, 184
Córdoba, 91, 98
Cornel, Antonio, 46
corregimientos, 10
Correo de Madrid, 26
cortejo, 18, 20, 23, 36
Cortes, 81, 124, 155, 157–9, 167, 169–70, 173–4, 180–2, 184, 194–5
Cortes del Norte, 103, 105
Cortes of Aragón, 92
Corunna, see La Coruña, Retreat to Corunna
Costa de Asturias y Santander, 90
Council of Castile, 62, 65, 104–6, 135
Coupigny, Marqués de, 98–101, 129
cuerpo político, 53, see also Intendance
cuerpos facultativos, 52
Cuesta, Gregorio, see García de la Cuesta, Gregorio

Dalrymple, Hew, 85, 88
Daoiz, Luis, 77
Denmark, 52, 54, 56, 89, 130, 142
despoblados, 172
Díaz Porlier, Juan, 162, 178, 197

Directory, 40, 46
División de Mallorca, 184
Dos de Mayo, 76–7, 82–5, 87
Doyle, Charles, 104–5, 167
Dupont de l'Etang, Pierre, 98–102
Durán y Barazábal, José Joaquín, 162, 178

Ebro, 63, 94, 101, 117, 121, 124–7
Echávarri, Pedro Agustín, 91, 98
efectivos, 21
El Duende de los Cafés, 184
El Empecinado, *see* Martín Díez, Juan
El Escorial, 62–3, 66
El Español, 115
El Ferrol, 57, 81
Elió, Francisco, 181, 183–4, 196
El Redactor General, 159
Elvas, 24, 47, 103
engineers, 3, 7, 17, 24, 41, 45, 52–3
Enlightenment, 29, 75, 156
Escoiquiz, Juan de, 56
Espeleta, Conde de, 90
Espinosa de los Monteros, 130, 137
Espoz y Mina, Francisco, 162–3, 166, 178, 197
estado llano, 21
Estado Mayor General, 171, 177, *see also* general staff
Extremadura, 84, 103, 135

Falkland Islands, 10
Family Compact, 5, 8–9, 14, 27–8, 37, 39–40
Felipe V, 2, 14, 18
Fernández de Córdoba, Luis, 198
fernandinos, 57, 62, 64, 66–7, 82
Fernando VII,
 abdication, 76, 79
 and Affair of El Escorial, 62–3, 66
 and army, post-1814, 178, 195–9
 and Cuesta, 91
 and Motín de Aranjuez, 66–7
 and revolution of 1820, 198
 and uprising, 76, 82–3, 85, 93
 enters Madrid, 75
 hatred of Godoy, 56
 popularity, 57
 release and restoration, 182–5, 194–5
 seeks Napoleon's help, 62
Figueras, 38, 64, 94, 101
Flórez Estrada, Alvaro, 93
Floridablanca, Conde de, 106, 116
Fontainebleau, Treaty of, 50, 58, 62
foreign troops, 3, 9–10, 13, 15, 18, 25, 38, 43–5, 89
France, 39–40, 46, 52, 54–6, 62–3, 78, 83, 163, 168–9, 174–5, 184
Frederick the Great, 5, 52
freemasonry, 196–7
French Revolution, 18, 29, 36, 40, 67, 75, 78, 156, 169
Freyre, Manuel, 182, 184
fuero militar, 3, 20, 25, 47, 82, 95, 172, 179

Galicia, 12, 81, 93–5, 103, 105, 133–4, 137–8, 142, 154, 166
Gamonal, 131
García de la Cuesta, Gregorio,
 and Talavera campaign, 139
 and uprising, 85–8, 90
 arrests deputies, 105–6
 establishes dictatorship, 90–1
 opposes civilian rule, 105
 opposes Godoy, 62
 opposes Junta Central, 135
 raises army, 95
 rivalry with Blake, 105
Garciny, Ignacio, 92
Gayán, Ramón, 162, 178
Gazeta de Valencia, 137
generalato, 19, 87–8, 105, 115, 177
Generalkriegskomissariat, 1
general staff, 4, 53, 124, 167, 171, *see also* Estado Mayor General
Gerona, 98, 198
Gibraltar, 8, 85, 160
Girón, Pedro Agustín, 50, 93
Godoy, Diego de, 66
Godoy, Manuel de,
 and army, 36, 38, 40–5, 47–54,

Index

56, 58–62
and Fernando VII, 56
and French invasion, 64
and *ilustrados*, 45, 55
and María Luisa, 18, 36, 45, 52, 55–7, 61–2
and Treaty of Fontainebleau, 58
appointed Generalísimo, 47
at Bayonne, 76, 83
complains of beggars, 78
crushes Valencian revolt, 47–8
downfall, 65–7, 107
financial policy, 46
foreign policy, 36–7, 39–40, 46, 55–8
imprisons Montijo, 58
made Príncipe de la Paz, 39
personal shortcomings, 54–5
reformism, 40–1
resigns as Secretary of State, 46
rise to prominence, 18, 36
supporters purged, 82–3, 127
takes command, 47
unpopularity, 57, 59, 61, 63, 81
González Llamas, Pedro, 174
grado system, 19
Graham, Thomas, 161
Granada, 49, 85, 102–3, 135
Grande Armée, 81, 126
grandees, 2, 20, 58, 136, *see also* aristocracy, *grandeza*, *hidalguía*, *hijosdalgo*, magnates, nobility, *titulados*
grandeza, 2, 17, 19, 65, *see also* aristocracy, grandees, *hidalguía*, *hijosdalgo*, magnates, nobility, *titulados*
Great Britain, 10, 39–40, 46, 55–7, 63, 88, 97, 139–40, 154, 164, 169, 174
Gribeauval system, 6
Guadalquivir, 98–100
Guardia Civil, 25
Guardias de Corps, *see* regiments
Guardias de Infantería, 3, 18, 59, 66
guerrilla bands, 134, 161, *see also* guerrillas, *partidas*
guerrillas, 137, 139, 141, 161–3, 166, 169, 171, 175–6, 178, 199, *see also* guerrilla bands, *partidas*
Guervos, Francisco de Paula, 196
Guillelmi, Jorge Juan, 83, 92
Guipúzcoa, 38, 85

hidalguía, 2, 15–16, 19, 21, 49, 58, *see also* aristocracy, grandees, *grandeza*, *hidalguía*, magnates, nobility, *titulados*
hijosdalgo, 11, 15, 18, 21, 26, 29, 196, *see also* aristocracy, grandees, *grandeza*, *hidalguía*, magnates, nobility, *titulados*
Huesca, 163

ilustrados, 23, 27, 45, 55
Infantado, Duque del, 56, 62, 104–5, 132, 135, 143, 158, 170, 182–3
infantry, 3, 5–6, 9, 37–8, 43–4, 48, 50–1, 121–2, 167
Informe sobre la ley agraria, 58
Informes sobre Cortes, 155
Inquisition, 20, 157, 170, 182, *see also* Church, religious orders
Inspectors General, 3, 17, 134
Intendance,
French, 1
Spanish, 7, 25, 54, 117, *see also cuerpo político*
Irun, 83, 127
Italy, 56

Jaca, 97
Jackson, George, 116, 126, 130
Jaén, 103
Jaureghui, Gaspar, 162
jefes políticos, 171, 173, 179
Jena, 102
Jovellanos, Gaspar Melchor de, 45, 58, 116, 136, 156
junkers, 14
Junot, Jean Andoche, 58
Junta Central, *see* Junta Suprema

Central de Gobierno
Junta de Constitución y Ordenanzas del Ejército, 41, 44, 53, 59–60
junta de generales, 179
Junta de Generales y Ministros, *see* Junta de Constitución y Ordenanzas del Ejército
Junta de Gobierno, 76–7, 82, 85
Junta General de Guerra, 107, 131
Junta of Asturias, 103, 142
Junta of Cádiz, 155
Junta of Catalonia, 90, 95, 103
Junta of Extremadura, 103, 135
Junta of Galicia, 94, 103, 105, 142
Junta of Granada, 103
Junta of Jaén, 103
Junta of León, 87
Junta of Murcia, 104
Junta of Old Castile, 91, 103, 105
Junta of Seville, 87, 90, 94–5, 98, 102–4, 125, 134–5, 143–4
Junta of Valencia, 118
Junta Suprema Central de Gobierno,
  and guerrillas, 141
  and La Romana, 134, 142–3
  and political reform, 136, 143, 155
  campaigns, 129–32, 138–9
  character, 115–18, 124–5
  collapse, 115, 144–5, 154–5
  flees to Seville, 133–4
  formation, 104, 106, 115
  military policy, 107, 117, 119, 126, 134, 136, 142, 145
  opposition to, 124, 135–6, 142–4
  relations with British, 142

La Carolina, 100
La Coruña, 78, 81, 85, 89, 119, 133, 197–8
Lacy, Luis, 197
La Peña, Manuel, 158
Las Cabezas de San Juan, 198
Latin America, 154, 164, *see also* America, South America, Spanish Empire
Leith, James, 54
León, 12, 85, 87, 130, 134
Lérida, 90, 159
Lerín, 163
leva, 12–13, 25, 43, 48
liberals,
  and Latin America, 164
  anti-militarism, 154–5, 195
  ascendancy, 155–7
  military policy, 158–9, 168–75, 180, 184–5
  unpopularity, 182–3, 195
light troops, 6, 37–8, 43, 45, 48, 50–1
lines of Torres Vedras, 159
Logroño, 127
London, 79
Longa, Francisco, 162, 178
López Ballesteros, Francisco, 160–1, 168–9, 181
Louis XIV, 2, 18
Louis XVI, 37

Madrid, 10, 12, 18, 23–5, 36–7, 39, 53, 56–7, 64–6, 76–8, 83, 85, 94, 96, 98–101, 104, 126–7, 130, 132–3, 137–9, 165, 182, 184, 198
magnates, 2, 58, 65, *see also* aristocracy, grandees, *grandeza, hidalguía, hijosdalgo*, nobility, *titulados*
Mahón, Duque de, 85
majos, 23
Málaga, 89, 160
Mallén, 98
Mallorca, 88
mando único, 158, 171, 199
Manifiesto de las Persas, 194
María Luisa, 18, 36, 40, 46, 52, 55–7, 59, 61–2, 67, 76
Marie Antoinette, 37
Martín Díez, Juan, 196
mayorazgos, 58
Medellín, 121
Medina de Río Seco, 105
Memorial Militar y Patriótico del

Index

Ejército de la Izquierda, 136
Mengibar, 100
Menorca, 57, 88
Merino, Jerónimo, 178
Mesta, 156
Mexico, 164
Miláns del Bosche, Francisco, 197
Milicias Honradas, 125
military academies, 6, 16, 22, 41, 49, 52–3, 134, 177
military dictatorships, 90–2, 168–9
military orders, 22, 156
Mina, Marqués de la, 24
Ministry of Finance, 3
Ministry of War, 3, 117
miqueletes, 6, 37
Miranda de Ebro, 126
Molíns de Rey, 132
Monte Pío Militar, 22
Montijo, Conde de,
  and Castaños, 129
  and coup of 1814, 183
  and intrigues against Junta Central, 135, 143–4
  and Motín de Aranjuez, 64–6
  and plots against Fernando, 198
  and uprising, 78, 87–8
  imprisoned by Godoy, 58
  joins *fernandinos*, 56
Moore, John, 133, 142
Morillo, Pablo, 182
Morla, Tomás de, 6, 40, 42, 62, 89–90
Motín de Aranjuez, 36, 58–9, 65–7, 135, 194
Motín de Esquilache, 25, 66
Murat, Joachim, 64, 66, 76–7, 82, 87
Murcia, 104, 161

Napoleon, 86, 88, 102, 137, 151, 196
  and war in Spain, 101, 124–6, 131, 133, 144, 159, 161, 163, 165
  Iberian policy, pre-1808, 46, 57–8, 62
  intervention in Spain, 63–5, 76

releases Fernando, 182
National Guard, 173
Navarre, 6, 12, 162–3, 165, 197
navy, 8, 39, 42
nobility, 1–2, 11, 15–18, 20, 49, 57–8, 78, 135, 155–6, 172, 177, 185, *see also* aristocracy, grandees, *grandeza*, *hidalguía*, *hijosdalgo*, magnates, *titulados*
Normandy, 52
notables, 20–1, 26, 28–9, 47, 79, 81–2, 84, 87, 90–1, 95–6, 107, 176, *see also* caciques

Ocaña, 143–4
O'Donnell, Carlos, 93
O'Donnell, Enrique, *see* Abisbal, Conde del
O'Donnell, José, 183
O'Farrill, Gonzalo, 46
officer corps,
  and conduct of war, 123–4, 137–8
  and liberals, 177–82, 184–5, 195
  and restoration, 195–9
  and uprising, 79, 82, 88–9
  composition, 2, 14–17, 19–20, 49, 95, 119, 176–7, 185, 195–6, 199
  foreign links, 5
  internal tensions, 3, 15, 21–2, 29, 178–9, 185
  pay and conditions, 17–18, 46, 60, 174, 196
  privileges, 2, 20, 107, 155–6, 178, 180, 185
  relations with British, 181
  training and quality, 22–4, 49, 118–20
Old Castile, 86–7, 90–1, 95, 103, 105, 126, 131, 133–4, 137, 162, 166, *see also* Castile, Castiles
Oporto, 85
Ordenanzas, 5, 21, 120, 134, 172, 174

Order of Carlos III, 22
O'Reilly, Conde de, 5, 8, 15, 24
Osuna, Duque de, 183
Oviedo, 78, 97, 142, 159

Palacio, Marqués del, 90, 158, 168
Palafox brothers, 66
Palafox, Francisco, 129, 131, 135–6, 143–5
Palafox, José,
   and campaigns of 1808, 126–7, 129–33
   and revolt in Aragón, 79, 83, 89
   establishes dictatorship, 91–3
   organises army, 95
   political aspirations, 103, 127, 135
   returns to Spain, 182–3
   snubbed by Junta Central, 106
palafoxistas, 129, 131–2
Pamplona, 63, 94, 126–7, 162, 197–8
Pardo de Figueroa, Benito, 40, 45
partidas, 161, 163, 175–6, see also guerrilla bands, guerrillas
Perpignan, 38
Portugal, 7, 24, 46–7, 52, 56, 58, 63–4, 89, 103, 137, 144, 154, 159
press, 102, 127, 137, 174, 195
Procurador General de la Nación y del Rey, 170
pronunciamientos, 169, 178, 183, 199
provincial juntas, 88, 90, 94–5, 97, 102–4, 106–7, 117–18, 134, 136, 141–2, 145, 158
provincial militia, 3, 10, 12, 16, 41–2, 44–5, 47–8
Prussia, 5, 42, 57
Puerto Rico, 57
Pyrenees, 37, 166, 181, 183, 197

Quintanilla, Marqués de, 105–6
Quiroga, Antonio, 197

Reding, Teódoro, 98–101
Regency, 144–5, 155, 157, 164–7, 170–1, 173, 182
regiments,
   Borbón, 38
   Brabante, 13
   Bruselas, 13
   Campo Mayor, 50
   Carabinieros Reales, 3, 18, 61
   Cazadores de Barbastro, 38
   Flandés, 13
   Gardes Françaises, 18
   Gerona, 37
   Guardias de Corps, 3, 17–19, 36, 59, 61–2, 66, 77, 83
   Guardias de Honor del Generalísimo-Almirante, 59, 61, 66
   Guardias Españolas, 18
   Guardias Walonas, 15, 25, 59, 67
   Husares de María Luisa, 38, 52
   Husares Españoles, 38
   Jaén, 38
   Lanceros de Castilla, 166
   Lanceros de Jérez, 96
   Légion Portugaise, 81
   Málaga, 37
   Milán, 13
   Navarra, 81
   Ordenes Militares, 38
   Preux, 89
   Primer de Barcelona, 38
   Reding *mayor*, 89
   Segundo de Barcelona, 38
   Segundo de Voluntarios de Aragón, 38
   Soria, 196
   Tarragona, 37
   Voluntarios de Castilla, 38
   Voluntarios de la Corona, 38
   Voluntarios del Estado, 38
   Voluntarios de Navarra, 50
   Voluntarios de Valencia, 38
   Voluntarios Distinguidos de Cádiz, 95, 169, 175
   Zapadores-Minadores, 52
Reinosa, 130
religious orders, 156–7, see also Church, Inquisition
répresentatives-en-mission, 94

Index

Resguardo, 22, 79, 91
Retreat from Moscow, 163
Retreat to Corunna, 133
Revolutionary Wars, 29, 37–9, 43–5, 53, 55, 78, 169, 175
Ricardos, Antonio, 37–8
Riego, Rafael, 197–8
Rivas, Duque de, 17
Romana, Marqués de la,
  accepts Cortes, 158
  and uprising, 89
  commands Spanish forces in Denmark, 81
  conspires against Junta Central, 135, 143–5
  division of, 54
  in Galicia, 134–8
  regains Army of the Left, 144
  replaces Castaños and Blake, 130
  returns from Denmark, 130
  suppresses Junta of Asturias, 142
  suppresses Valencian revolt, 47
Rome, 26, 168
Ronda, 93, 160
Rousillon, 37
Royal Guards, 9, 15, 18–19, 56, 58–9, 66–7, 172, 177, 179, see also Carabinieros Reales, Guardias de Corps, Guardias de Honor del Generalísimo-Almirante, Guardias de Infantería, Guardias Españolas, Guardias Walonas
Royal Navy, 39, 89

Salamanca, 133, 163
San Carlos, Duque de, 182–3
Sánchez, Julián, 166
Sancho, Vicente, 173, 177
San Ildefonso, Treaty of, 40, 57
San Juan, Benito, 132
San Lúcar de Barrameda, 184
San Marcial, 121
San Miguel, Evaristo de, 197
San Roque, 45
San Sebastián, 64, 85, 94
Santa Cruz de Tenerife, 57

Santander, 97, 162
Santo Domingo, 39
Segovia, 6, 53, 85, 106
señoríos, 22
señoríos (Basque), 6, see also Basque country, Basque provinces
serviles, 157, 176, 178, 185, 195
Seven Years' War, 5–6
Seville, 7, 64, 78–9, 83–5, 87, 90, 94–5, 98, 102–4, 119, 125, 131, 134–5, 143–4
Sierra Morena, 37, 100, 144
Sigüenza, 131
Socorro, Marqués del, 24, 64, 66, 81, 83–5, 87–9, 102
somatenes, 6, 37, 95–6, 101–2
Somosierra, 132
sorteo, 10–13, 37–8, 42–3, 47–8, 125
Sos, 163
South America, 6, 64, see also America, Latin America, Spanish empire
Spanish empire, 63, 140, 164, see also America, Latin America, South America
Spanish uprising, 75, 77–94, 102, 107, 134, 158
Suchet, Louis Gabriel, 162–3, 166
Supreme Council of War, 3, 24, 54, 106, 119
Switzerland, 9, 13
Sydenham, Thomas, 176

Tafalla, 163
Tagus, 64, 133
Talavera, 121–2, 137–8, 142–3
Tamames, 121
Tap y Núñez, Nicolás, 84–5
Tarragona, 90, 159, 198
tercios, 4
Tercios de Miqueletes, 95
Thirty Years' War, 1
Tilly, Conde de, 85, 103
titulados, 17, see also aristocracy, grandees, *grandeza*, *hidalguía, hijosdalgo*, magnates, nobility

Toreno, Conde de, 36, 116, 140
Torre del Fresno, Conde del, 84–5, 89
Tortosa, 89, 159
Trafalgar, 57, 87
trienio liberal, 199
Trinidad, 57
Trouillas, 38
Tudela, 98, 127, 131–2

Uclés, 135

vagos, 12, 37, 48
Valdés, Antonio, 105–6
Valdés, Cayetano, 184
Valencia, 6, 45, 47–8, 78–9, 81, 85, 91, 98, 118, 135, 143, 159, 163, 166, 169, 183, 196
vales reales, 46, 55, 60
Valladolid, 49, 86, 91
Valls, 121
Vedel, Dominique, 99–101
Velarde, Pedro, 77
Venegas, Francisco Xavier, 139
Villacampa, 162, 178
Villafranca de Panades, 89
Vitoria, 126, 166
Vizcaya, 48, 96, 129

War of the Oranges, 7, 42, 46–7, 52–3, 59, 61
Wellesley, Arthur, *see* Wellington, Duke of
Wellesley, Henry, 118, 121, 143, 155, 194–5
Wellesley, Marquess of, 116, 143
Wellington, Duke of, 115, 154–5, 162–3, 165–6, 181
  and coup of 1814, 184
  and liberals, 170–1, 174
  and *serviles*, 178, 182
  and strategy, 142, 159, 161
  and Talavera campaign, 139
  appointed commander-in-chief of Spanish army, 168–9
  views on guerrillas, 162
  views on Junta Central, 142
  views on Spaniards, 124
  views on Spanish army, 118, 122–3, 181, 183
  views on uprising, 79, 81
Whittingham, Samuel Ford, 120, 184

Zamora, 49
Zaragoza, 78–9, 83, 85, 91–3, 98, 106, 126, 131–2, 135, 198